Satan's Counterfeit Prophecy

Heidi Heiks

TEACH Services, Inc.
P U B L I S H I N G
www.TEACHServices.com • (800) 367-1844

Copyright © 2013 TEACH Services, Inc.
ISBN-13: 978-1-4796-0250-6 (Paperback)

Library of Congress Control Number: 2013946720

Published by

TEACH Services, Inc.
P U B L I S H I N G
www.TEACHServices.com • (800) 367-1844

Dedicated to my Beloved Son

Corey Heiks

CONTENTS

FOREWORD

Since the attacks on the World Trade Center and the Pentagon on September 11, 2001, Islam has received renewed attention in the Western world. Literally hundreds of books and articles have been written on the religion of Islam, Islamic fundamentalism, jihad terrorism, and their threat to Western societies.

Many of these books and articles have been written by theologians and Bible scholars, including some Seventh-day Adventists, who believe that current events involving Moslems are a fulfillment of prophecy. This is really nothing new; as far back as Nicholas of Cusa (15th century) Moslems were seen as fulfilling parts of the prophecies of Daniel and Revelation. Cusa thought the first beast of Revelation 13 might apply to Mohammed.[1] In 1529, Martin Luther identified the Little Horn in Daniel 7 as the Turk or the Mohammedan kingdom.[2] At other times he applied the symbol of the Little Horn to the papacy.[3] In the 17th century some Bible students saw in the fifth and sixth trumpet the Moslems and Turks,[4] because in 1529 and 1683 the Turks attempted to conquer Europe. Both times they were stopped at the gates of Vienna.

The interpretation of the fifth and sixth trumpets with the Moslems and Turks became the standard interpretation of Bible scholars in the 18th and 19th centuries.[5] In the New World as well as the Old, expositors usually saw in the first four trumpets the barbarian invasions of the Roman Empire and in the fifth and sixth the Saracens (another name for Moslems) and Turks. Thus it is not surprising that the Millerites, especially Josiah Litch, did the same. They had behind them centuries of exposition representing many faiths and nationalities.

For Josiah Litch the "fallen Star" in Revelation 9:1 was Mohammed, and the symbolic "locusts" (vs. 3), the Moslem horsemen. The "five months" (vs. 5) of torment were for him 150 years, which referred to the period of the Turkish torment of the Greeks from 1299 to 1449. All of this had, of course, been previously presented again and again by others.

The symbolic "hour, day, month, and year" under the sixth trumpet (Rev 9:15) was widely acknowledged as representing 391 years and fifteen days. Adding this time period to 1449 brought Litch to August 1840,[6] when the Sultan in Constantinople, he believed, would voluntarily surrender his independence into the hands of the Christian powers. This prediction, made in 1838, attracted considerable attention when Turkey became prominent in the news in 1840.

Not surprisingly, Uriah Smith in 1867 introduced this interpretation of the trumpets into the Seventh-day Adventist Church in his book *Thoughts, Critical and Practical, on the Book of Revelation.* It became the standard interpretation of the trumpets of Revelation in the church until

---

[1] Le Roy Edwin Froom, *The Prophetic Faith of Our Fathers*, 4 vols. (Washington, D.C.: Review and Herald, 1950-1954), 2:136.

[2] Ibid., 2: 268.

[3] Ibid.

[4] Ibid., 2:274, 276.

[5] Among these interpreters we find the names of John Wesley, Edward Irving, and Henry Drummond.

[6] Josiah Litch, *The Probability of the Second Coming of Christ About A. D. 1843. Shown By a Comparison of Prophecy and History, Up to the Present Time, and an Explanation of Those Prophecies Which Are Yet To Be Fulfilled* (Boston: David H. Ela, 1838), 157; cited in P. Gerard Damsteegt, *Foundations of the Seventh-day Adventist Message and Mission* (Grand Rapids, MI: Eerdmans, 1977), 28.

recent times. Many members around the world still hold this view and believe that any deviation from it constitutes an apostasy from the faith.

Smith developed the idea that the demise of the Ottoman/Turkish Empire would herald the Second Coming. During the first World War, therefore, when Turkey, which supported Germany and Austria, came to an end, many Adventists expected the Second Advent at that time.

In this book, Heidi Heiks has assembled a large amount of historical material showing that the traditional interpretation of the fifth and sixth trumpets in Revelation 9 is exegetically and historically not defensible. The assumed dates for the beginning and ending of the 150 and 391 years are not confirmed by the historical events. He also provides an explanation for a statement in *The Great Controversy*, page 334, where Ellen White seems to support Litch's interpretation of the trumpets. Litch himself later abandoned his interpretation, severed all connections with Adventists, and became a futurist, expecting all the prophecies in Revelation to be fulfilled in the future, immediately preceding the Second Advent.

Heidi Heiks is to be commended for spending much time and energy in collecting the many historical and theological sources found in this volume, some of which had to be first translated into English. While the book is not an easy read, it is hoped that it will contribute to a better understanding as to why the traditional interpretation can no longer be defended and why a more spiritual interpretation of the trumpets in the book of Revelation is preferable.

Gerhard Pfandl, Ph.D.
Associate Director
Biblical Research Institute
General Conference of Seventh-day Adventists

ACKNOWLEDGMENTS

I want to thank David Trim, director, and associates at Archives, Statistics, and Research of the General Conference of Seventh-day Adventists for all their kind and courteous help, and for giving me unrestricted access to all documents. I am indebted to Pastor Stephen P. Bohr of Secrets Unsealed, Fresno, CA, for permission to use his excellent commentary on the sixth trumpet of Revelation 9:13-21. And many thanks to Jean Handwerk, who has proven herself again as an excellent copyeditor with her innumerable suggestions that I have incorporated into this thesis. My deepest gratitude and appreciation go to my wife Robin, who has fully supported me in another demanding endeavor. And there is no doubt in my mind that heaven not only inspired the idea for this book, to prepare a people for our Lord's return, but opened the necessary doors to make it possible.

INTRODUCTION

It is time the alarm be sounded again. The enemy has broken into our ranks on a new front. Satan's latest "north wind" of doctrine is attempting to defeat understanding about the identity of his right-hand man and the great controversy theme by introducing Islam into Biblical prophecy. However, a clear road map, a "more sure" guide, has been given to a people looking for Jesus' Second Advent. Islam is nowhere to be found on that prophetic chart.

This new "north wind" is based upon two things: first, the writings of Josiah Litch, and secondly, the misread statement of Ellen White's in *The Great Controversy*, 334-5. It is true that Islam hindered the expansion of the papacy, as history attests, but its adherents were never part of any Bible prophecy then or now, as this book will prove. Our primary purpose, therefore, will be to thoroughly scrutinize the very prophetic foundation upon which the interpretation involving Islam has been built, in order to show the reader that those claims cannot withstand investigation from the primary sources. This study is more about what the fifth and sixth trumpets of Revelation are not, rather than what they are. After all, it is premature to speak of what they are, when the generally-accepted view is built upon a platform of error. It is this fog of error that must first be lifted before we, as a church, can move forward, united in our message to the world as we rightly present the warning messages of the trumpets of Revelation to a dying world. This study comes at a critical time, as the sixth trumpet of Revelation has its application in force in this present period of earth's history, and will continue so until the close of probation, as we will prove. I find myself in complete harmony with Pastor Bohr's exposition of the sixth trumpet of Revelation; that is why the reader will find that excellent work inserted as Chapter 6, along with my editorial comments. The seventh trumpet of Revelation, as will be shown, is when Jesus receives his kingdom. The administration of the seven last plagues will follow, climaxing with the second coming of Christ in the clouds of heaven.

Satan has been sending forth misguided men who have presented a false, "horizontal" or earth-bound conflict (wars and rumors of wars, pagans fighting pagans: Matt. 24:6-8) to precede and overshadow the genuine, "vertical" or earth-against-heaven great-controversy conflict (Matt. 24:9-14) that Scripture tells us is to take place. Acceptance of either a false prophetic fulfillment or a false supposedly-prophesied conflict will, in turn, discredit true Seventh-day Adventism when it is proved (as it surely will be) that the "so-called" SDA Islam prophecy has failed. Its interpretation will be ridiculed by the world. How will the masses then receive the true message (the Three Angels' Messages) when they perceive it coming from the same discredited source? Let us seriously think on these things! This is not to say Islam could not play a part in the horizontal picture (wars and rumors of wars) to develop the real issue to its fruition. But sometimes we all need to step out of the woods in order to see the forest-- in other words, so we can see the big picture. The big picture and the commission of Daniel and Revelation that has been clearly given for the Seventh-day Adventist Church from her conception has to do with Rome, because the central issue is over the commandments of God versus the commandments of men. And behind that lies the origin of all conflict: the government and authority of God, challenged by Satan and his government.

"The world is filled with storm and war and variance. Yet under <u>one head</u>--the <u>papal power</u>--the people will <u>unite</u> to oppose God in the person of His witnesses."[7]

"<u>Romanism in the Old World</u> and <u>apostate Protestantism in the New</u> will pursue a similar course toward those who honor all the divine precepts."[8]

"It is a <u>backsliding church</u> that lessens the distance between <u>itself</u> and the <u>Papacy</u>."[9]

"Satan will so mingle his <u>deceptions</u> with truth that <u>side issues</u> will be created to <u>turn the attention of the people from the great issue</u>, the test to be brought upon the people of God in these last days…. The truth for this time, the third angel's message."[10]

There is no mistake, then, how our prophetic chart really reads! It is Rome, not Islam, that that is portrayed in those prophecies. Our God is truly amazing, for His counsels reveal how much he really cares about each and every one of us. He has told us beforehand that Satan's "side issues" would arise to try to turn our attention to horizontal issues when recognition of pressing vertical issues is needed, and especially at such a time as this. But Satan's deceptions by no means stop there. Further instruction has been given us for the detection of Satan's "North wind" side-issues prophecies:

"The Bible contains all the principles that men need to understand in order to be fitted either for this life or for the life to come. And these principles may be understood by all. No one with a spirit to appreciate its teaching can read a single passage from the Bible without gaining from it some helpful thought. But the most valuable teaching of the Bible is not to be gained by occasional or disconnected study. Its great system of truth is not so presented as to be discerned by the hasty or careless reader. Many of its treasures lie far beneath the surface, and can be obtained only by diligent research and continuous effort. The truths that go to make up the great whole must be searched out and gathered up, "here a little, and there a little." Isaiah 28:10. When thus searched out and brought together, they will be found to be perfectly fitted to one another. Each Gospel is a supplement to the others, <u>every prophecy an explanation of another</u>, <u>every truth a development of some other truth</u>. The types of the Jewish economy are made plain by the gospel. Every principle in the word of God has its place, every fact its bearing. And the complete structure, in design and execution, bears testimony to its Author. Such a structure no mind but that of the Infinite could conceive or fashion."[11]

---

[7] Ellen White, *Testimonies for the Church* (Nampa, ID: Pacific Press, 1948), 7:182. [Emphasis mine]
[8] Ellen White, *The Great Controversy* (Nampa, ID: Pacific Press, 1911), 616. [Emphasis mine]
[9] Ellen White, *Signs of the Times*, Feb. 19, 1894. [Emphasis mine]
[10] Ellen White, *Manuscript Releases* (Silver Spring, MD: E. G. White Estate, 1990), 9:290-291. [Emphasis mine]
[11] Ellen White, *Education* (Mountain View, CA: Pacific Press, 1903), 123. [Emphasis mine]

"The books of Daniel and the Revelation are <u>one</u>. One is a <u>prophecy</u>, the other a <u>revelation</u>; one a book <u>sealed</u>, the other a book <u>opened</u>."[12]

In other words, what you find being discussed in the book of Daniel, you will also find in the book of Revelation, following the rule of repetition and enlargement. These two books never depart from the true conflict, the "vertical" great-controversy theme. The contents of Chapter 6 will show our presentation to be conclusive, but we will give just a very small sample here to stress the importance of what we are really contemplating here. In Revelation 16:13-14 we are told that the papacy (the beast), apostate Protestantism (the false prophet), and the dragon (the civil power, comprised of kings, rulers and governors--see Rev. 19:19-20 and TM 39), spearheaded by demons, will be released at a fixed point in time designated by heaven to go forth unto the kings of the earth and of the whole world:

> Rev 16:13 "And I saw <u>three</u> unclean <u>spirits</u> like frogs *come* <u>out of the mouth</u> of the dragon, and <u>out of the mouth</u> of the beast, and <u>out of the mouth</u> of the false prophet."
> Rev 16:14 "For they <u>are the spirits of devils</u>, working miracles, *which* go forth unto the kings of the earth and of the whole world, to gather them to the battle of that great day of God Almighty."

This development of one truth upon another then another will be traced in our presentation. The reader will readily see with whom heaven has designated we will be contending at the front lines of the genuine "vertical" conflict. It will not be Islam.

> Eph. 6:12 "For we wrestle not against flesh and blood, but against principalities, against powers, against the rulers of the darkness of this world, against spiritual wickedness in high *places*."

The horizontal or earth-limited conflicts such as those involving the Islamic world today— described as "wars and rumors of wars"-- is neither our focus nor the Bible's. To illustrate the development of one truth upon another truth that we have followed in our study and presentation, notice from the previous underlining of Revelation 16:13-14 and the underlining of the following texts that the two are minutely interlocked with each other:

> Rev 9:17 "And thus I saw the horses in the vision, and them that sat on them, having breastplates of fire, and of jacinth, and brimstone: and the heads of the horses *were* as the heads of lions; and <u>out of their mouths</u> issued fire and smoke and brimstone.
> Rev 9:18 "By these <u>three</u> was the third part of men killed, by the fire, and by the smoke, and by the brimstone, which issued <u>out of their mouths</u>."

Now let's look at the prophecy of Revelation 16:13-14 again. God has designated this final, global unifying work of demons to take place at a time known only to Himself. He has not revealed the point in time at which this occurs.

---

[12] Ellen White, *Manuscript Releases* (Silver Spring, MD: E. G. White Estate, 1993), 19:320. [Emphasis mine]

Rev 16:13 "And I saw three unclean spirits like frogs *come* out of the mouth of the dragon, and out of the mouth of the beast, and out of the mouth of the false prophet.

Rev 16:14 "For they are the spirits of devils, working miracles, *which* go forth unto the kings of the earth and of the whole world, to gather them to the battle of that great day of God Almighty."

Heaven's specific timing of the "going forth" of verse 14, and the demonic activity described in that same verse, have also been presented in Revelation 9:15, with further specifications given in that chapter:

Rev 9:15 "And the four angels were loosed, which were prepared for an hour, and a day, and a month, and a year, for to slay the third part of men."

Looking at the big picture through the prophetic lens given us in the writings of Ellen White will help bring some closure to what this is really all about—as to the true conflict that heaven has been pointing to all along:

"Through the two great errors, the immortality of the soul and Sunday sacredness, Satan will bring the people under his deceptions. While the former lays the foundation of spiritualism, the latter creates a bond of sympathy with Rome."[13]

"Satan has long been preparing for his final effort to deceive the world. The foundation of his work was laid by the assurance given to Eve in Eden: 'Ye shall not surely die.' 'In the day ye eat thereof, then your eyes shall be opened, and ye shall be as gods, knowing good and evil.' Genesis 3:4, 5. Little by little he has prepared the way for his masterpiece of deception in the development of spiritualism. He has not yet reached the full accomplishment of his designs; but it will be reached in the last remnant of time. Says the prophet: 'I saw three unclean spirits like frogs; ... they are the spirits of devils, working miracles, which go forth unto the kings of the earth and of the whole world, to gather them to the battle of that great day of God Almighty.' Revelation 16:13, 14. Except those who are kept by the power of God, through faith in His word, the whole world will be swept into the ranks of this delusion. The people are fast being lulled to a fatal security, to be awakened only by the outpouring of the wrath of God."[14]

Here is what is called a "no-brainer." If the two great religious errors consist of the immortality of the soul and Sunday sacredness—if those two weapons of warfare in the enemy's arsenal will round up the global masses at a specified time designated by heaven, shall we not expect that the enemy will stop at nothing to keep his battle plan from being exposed? Since Eden, deception has been his

---

[13] Ellen White, *The Great Controversy* (Nampa, ID: Pacific Press, 1911), 588. [Emphasis mine]
[14] Ibid., 561-2. [Emphasis mine]

most successful method, and we may rightly anticipate the same method today. His deceptions naturally would come in two main structured formats before breaking off into multiple avenues:

1. Deception on what the Scriptures actually teach on the two topics;

2. Deception on what the Scriptures reveal regarding the means and methods to be used to implement that battle plan of the delusionary teachings of the Scriptures on both accounts.

Though both aspects of the enemy's plan are fully exposed in the Scriptures, as we will show, our concern in this study will be confined to the pertinent issues surrounding the immortality of the soul.

I wish to stop here and relate a personal experience I had shortly after I joined the Seventh-day Adventist Church in the early 80s. I remember very well the account I am about to share because it was burned into my mind for infinity. Where I lived at the time, there was an old military surplus store that I liked to go into now and then, just to look around. In time I became good friends with the owners. I always like to talk spiritual things when given the opportunity, which I did with them. It was not till much later that the Mrs. informed me she was a Mormon. I must admit I was quite surprised-- not that she was a Mormon, but because in my mind her actions belied any religious beliefs. She smoked cigarettes, had a sailor's tongue, wore military dress, and liked to show off her 357 snub nose pistol she carried in her purse. She let people know she wouldn't hesitate to use it.

At the time I did contract work. One day she asked if I would come to her house and give them an estimate. I agreed and, when the time came, I made my way there and we discussed her project. She then changed the subject and started to ask me some of my beliefs. Then it turned to the state of the dead. I told her the Bible says the dead "know not anything," and therefore those who attend séances, thinking they are talking to dead relatives or friends, are in fact speaking to demons.

I never saw a person change demeanor so fast in my life. She instantly became aggressive, poking my chest like a man raving mad and shouting that I had no idea what I was talking about. Cursing, she told me, "I don't care what that book says or what anybody else says, because I know who I talked to and what I saw! Are you actually trying to tell me that I did not speak to my mother?"

I stepped back, put my hands up, and tried to apologize, as it was obvious that this conversation, along with any other spiritual talk, was over. So was the friendship, because she never ever had anything to do with me again.

I made it out the door alive, but the lesson to be learned from my experience is this: As Seventh-day Adventists, we need to realize that with Satan, yes, Sunday sacredness is the objective, but the *means* of getting all on board that train is spiritualism, the belief in the immortality of the soul. Before the universal onslaught of demon activity foretold in the book of Revelation is to be launched, if by then the masses have not been brought abreast of the truth of the state of the dead as we, as a church, know it to be, according to the scriptures, then as a church we will have fallen short. Our efforts in giving the final warning message will be greatly restricted, our successes will be fewer, and our persecution will be a hundredfold more intense. Consider the following, please:

> "We have great and solemn truths to give to the world, and they are to be proclaimed in no hesitating, limping style. <u>The trumpet is to give a certain sound</u>. Some will come to hear the strange message out of curiosity; others with a longing to receive true knowledge, asking the question, 'What shall I do that I may inherit eternal life?' (Mark 10:17). Thus men came to Christ. And mingling with His hearers

were [evil] angels in the form of men, making their suggestions, criticizing, misapplying, and misinterpreting the Saviour's words....

"In this time evil angels in the form of men will talk with those who know the truth. They will misinterpret and misconstrue the statements of the messengers of God."[15]

"<u>Satanic agencies</u> in <u>human form</u> will take part in this last great conflict to oppose the building up of the kingdom of God. And <u>heavenly angels</u> in <u>human guise</u> will be on the field of action. The two opposing parties will continue to exist till the closing up of the last great chapter in this world's history."[16]

"Spiritual beings sometimes appear to persons in the form of their deceased friends, and relate incidents connected with their lives, and perform acts which they performed while living. In this way they lead men to believe that their dead friends are angels, hovering over them, and communicating with them. Those [demons] who thus assume to be the spirits of the departed, are regarded with a certain idolatry, and with many their word has greater weight than the Word of God."[17]

"I saw the rapidity with which this delusion [spiritualism] was spreading. A train of cars was shown me, going with the speed of lightning. The angel bade me look carefully. I fixed my eyes upon the train. It seemed that the whole world was on board. Then he showed me the conductor, a fair, stately person, whom all the passengers looked up to and reverenced. I was perplexed and asked my attending angel who it was. He said, 'It is Satan. He is the conductor, in the form of an angel of light. He has taken the world captive.... And they are all going with lightning speed to perdition.'"[18]

"The miracle-working power manifested through spiritualism will exert its influence against those who choose to obey God rather than men. Communications from the spirits will declare that God has sent them to convince the rejecters of Sunday of their error, affirming that the laws of the land should be obeyed as the law of God. They will lament the great wickedness in the world and second the testimony of religious teachers that the degraded state of morals is caused by the desecration of Sunday. <u>Great will be the indignation excited against all who refuse to accept their testimony</u>."[19]

"Christ shows that without the controlling power of the Spirit of God, humanity is a terrible power for evil, to hurt and destroy humanity. When men banish this Spirit, unbelief and hatred of reproof stir up satanic influence. Principalities and powers, the rulers of the darkness of this world, and spiritual wickedness in high places, will <u>unite</u>

---

[15] Ellen White, *Selected Messages* (Hagerstown, MD: Review and Herald, 1980), 3: 410-411. [Emphasis mine]

[16] Ellen White, *Maranatha* (Hagerstown, MD: Review and Herald, 1976), 167. [Emphasis mine]

[17] Ellen White, *Patriarchs and Prophets* (Nampa, ID: Pacific Press, 1958), 684-5. [Emphasis mine]

[18] Ellen White, *Early Writings* (Hagerstown, MD: Review and Herald, 1882, 1945), 263. [Emphasis mine]

[19] Ellen White, *Maranatha* (Hagerstown, MD: Review and Herald, 1976), 167. [Emphasis mine]

in a desperate companionship. They will be leagued against God in the person of his saints. By misrepresentation and falsehood, they will demoralize both men and women who, to all appearances, believe the truth. False witnesses will not be wanting in this terrible work. But Christ gives the assurance: 'There shall not a hair of your head perish. In your patience possess ye your souls.' Christ will restore the life taken; for he is the Life-giver: he will beautify the righteous with immortal life."[20]

The intensity of the real conflict is now before the reader in bold relief, and the less we have to say about Islam, the better. We all know that to be forewarned is to be forearmed. Now, before the restraints are entirely let go, heaven is giving us this last opportunity to see if we really believe what we proclaim. Do we comprehend the urgency of the message in this hour of earthly history? Light and understanding in God's word are never given to His people for their mere entertainment. Today-- not tomorrow, but *today*-- as a church-- a new and earnest effort needs to be made to address this critical lack of understanding among the world's population.

Deception, we have been told over and over again (Matt. 24:3-4, Rev. 13:14, Rev. 16:14), is the game plan of the enemy. *Self*-deception is without argument the greatest deception of all. Since the very nature of our study is the exposure of deception, Ellen White has given us all a meter stick, if you will, for self-inventory-- to see for ourselves if we are self-deceived and to which camp we really belong, as this will determine what we see or do not see:

Lessons from the Christ-Life

Mrs. E. G. White

"What a contrast to the reception given to Christ by the Jewish leaders was the reception given to Him by Simeon! The Jews lived in daily expectation of seeing the long-looked-for Messiah. They talked of His coming, and with proud ambition built hopes of worldly greatness on the prospect. But when He came, meek and lowly, a man of sorrows and acquainted with grief, they hid their faces from Him.

"Simeon no sooner saw the infant in the priest's arms than he was divinely impressed. Taking Him in his arms, he blessed Him, and said, 'Lord, now lettest thou thy servant depart in peace, according to thy word: for mine eyes have seen thy salvation, which thou hast prepared before the face of all people; a light to lighten the Gentiles, and the glory of thy people Israel.'

"Simeon realized that he held in his arms One who was the Way, the Truth, and the Life. There was at this time nothing in Christ's outward appearance to give him this assurance, but Simeon had lived in the atmosphere of heaven. The bright beams of the Sun of righteousness gave him spiritual discernment. His one desire had been to see Christ. The purity of his life corresponded to the light he had received, and he was prepared for the revelation of the great truth that this helpless infant was the Lord's anointed, even the Messiah. Joy and exultation transfigured his face as he held in his arms God's most precious gift to men. His illumined mind received the light flowing from the Source of all light. He saw that Christ was to be the hope of the

---

[20] Ellen White, *Review and Herald*, December 7, 1897. [Emphasis mine.]

Gentiles as well as of the Jews. The walls of tradition built up by Jewish prejudice did not exist in his mind. He realized that the Messiah was to bring redemption to all.

"Turning to the Jews, we see the other side. The scribes and Pharisees had separated themselves from God by their national pride. There were in Judea schools of learning, and the leaders of these schools were filled with self-exaltation. They thought that they had all the light that had ever been given to the world. They looked for the Messiah to come as a temporal prince, to exalt the Jewish nation above all other nations on the earth. As their self-confidence increased, their dependence on God decreased. They walked in their own ways, and were filled with self-sufficiency and self-righteousness. They professed to be the expositors of Scripture, but they misinterpreted and misapplied its teachings. Instead of reflecting light to the people, they cast a shadow upon them. The voice of God speaking to them through His Son was to them the voice of a stranger.

"The least difference of opinion expressed by Christ was an occasion for the Jews to resist and denounce Him. At times they charged Him with working miracles through Beelzebub, the prince of the devils. The least mention of Christ as a light to lighten the Gentiles roused to fury the national prejudice. The worst passions of the heart were stirred; for the Pharisees had taught the Jewish people to despise and hate the Gentiles. Were their commands and traditions to be treated with indifference, and, worse still, to be brushed away as error? Was this man, the son of a carpenter, to be accepted as knowing more than the priests and rulers? They would show him that he could not take the people from them. They determined to put him to death.

"Why should there be such a difference between the reception of Christ by the Jewish teachers and His reception by Simeon?--Because the spiritual condition of the two was different. The Jews were guided and controlled by pride and selfishness. Simeon revered God, and walked in the way of the Lord. He listened constantly for the voice of God, and he was enlightened by the Holy Spirit. Those who wait on the Lord will, like Simeon, receive divine illumination.

"Simeon and the priests represent two classes,--those who are guided by the Spirit of God because they are willing to be instructed, and those who, refusing to receive the light which would lead them into all truth, are guided by the spirit of the power of darkness, and are daily being led into deeper darkness.

"By divine illumination Simeon understood Christ's mission. The Holy Spirit impressed his heart. But the priests and rulers were imbued with the spirit of the enemy of God; and today the same spirit influences human minds, controlling with power the hearts of men, and making of none effect the appeals of the Spirit.

"The Jewish leaders claimed to be the expositors of prophecy; but while their hearts were filled with envy, evil-surmisings, and selfish pride, they could not distinguish between the voice of the true Shepherd and the voice of a stranger. They strengthened one another in resistance. The same thing is done in our day. The same resistance of truth will be shown by those who stubbornly refuse to receive the cautions and reproofs which the Lord sends. But those who reject the word of God for tradition will not be able to stand amid the perils of the last days.

"The Jews virtually said, as did Pharaoh, 'Who is the Lord, that I should obey His voice?' The same power that had made itself felt all over the land of Egypt was striving with the Jews. But they refused to bow before it, and their hearts grew harder.

The same voice is speaking to men and women today. We are in danger of falling into the error into which the Jews fell. God warns us not to do as they did.

"If our hearts are open to receive the light of truth, we shall see what Jesus is to our world. But too often that which would be to the people of God the very light and blessing they need is rejected because of blindness of mind and hardness of heart. Many walk in darkness, and can see no light. To them truth seems to be error. The voice of One coming in the name of the Father is ignored. They prepare the way for Satan to bring them strong delusions, that they may believe a lie. God's word declares, 'Of your own selves shall men arise, speaking perverse things, to draw away disciples after them.'

"God stands ready to bestow rich blessings upon men; but few will bend from their selfishness to receive the gracious gift. From age to age there is acted over the same rejection of light that grieved the heart of Christ when He was on earth. There is seen the same refusal to hear the voice of God through His appointed agencies, because the message borne does not sanction human theories. Christ is as really rejected today by the rejection of His messages of warning and reproof as when He stood in this world a man among men."[21]

The following statement reiterates that warning:

"But those who reject the word of God for tradition will not be able to stand amid the perils of the last days."[22]

Again we have been admonished on this vital point:

"We shall be attacked on every point; we shall be tried to the utmost. We do not want to hold our faith simply because it was handed down to us by our fathers. Such a faith will not stand the terrible test that is before us."[23]

The qualities of a good teacher are, first, that he himself is teachable and, secondly, that he transforms empty minds into open minds. Hence, the following counsel will always be in the back of his mind:

"We have many lessons to learn, and many, many to unlearn. God and heaven alone are infallible. Those who think that they will never have to give up a cherished view, never have occasion to change an opinion, will be disappointed. As long as we hold to our own ideas and opinions with determined persistency, we cannot have the unity for which Christ prayed."[24]

The purpose of this book, then, is to separate the word of God from the traditions of the fathers, facts from fiction, truth from error, and to expose one of the greatest perversions of truth to mislead

[21] Ellen White, *Review and Herald* (Battle Creek, MI) April 2, 1901.
[22] Ibid.
[23] Ellen White, *Review and Herald* (Battle Creek, MI) April 29, 1884.
[24] Ibid., July 26, 1892.

humanity, conceived by one of Satan's most loyal subjects and unwittingly promoted by one of the pioneers in Adventism. Josiah Litch's prediction for the fifth and sixth trumpets of Revelation rested <u>entirely</u> on a single date in the writings of a cultured despiser of religion, Edward Gibbon:

> "God intends that improvement shall be the lifework of all His followers and that it shall be guided and controlled by correct experience. The true man is one who is willing to sacrifice his own interest for the good of others and who exercises himself in binding up the brokenhearted. The true object of life has scarcely begun to be understood by many, and that which is real and substantial in their life is sacrificed because of cherished <u>errors</u>.... <u>Gibbon the skeptic</u>, and many others whom God endowed with giant minds, and whom the world called great men, rallied under the <u>banner of Satan</u> and used the gifts of God for the <u>perversion of truth</u> and the <u>destruction of the souls of men</u>. Great intellect, when made a minister of vice, is a curse to the possessor and to <u>all who come within the circle of its influence</u>."[25]

Ellen White exposed Edward Gibbon more widely in the *Review and Herald*, Jan. 8, 1880, when the world was still joyfully raving over the man's literary attainments. (It would be another year before Uriah Smith's book *Daniel and The Revelation* would be published in its new combined format--as we knew it pre-1944.) Her admonition has always fallen on deaf ears, even with her additional input:

> "The '<u>woe, woe, woe!</u>' was <u>pronounced upon a church</u> who walked in the sparks of their own kindling, who did not derive their light and power from the great central Light, the Sun of Righteousness, and diffuse that light and glory to those who were in darkness. By absorbing and diffusing the light, they cause their own light to burn brighter. The one who receives light, but does not give it as God requires him to do, will become a receptacle of darkness."[26]

> "Those who have been self-indulgent and ready to yield to pride and fashion and display, will sneer at the conscientious, truth-loving, God-fearing people, and will, in this work, sneer at the God of heaven Himself. The Bible is disregarded, the wisdom of men exalted, and <u>Satan and the man of sin worshiped by the wisdom of this age, while the angel is flying through the midst of heaven crying</u> 'Woe, woe, woe, to the inhabiters of the earth.' (Revelation 8:13).

> "I have been shown that the hand of the Lord is stretched out already to punish those who will become monuments of divine displeasure and holy vengeance, for the day of recompense has come when men who exalted the man of sin in the place of Jehovah in worshiping an idol sabbath in the place of the Sabbath of the Lord

---

[25] Ellen White, *Testimonies for the Church* (Nampa, ID: Pacific Press, 1948), 4:519-520.
[26] Ellen White, *Pamphlets in the Concordance* (Payson, AZ: Leaves of Autumn Books, 1983), 1:320 (028, 3). [Emphasis mine]

Jehovah will find it a fearful thing to fall into the hands of the living God, for he is a consuming fire."[27]

"Then, to add insult to injury, many have been led to believe the lie that Ellen White turned about-face and endorsed the prediction of Josiah Litch when she wrote, 'In the year 1840 another remarkable fulfillment of prophecy excited widespread interest.... The event exactly fulfilled the prediction." (GC 334-5.) However, Litch's prophetic foundation rested entirely on a single date from Edward Gibbon, whom she so adamantly and wholeheartedly discredited as standing "under the banner of Satan." Even our critics, including Desmond Ford, have mistakenly accused her of supporting Josiah Litch's interpretation of Revelation 9. Robert W. Olson, from the Ellen G. White Estate, wrote about that error in understanding:

55. REVELATION 9 AND JOSIAH LITCH

"Ford states, 'Litch's application of Revelation 9:15 to August 11, 1840, was quite wrong, as he himself admitted in later years.' 'Ellen White accepted the prophetic conclusions of Josiah Litch regarding August 11, 1840.' (Ford, pgs, 659-660, 584). Did Mrs. White say much about the seven trumpets?

"No. This is the only known reference to Revelation 9 in all of Ellen White's writings and it appears, not in connection with an exegetical study of the Bible, but as part of her description of the Millerite movement. On the basis of his interpretation of Rev. 9:15, Josiah Litch predicted in 1838 that the Ottoman power would be broken in 1840. On August 1, 1840, he predicted that it would occur on August 11. What took place on that date confirmed the faith of multitudes in the Millerite interpretation of Scripture and gave the advent movement great impetus.

"If Ellen White, in the *Great Controversy*, pp. 334-335, means that John the Revelator's prophecy was fulfilled on August 11, 1840, she would be giving support to Litch's interpretation of Revelation 9:15. If she simply means that Josiah Litch's prediction was fulfilled, then she is not necessarily supporting Litch's interpretation of the text...."[28]

Robert Olson was absolutely correct when he said Ellen White's *Great Controversy* statement about Litch's prediction and its fulfillment did not stem from an exegetical study of God's word, but was simply a description of an occurrence during the Millerite movement, an inspired and accurate accounting of an incident in Advent history. Here is her statement in full:

"In the year 1840 another remarkable fulfillment of prophecy excited widespread interest. Two years before, Josiah Litch, one of the leading ministers preaching the second advent, published an exposition of Revelation 9, predicting the fall of the

---

[27] Ellen White, *1888 Materials* (Washington, DC: Ellen White Estate, 1987), 2:485. [Emphasis mine]
[28] Robert W. Olson, *ONE HUNDRED AND ONE QUESTIONS ON THE SANCTUARY AND ON ELLEN WHITE*, (Washington, D. C.: Ellen G. White Estate, 1981), 50. [Emphasis mine]

Ottoman Empire. According to his calculations, this power was to be overthrown 'in A.D. 1840, sometime in the month of August;' and only a few days previous to its accomplishment he wrote: 'Allowing the first period, 150 years, to have been exactly fulfilled before Deacozes ascended the throne by permission of the Turks, and that the 391 years, fifteen days, commenced at the close of the first period, it will end on the 11th of August, 1840, when the Ottoman power in Constantinople may be expected to be broken. And this, I believe, will be found to be the case.'--Josiah Litch, in *Signs of the Times*, and *Expositor of Prophecy*, Aug. 1, 1840.

"At the very time specified, Turkey, through her ambassadors, accepted the protection of the allied powers of Europe, and thus placed herself under the control of Christian nations. The event exactly fulfilled the prediction. (See Appendix.) When it became known, multitudes were convinced of the correctness of the principles of prophetic interpretation adopted by Miller and his associates, and a wonderful impetus was given to the advent movement. Men of learning and position united with Miller, both in preaching and in publishing his views, and from 1840 to 1844 the work rapidly extended."[29]

The title of the chapter in *The Great Controversy* from which this quote is taken is called "An American Reformer." It is all about the man William Miller and "his views." Josiah Litch admitted that the leading ideas for his own understanding of the seven trumpets of Revelation came directly from the works of William Miller:

"The writer would here acknowledge himself indebted to Mr. William Miller's valuable Lectures, for the leading ideas of the following pages. Although the views of Mr. M. may not be correct on every point, yet, so far as his calculation of time is concerned, the writer can but consider his plan irrefutable...."[30]

It is indisputable that Ellen White did no more than recount, without partiality, a notable incident involving Josiah Litch that occurred in the Millerite movement. In so doing, her own word choice indicates her neutral position, neither supporting nor criticizing Josiah Litch or William Miller. Who has the authority to change Ellen White's writings to say or imply "his views" means "my views" or "our views"? Once again, confusion on this matter is the result of misreading Ellen White's writings. To say otherwise is to make Ellen White out to be a false prophet, which would play directly into the hands of our critics, as this book will fully demonstrate. In its comparison of Scripture with Scripture, in its consultation of the writings of Ellen White, and in its utilization of primary sources, this book will unmask one of the greatest cover-ups by Satan and his host to be found in all the book of Revelation. Let us begin.

And yet she calls it a "remarkable fulfillment of prophecy." That can't be explained away.

---

[29] Ellen White, *The Great Controversy* (Nampa, ID: Pacific Press, 1911), 334-5. [Emphasis mine]
[30] Josiah Litch, *The Probability of the Second Coming of Christ About A.D. 1843* (Boston: David H. Ela, 1838), preface.

1

August 11, 1840: What Really Happened?

Our sole attention in chapter 1 will be the historical events that were recognized and recorded by Josiah Litch. The following excerpts are taken directly from primary sources; they are Joshua Litch's own definitive statements about events occurring on or terminating on August 11, 1840, that he considered to mark fulfillment of the 6th trumpet, according to Millerite understanding. Largely unknown to many Seventh-day Adventists, but correctly understood by our critics,[31] Josiah Litch shifted ground for his prophetic interpretation four different times when he identified four different events for the fulfillment of Aug. 11, 1840. Three of those historical events found their alleged fulfillment after that date. The fourth and final event that Litch believed would occur on August 11, 1840, in fulfillment of prophecy, did not occur until the year 1842, as we will show from the primary sources.

Josiah Litch's four failed prophetic expectations follow in succession, as marked. The first was published in 1838. Page numbering of the original will be in brackets throughout; all other emphasis is in the original:

The Probability of the Second Coming of Christ about A.D. 1843

Josiah Litch

"...But when will this power be overthrown? [The Turks or Turkey, of which the Ottoman Empire was composed] According to the calculations already made, that the five months ended 1449, the hour, fifteen days, the day, one year, the month, thirty years, and the year, three hundred and sixty years; in all, three hundred and ninety-one years and fifteen days, will end in A.D. 1840, sometime in the month of August. The prophecy is the most remarkable and definite, (even descending to the days) of any in the Bible, relating to these great events. It is as singular as the record [158] of the time when the empire rose.... *There shall be time no longer.* This scene is to take place immediately after the end of the three hundred and ninety-one years and fifteen days, or the drying up the great river Euphrates. There [159] shall be no more season of mercy; for in the days of the seventh angel, when he shall begin to sound, the mystery of God shall be finished. The great mystery of salvation by faith shall be ended, and the year of his redeemed will come.

---

[31] Ronald L. Numbers and Jonathan M. Butler, *The Disappointed Millerism and Millenarianism in the Nineteenth Century*, See Chapter 5: Eric Anderson, *The Millerite Use of Prophecy* (Knoxville: Univ. of Tennessee Press, 1993), 78-91. See also Kai Arasola, *The End of Historicism, Millerite Hermeneutic of Time Prophecies in the Old Testament* (University of Uppsala, Faculty of Theology, 1989), 146-155.

"Reader, are you prepared for that event? Have you on a wedding garment? Have you your lamp trimmed and oil in your vessel? O be wise NOW, *for* THEN *the* MASTER *will have shut the* DOOR." [32]

In this written work by Josiah Litch in 1838, we have two major events that were predicted to take place:

(1) 1. The Turks or Turkey, comprising the whole of the Ottoman Empire, would come to its end sometime in the month of August, 1840. Litch's more specific prediction for the 11th of August was not yet given.

2. The close of probation for all of humanity would take place at the same time. The event that would put the finishing touch on the Millerite prediction for the 6th trumpet's fulfillment in August of 1840 would occur on August 1, 1840:

SIGNS OF THE TIMES
August 1, 1840

[69] "THE CLOSING-UP OF THE DAY OF GRACE.

"As there has been much enquiry of late on the subject of the closing up of the day of grace, or probation, we here give the scriptures on which this opinion is founded, with some remarks and leave our readers to judge for themselves.... When the sixth Trumpet hath ceased to sound, the seventh begins, and 'in the days of the voice of the seventh angel, when he shall BEGIN to sound, the mystery of God, or dispensation of grace shall be finished.' It would appear from this, that upon the fall of the Turkish empire which will take place on the closing up of the 'sixth vial' and 'trumpet,' that the day of probation will close. Again, Rev. xi. 15. 'And the seventh angel sounded; and there were great voices in heaven, saying, the kingdom of this world are become the kingdoms of our Lord and of his Christ; and he shall reign forever and ever.' This most certainly closes up the gospel dispensation, and brings us to the glorified state; for we are to 'reign forever and ever.' This will take place when the seventh angel shall sound. Here we have this most solemn and momentous subject, as brought to view in the book of Revelation. There is one other passage that we quote, which has an important bearing upon this subject. Mat. Xxv. 10-12. 'And while they went to buy, the bridegroom came; and they that were ready went in with him to the marriage, and the DOOR WAS SHUT.' We learn that preparation was made by the wise, when the midnight cry was given, but the foolish deferred the matter until it was too late; for while they went to buy, the bridegroom came, 'and the door was shut.' Afterwards, the foolish virgins came, saying, 'Lord, Lord, open unto us. But he answered and said, Verily I say unto you, I know you not.' This is the time referred to in Rev. xxii. 11, 'He that is unjust, let him be unjust still, and he which is filthy, let him be filthy still; and he that is righteous, let him be righteous still; and he that is holy, let him be holy still.' ...Allowing the first period of 150 years to have been

---

[32] Josiah Litch, *The Probability of the Second Coming of Christ about A.D. 1843* (Boston: David H. Ela, 1838), 153-159.

exactly fulfilled before Deacozes ascended the throne by permission of the Turks, and that the 391 years 15 days commenced at the close of the first period, it will end in the 11th of August, 1840, when the Ottoman power in Constantinople may be expected to be broken. And this, I believe, will be found to be the case.

"But still there is no positive evidence that the first period was exactly, to a day, fulfilled; nor yet that the second period began, to a day, where the first closed. If they began and ended so, the above calculation will be correct. If they did not, then there will be a variation in the conclusion; but the evidence is clear that there cannot be a year's variation from the calculation; we must wait patiently for the issue.

"But what, it is asked, will be the effect on your own mind, if it does not come out according to the above calculation? Will not your confidence in your theory be shaken? I reply, not at all. The prophecy in hand is an isolated one; and a failure in the calculation does not necessarily affect any other calculation. But yet, whenever it is fulfilled, whether in 1840, or at a future period, it will open the way for the scenes of the last day. Let no man, therefore, triumph, even if there should be an error of a few months in our calculation on this prophesy.   L.

"EVENTS TO SUCCEED THE SECOND WOE.

"The question is often asked, Do you believe with Mr. Miller that the day of grace will close in the month of August? To this, I reply, It is impossible for me to tell what will come in the month of August. If the foregoing calculations are correct, however, and the Ottoman power falls, we shall be brought to a point where there is no certainty that the day of grace will be continued for one hour. For when the second woe is past, the third woe cometh quickly. And when the seventh trumpet sounds, the day of grace will be past. Hence, when any one can prove to me satisfactorily how long a period 'Quickly' is, as used in Rev. xi. 14, I will tell them how long the day of grace will last after the fall of the Ottoman empire, and not before. Every one must be his own judge on this point. But this I affirm, it will be a fearful experiment for any one to try, to put off the work of salvation until the 11th of August, or any other time. There is no safety except in Christ."[33]

We will now condense and clarify the position of Litch that was just quoted. Please note that all that Josiah Litch wrote before August 11, 1840, is under **(1).**

(1) 1. On August 1, 1840, Josiah Litch for the first time publically predicted the precise day of August 11, 1840, for the fall of Turkey or the Ottoman Empire.

2. The close of probation was still proclaimed for August 11, 1840, as well, but Litch now gave himself up to a year's fallback cushion in case he would be mistaken in some particulars.

With the passing of August 11, 1840, and with no evidence that Turkey had fallen or that probation had closed, the brethren waited until November 1, 1840, to address the embarrassment:

SIGNS OF THE TIMES
November 1, 1840

---

[33] Josiah Litch, Events to Succeed the Second Woe, *Signs of the Times*, Boston, August 1, 1840.

[117] "Mr. Miller, in his 8th lecture, makes the following remarks, 'And whoever lives until the year 1839 will see the final dissolution of the Turkish empire, for then the sixth trumpet will have finished its sounding; which, if I am correct, will be the final overthrow of the Ottoman power. And then will the seventh trump and last woe begin, under which the kingdoms of the earth and the anti-christian beast will be destroyed, the powers of darkness chained, the world cleansed, and the church purified.'

"The following remarks of Bro. Litch on this question will be read with interest.

"DEAR BROTHER HIMES – I seize a few moments to say the news from the east is most thrilling on the public mind, so far as I have opportunity of witnessing.

"What a prospect! nothing short of one universal blaze of war all over the old world can be anticipated. It must and will come, and for it the nations are mustering. Well, so be it.

"'The plague, and death, and din of war, our Savior's swift approach declare, And bid our hearts arise; Earth's basis shook, confirms our hope, Its cities fall, but lifts us up, To meet him in the skies.'"

"The world have, since the 11th of August, had a strong disposition to triumph, as though they were past all danger, and could give full scope to their opposition to the doctrine of Christ's near approach. But what will they say now? The calculation on the prophetic periods of Revelation, 9th chapter, were, that they would end August 11th, and that up to that period the Ottoman power would stand; but that that time would seal its doom.

"Now what are the facts? Why, that on the 15th of August, the Sultan, by his ambassador, presented to the Pacha of Egypt the ultimatum of the four powers. He replied by an oath of God, or in other words, in the name of God, he signed the death warrant of the Ottoman power.

" 'AN OATH BY GOD. I will not give up one foot of the land I possess, and if the powers make war upon me, I will turn the empire upside down, and be buried in its ruins.' MEHEMET ALI.

"What is the result of that decision? What do the politicians say is the result of it? Why, a war of the most destructive character the world ever witnessed. Beyrout already in ruins, and the hosts of Europe, Asia and Africa, mustering for still more dreadful scenes of slaughter and blood.

[118] "And well Mehemet knew that a war once begun on that question, would never end until Turkey was in ruins. That must be the result of the war. Finally, it is a very striking fulfilment of the calculation; for that decision was but four days after the 11th of August, the period fixed for the termination or the prophecy. The like singular accuracy in the fulfilment of a prophetic period cannot be found in history. Will men lay it to heart? J. LITCH.

"The time was given as near as it could be, unless the prophet had descended to reckon by minutes. An hour, a day, a month, and a year. An hour is fifteen days. The Ottoman power was given into the hands of the four powers just four days after the expiration of the time given by the prophet. He could not give it more definite without descending to minutes. The four days would make just 16 minutes, so we have the fulfilment as near as it could be given in prophetic times. ED."[34]

(2) 1. Litch now said that "war" was most likely, which would destroy Turkey and fulfill the prophecy.

2. Litch shifted to August 15, 1840, for the fulfillment of the prophecy by declaring the act of the Sultan's ambassador in presenting to the pacha of Egypt the ultimatum of the four powers had met its fulfillment: "...For that decision was but four days after the 11th of August, the period fixed for the termination of the prophecy."

SIGNS OF THE TIMES
February 1, 1841

[161] "THE NATIONS.

"And the sixth angel poured out his vial upon the great river Euphrates, and the water thereof was dried up.

"We have had numerous questions propounded relative to the fall of the Ottoman power within the three last months, both by the friends and opponents of our cause. As we wish to give a full and distinct answer to them all, we present the following article for the satisfaction of that class of our readers. They will not only find all their questions answered, but we hope their faith in the word of God will be confirmed. "THE ELEVENTH OF AUGUST, 1840. FALL OF THE OTTOMAN EMPIRE.

"The time and event above named have excited deep interest in the public mind for more than a year past. It is therefore proper that the whole subject should be carefully reviewed, and the exact state of the care presented.

"Has, then, or has not, THE ORIGINAL CALCULATION IN REFERENCE TO THE 11TH OF AUGUST AND THE OTTOMAN EMPIRE BEEN ACCOMPLISHED!

"The calculations are founded on the 9th chapter of Revelation. Therefore, without entering into a very minute exposition of the chapter, it will be sufficient to give the outline of the views entertained in reference to it.

"1. The fifth trumpet is believed to have introduced the Mohamedan delusion, and the time of its sounding to be divided into two periods. The first devoted to the general spread and establishment of the Mohamedan religion; the second to the wearing out and tormenting of the Greek kingdom, under Othman and his successors, but without conquering it. The period of torment was to be five (prophetic) months, or 150 years, beginning when the Mohamedan powers, of which the Ottoman empire was composed, had a king over them and began under him their assault on the Greeks. But from the time of Mahomet to the days of Othman, they were divided into various factions, under different leaders. Othman gathered those factions and consolidated them into an empire, himself the chief.

---

[34] *Signs of the Times*, Boston, November 1, 1840.

"2. The sixth trumpet changed the nature of the war carried on between the Turks and Greeks from torment to death, political death, which was to take place at the end of the five months, or 150 years.

"With these general remarks I will present the original calculation made on these prophetic periods, that the reader may have distinctly before him what we were to anticipate, and compare it with what has actually taken place. Let it be borne in mind, this was not written in 1840 and after the 11th of August, and so adapted to meet the events of that day; but it was written in May, 1838. It may be found in a book entitled 'CHRIST'S SECOND COMING,' by J. Litch, published by D.H. Ela, Boston. p. 153-158....

"The truth is, the Ottoman power in Constantinople was impotent, and could do nothing toward sustaining itself; and it has been since the 11th of August, entirely under the dictation of the great Christian powers of Europe. Nor can it longer stand at all, than they hold it up. Finally, the *London Morning Herald* is right when it says (See the *Signs of the Times*, Jan. 1, 1841.) 'The Ottoman government is reduced to the rank of a puppet, and that the sources of its strength are entirely dried up.'

"In conclusion: I am entirely satisfied that on the 11th of August, 1840, the Ottoman power according to previous calculation, DEPARTED TO RETURN NO MORE. I can now say with the utmost confidence, 'The second woe is past and behold the third woe cometh quickly.' 'Blessed is he that watcheth and keepeth his garments, lest he walk naked and they see his shame.'" L.[35]

(3) By 1841 it was clear that war was not in the making, so Litch shifted ground again and said the fall of Turkey was a voluntary surrender of Turkish supremacy in Constantinople to the Christian powers.

Prophetic Exposition; or a Connected View of the Testimony of the Prophets Concerning the Kingdom of God and the Time of Its Establishment

Josiah Litch

"....WHEN DID MAHOMMEDAN INDEPENDENCE IN CONSTANTINOPLE DEPART?

"In order to answer this question understandingly, it will be necessary to review briefly the history of that power for a few years past.

"For several years the Sultan has been embroiled in war with Mehemet Ali, Pacha of Egypt. In 1838 there was a threatening of war between the Sultan and his Egyptian vassal. Mehemet Ali Pacha, in a note addressed to the foreign consuls, declared that in future he would pay no tribute to the Porte, and that he considered himself independent sovereign of Egypt, Arabia, and Syria. The Sultan, naturally incensed at this declaration, would have immediately commenced hostilities, had he not been restrained by the influence of the foreign ambassadors, and persuaded to delay. This

---

[35] *Signs of the Times*, Boston, February 1, 1841.

war, however, was [193] finally averted by the announcement of Mehemet, that he was ready to pay a million of dollars, arrearages of tribute which he owed the Porte, and an actual payment of $750,000, in August of that year.

"In 1838 hostilities again commenced, and were prosecuted, until, in a general battle between the armies of the Sultan and Mehemet, the Sultan's army was entirely cut up and destroyed, and his fleet taken by Mehemet and carried into Egypt. So completely had the Sultan's fleet been reduced that, when hostilities commenced in August, he had only two first-rates and three frigates, as the sad remains of the once powerful Turkish fleet. This fleet Mehemet positively refused to give up and return to the Sultan, and declared, if the powers attempted to take it from him, he would burn it.

"In this posture affairs stood, when, in 1840, England, Russia, Austria and Prussia interposed, and determined on a settlement of the difficulty; for it was evident, if let alone, Mehemet would soon become master of the Sultan's throne.

"The following extract from an official document, which appeared in the *Moniteur Ottoman*, August 22, 1840, will give an idea of the course of affairs at this juncture. The conference spoken of was composed of the four powers above named, and was held in London, July 15th, 1840: --

"'Subsequent to the occurrence of the disputes alluded to, and after the reverses experienced, as known to all the world, the ambassadors of the great powers at Constantinople, in a collective official note, declared that their governments were unanimously agreed upon taking measures to [194] arrange the said differences. The Sublime Porte, with a view of putting a stop to the effusion of Mussulman blood, and to the various evils which would arise from a renewal of hostilities, ACCEPTED *the intervention of the great powers.*'

"Here was certainly a voluntary surrender of the question into the hands of the great powers. But it proceeds: --

"'His Excellency, Sheikh Effendi, the Bey Likgis, was therefore despatched as plenipotentiary to represent the Sublime Porte at the conference which took place in London, for the purpose in question. It having been felt that all the zealous labors of the conferences of London in the settlement of the Pacha's pretensions were useless, and that the only public way was to have recourse to coercive measures to reduce him to obedience in case he persisted in not listening to pacific overtures, the powers have, together with the OTTOMAN PLENIPOTENTIARY, drawn up and signed a treaty, whereby the *Sultan offers* the Pacha the hereditary government of Egypt, and all that part of Syria extending from the gulf of Suez to the lake of Tiberias, together with the province of Acre, for life; the Pacha, on his part, evacuating all other parts of the Sultan's dominions now occupied by him, and returning the Ottoman fleet. A certain space of time has been granted him to accede to these terms; and, as the proposals of the Sultan and his allies, the four powers, do not admit of any change or qualification, if the Pacha refuse to accede to them, it is evident that the evil consequences to fall upon him will be attributable solely to his own fault.

"'His Excellency, Rifat Bey, Musleshar for foreign affairs, has been despatched in a government [195] steamer to Alexandria, to communicate the ultimatum to the Pacha.'"

"From these extracts it appears, --

"1. That the Sultan, conscious of his own weakness, did voluntarily accept the intervention of the great Christian powers of Europe to settle his difficulties, which he could not settle himself.

"2. That they (the great powers) were agreed on taking measures to settle the difficulties.

"3. That the ultimatum of the London conference left it with the Sultan to arrange the affair with Mehemet, if he could. The Sultan was to offer to him the terms of settlement. So that if Mehemet accepted the terms, there would still be no actual intervention of the powers between the Sultan and Pacha.

"4. That if Mehemet rejected the Sultan's offer, the ultimatum admitted of no change or qualification; *the great powers* stood pledged to coerce him into submission. So long, therefore, as the Sultan held the ultimatum in his own hands, he still maintained the independence of his throne. But that document once submitted to Mehemet, and it would be forever beyond his reach to control the question. It would be for Mehemet to say whether the powers should interpose or not.

"5. The Sultan did despatch Rifat Bey, in a government steamer (which left Constantinople Aug. 5), to Alexandria, to communicate to Mehemet the ultimatum.

"This was a voluntary governmental act of the Sultan.

"*The question now comes up,* WHEN WAS THAT DOCUMENT PUT OFFICIALLY UNDER THE CONTROL OF MEHEMET ALI?

[196] "The following extract of a letter from a correspondent of the *London Morning Chronicle* of Sept. 18, 1840, dated 'Constantinople, Aug. 27th, 1840,' will answer the question: --

"'By the French steamer of the 24th, we have advices from Egypt to the 16th. They show no alteration in the resolution of the Pacha. Confiding in the valor of his Arab army, and in the strength of the fortifications which defend his capital, he seems determined to abide by the last alternative; and as recourse to this, therefore, is now inevitable, all hope may be considered as at an end of a termination of the affair without bloodshed. Immediately on the arrival of the Cyclops steamer with the news of the convention of the *four powers,* Mehemet Ali, it is stated, had quitted Alexandria, to make a short tour through Lower Egypt. The object of his absenting himself at such a moment being partly to avoid conferences with the European consuls, but principally to endeavor, by his own presence, to arouse the fanaticism of the Bedouin tribes, and facilitate the raising of his new levies. During the interval of his absence, the *Turkish government steamer,* WHICH HAD REACHED ALEXANDRIA ON THE 11TH, WITH THE ENVOY RIFAT BEY ON BOARD, had been by his orders placed in quarantine, and he was not released from it till the 16th. Previous, however, to the Porte's leaving, and on the very day on which he had been admitted to pratique, the above-named functionary had had an audience of the Pacha, and had communicated to him the command of the Sultan, with respect to the evacuation of the Syrian provinces, appointing another audience for the next day, when, in the [197] presence of the consuls of the European powers, he would receive from him his definite answer, and inform him of the alternative of his refusing to obey; giving him the ten days which have been allotted him by the convention to decide on the course he should think fit to adopt.'"

"According to the foregoing statement, the ultimatum was *officially put into the power of Mehemet Ali, and was disposed of by his orders, viz., sent to quarantine,* ON THE ELEVENTH DAY OF AUGUST, 1840.

"But have we any evidence, beside the fact of the arrival of Rifat Bey at Alexandria with the ultimatum on the 11th of August, that Ottoman supremacy died, or was dead, that day?

"Read the following, from the same writer quoted above, dated 'Constantinople, August 12, 1840:' –

"'I can add but little to my last letter, on the subject of the plans of the *four powers*; and I believe the details I then gave you comprise everything that is yet decided on. The portion of the Pacha, as I then stated, is not to extend beyond the line of Acre, and does not include either Arabia or Candia. Egypt alone is to be hereditary in his family, and the province of Acre to be considered as a pachalic, to be governed by his son during his lifetime, but afterward to depend on the will of the Porte; and even this latter is only to be granted him on the condition of his accepting these terms, and delivering up the Ottoman fleet within ten days. In the event of his not doing so, this pachalic is to be cut off. Egypt is then to be offered him, [198] with another ten days to deliberate on it, before actual force is employed against him.

"'The manner, however, of applying the force, should he refuse to comply with these terms, -- whether a simple blockade is to be bombarded, and his armies attacked in the Syrian provinces, -- is the point which still remains to be learned; nor does a note delivered yesterday by the four ambassadors, in answer to a question put to them by the Porte, as to the plan to be adopted in such an event, throw the *least light* on this subject. It simply states that provision has been made, and there is no necessity for the Divan alarming itself about any contingency that might afterwards arise.'

"Let us now analyze this testimony.

"1. The letter is dated 'Constantinople, Aug. 12.'

"2. 'Yesterday,' the 11th of August, the Sultan applied, in his own capital, to the ambassadors of four *Christian nations,* to know the measures which were to be taken in reference to a circumstance vitally affecting his empire; and was only told that 'provision had been made,' but he could not know what it was; and that he need give himself no alarm '*about any contingency which might* AFTERWARDS ARISE!!' From that time, then, *they,* and not *he,* would manage that.

"Where was the Sultan's independence that day? GONE. Who had the supremacy of the Ottoman empire in their hands? *The great powers.*

"*According to previous calculation, therefore,* [199] OTTOMAN SUPREMACY *did depart on the* ELEVENTH OF AUGUST *into the hands of the great Christian powers of Europe.*

"Then the second wo [*sic*] is past, and the sixth trumpet has ceased its sounding; and the conclusion is now inevitable, because the word of God affirms the fact in so many words, '*Behold, the third wo* [sic] *cometh quickly.'* And 'in the days of the voice of the seventh angel, when he shall be finished....' But what will take place when the seventh angel sounds? I answer, Great voices will be heard in heaven, saying, 'The kingdoms of this world have become the kingdoms of our Lord and his Christ, and he shall reign forever and ever.' Nor is this event a mere spiritual reign over the kingdoms of this world; but the Revelator goes on to say, 'and thy wrath is come, and the time of the dead, that they should be judged; and that thou shouldest give reward unto thy servants the prophets, the saints, and them that fear thy name, small and great, and shouldest destroy them that destroy the earth.' This, then, is the consummation, when every one shall receive his retribution, according to what he has done.

"'The third wo [sic] cometh quickly.' It cannot be afar off; it is nigh, even at the door. Men may scornfully inquire, 'Where is the promise of his coming? for since the fathers fell asleep, all things continue as they were from beginning.' 'But the day of the Lord will come as a thief in the night.' There are abundant promises of his coming, and that speedily. But I do not expect another sign equal in strength and conclusiveness to the one now spread out before us in the present [200] article. The present calculation was before the world two years and more before the time of fulfillment; and the attention of the whole community was turned toward it. There are few persons, in New England at least, whose minds were not arrested and turned to the 11th of August; and vast multitudes were ready to say, ay, did say, if this event takes place according to the calculation, at the time specified, we will believe the doctrine of the *advent near.* But how is it with them now? Why, just as it was with the old Jews in the days of Christ; when he was every day performing the most stupendous miracles in their sight, they said to him, 'Master, we would see a sign of thee.' So now: men desire a sign from heaven. But let them be assured, they can never have a more convincing one than this; -- the last great prophecy with which a prophetic period is connected, except the concluding period, when Christ will come, has been filled up in the exact time, and has brought us to the very verge of eternity. There is no time to be whiled away in idleness or indifference by those who love the Lord Jesus Christ. They have a great work to do, both for themselves and others. Nor should the sinner delay to awake from his slumbers, and lay hold on eternal life. Grace be with all who love the Lord Jesus Christ."[36]

(4) 1. The new shift was the new proof in 1842; it was a diplomatic "document" or "note" that:

"The ultimatum was *officially put into the power of Mehemet Ali, and was disposed of by his orders, viz., sent to quarantine,* ON THE ELEVENTH DAY OF AUGUST, 1840."[37]

2. In addition to that, Litch claimed further proof:

"But have we any evidence, beside the fact of the arrival of Rifat Bey at Alexandria with the ultimatum on the 11th of August, that Ottoman supremacy died, or was dead, that day? ...'Yesterday,' the 11th of August, the Sultan applied, in his own capital, to the ambassadors of four *Christian nations,* to know the measures which were to be taken in reference to a circumstance vitally affecting his empire; and was only told that 'provision had been made,' but he could not know what it was; and that he need give himself no alarm *'about any contingency which might*

---

[36] Josiah Litch, *Prophetic Exposition; Or A Connected View Of The Testimony Of The Prophets Concerning The Kingdom Of God And The Time Of Its Establishment* (Boston: Joshua V. Himes, 1842), 192-200.
[37] Ibid., 197.

AFTERWARDS ARISE!!' From that time, then, *they,* and not *he,* would manage that.

"Where was the Sultan's independence that day? GONE. Who had the supremacy of the Ottoman empire in their hands? *The great powers.*

"According to previous calculation, therefore, [199] OTTOMAN SUPREMACY *did depart on the* ELEVENTH OF AUGUST *into the hands of the great Christian powers of Europe."[38]*

The "previous calculation" (*Signs of the Times,* February, 1, 1841) was in reference to the fall of Turkey in a voluntary surrender of Turkish supremacy in Constantinople to the Christian powers. Two prominent figures in the Advent movement were Uriah Smith and A. T. Jones. These gentlemen, along with other pioneers, continued to accentuate that understanding of the prediction made by Josiah Litch.

Daniel and the Revelation

Uriah Smith

"The sultan dispatched Rifat Bey on a government steamer to Alexandria, to communicate the ultimatum to the pasha. It was put into his hands, and by him taken in charge, *on the eleventh day of August,* 1840!"[39]

The Great Nations of To-Day

Alonzo Trevier Jones

A. T. Jones worded it this way:

"According to this statement, the ultimatum was officially put into the hands of Mehemet Ali on the ELEVENTH DAY OF AUGUST, 1840."[40]

The point not to be missed in the writings of these two authors is the claim that the fulfillment of the prophecy was in the ultimatum that was officially put into the hands of Mehemet Ali on the eleventh day of August, 1840. The reader now has an unbiased, factual account of what "really happened" on August 11, 1840!

---

[38] Ibid., 198-9.
[39] Uriah Smith, *Daniel and the Revelation* (Washington, D.C.: Review and Herald, 1897), 586.
[40] Alonzo Trévier Jones, *The Great Nations of To-Day,* (Battle Creek, Mich.: Review and Herald, 1901), 81.

2

Examining the Evidence: August 11, 1840?

In chapter 2 we will concentrate on the necessary primary historical documents referenced in chapter 1, along with other primary historical sources and data used among the Millerites. We will do so in order to examine whether the Millerite claims match the events of history for the declared fulfillment of the sixth trumpet of Revelation. Only by assuming nothing can we be fair and open to investigation. The related theological or scriptural issues will not begin to be addressed until chapter 3.

Hard-to-find primary historical documents that were foundational for the Millerite predictions have been placed in the appendices to enable the reader to reach an intelligent and unbiased conclusion for himself regarding the facts. Future references to all documents found in the appendices will be from the original pages. Again, page numbering of the original will be in brackets; all other emphasis is in the original.

The exposition that started it all among the Millerites was William Miller's published interpretation of the trumpets of Revelation. Though unknown to some, his work closely paralleled that of Protestant scholar Albert Barnes. Miller's book was entitled *Evidence from Scripture and History of the Second Coming of Christ, about the year 1843*. It would become the foundation for Josiah Litch's predictions. Although not referenced here we append this document for the benefit of the reader. See **Appendix I**.[41]

The work of Josiah Litch that was referenced in chapter 1, *The Probability of the Second Coming of Christ About A.D. 1843*, contained the basis for the prophetic understanding of the trumpets by Josiah Litch. This was our first referenced source in chapter 1, and is again referenced here and supplied in full for the reader in an appendix. See **Appendix II**.[42]

The second referenced document in chapter 1 that first gave the August 11, 1840, date may be found in **Appendix III**.[43]

The document that was first quoted in chapter 1 regarding the fall of Turkey in a voluntary surrender of Turkish supremacy in Constantinople to the Christian powers may be viewed in **Appendix IV**.[44]

The last document that we referenced in the previous chapter was a diplomatic document or note that in Litch's view fulfilled the prediction of the fall of Turkey in 1842. It can be found in **Appendix V**.[45]

---

[41] William Miller, *Evidence from Scripture and History of the Second Coming of Christ, about the year 1843; exhibited in a course of lectures.* (Boston, MA: 1842), 115-126. See **APPENDIX I**, pg. 171.

[42] Josiah Litch, *The Probability of the Second Coming of Christ About A.D. 1843.*, (Boston: Published by David H. Ela, No. 19 Washington Street, 1838.), Preface & pgs.146-159. See **APPENDIX II**, pg. 178.

[43] *Signs of the Times*, Boston, August 1, 1840. See **APPENDIX III**, pg. 185.

[44] *Signs of the Times*, Boston, February, 1, 1841. See **APPENDIX IV**, pg. 189.

[45] Josiah Litch, *Prophetic Exposition; Or A Connected View Of The Testimony Of The Prophets Concerning The Kingdom Of God And The Time Of Its Establishment.* (Boston: Joshua V. Himes, 1842), 161-200. See **APPENDIX V**, pg. 195.

We must all remember that participants in the 1844 movement believed that the sanctuary was the earth and that it was to be cleansed by fire at the Lord's second coming. Therefore, the "daily" had to be something earthly, as well. All prophecies had to be fulfilled before Jesus' return, and that is why the sixth trumpet had to have a forced fulfillment before that time, as well. For the moment we must set aside the fact that the Turkish nation is with us to this day. The first question that must be asked, in a review of the historical events mentioned in chapter 1 upon which Josiah Litch based his thrice-shifted claim of prophetic fulfillment, is this:

1. Does history confirm the "final dissolution" or "final overthrow" of the Turkish Empire on August 11, 1840? We shall now consult primary sources for our definitive answer:

> "And whoever lives until the year 1839 will see the final dissolution of the Turkish Empire, for then the sixth trumpet will have finished its sounding, which, if I am correct, will be the final overthrow of the Ottoman power. And then will the seventh trump and last woe begin, under which the kingdoms of the earth and the anti-Christian beast will be destroyed, the power of darkness chained, the world cleansed, and the church purified."[46]

> "But when will this power [Turkey] be overthrown? According to the calculations already made, that the five months ended 1449, the hour, fifteen days, the day, one year, the month, thirty years, and the year, three hundred and sixty years; in all, three hundred and ninety-one years and fifteen days, will end in A.D. 1840, some time in the month of August. The prophecy is the most remarkable and definite, (even descending to the days) of any in the Bible, relating to these great events. It is as singular as the record [158] of the time when the empire rose. The facts are now before the reader, and he must make what disposition of them he thinks best. The sixth woe yet continues, and will till the great river Euphrates is dried up, and the seventh trumpet sounds."[47]

These two proclamations by Miller and Litch were open-ended and supplied no specified event that would signal the cause of its demise. Neither did Litch's *Signs of the Times* article of August 1, 1840. Nonetheless, Miller's descriptive language clearly revealed his anticipation of the "final dissolution" or the "final overthrow" of the Turkish Empire and with Litch following in his train, the reader is left with no doubt that the Millerites were awaiting the absolute end of Turkey. They expected it never to be viewed upon the pages of history again.

However, we saw how all of that changed, when in chapter 1 we read Litch's three definitive shifting events after August 11, 1840, that were numbered from 2 to 4 in bold. In *Signs of the Times* of November 1, 1840, regarding what we called No. 2, Litch shifted to August 15, 1840, for the fulfillment of the prophecy by declaring that the act of the Sultan's ambassador in presenting to the pacha of Egypt the "ultimatum" of the four powers met the test of fulfillment. That decision of Litch's was but four days after the 11th of August, the period date first fixed for the termination of

---

[46] William Miller, *Evidence from Scripture and History of the Second Coming of Christ, about the year 1843; exhibited in a course of lectures.* (Boston, MA: 1842), 124.
[47] Josiah Litch, *The Probability of the Second Coming of Christ About A.D. 1843.,* (Boston: David H. Ela, No. 19 Washington Street, 1838), preface & pgs.157-158.

the prophecy. Litch's third shift (No. 3 in chapter 1) in understanding involved both the prophecy's closing event and its date. He specified in *Signs of the Times* of February, 1, 1841, that the fall of Turkey officially occurred in a voluntary surrender of Turkish supremacy in Constantinople to the Christian powers, returning to August 11, 1840, for its fulfillment. The fourth shift (chapter 1's No. 4) came in 1842, when Litch claimed proof of a diplomatic "document" or "note" that:

> "The ultimatum was *officially put into the power of Mehemet Ali, and was disposed of by his orders, viz., sent to quarantine,* ON THE ELEVENTH DAY OF AUGUST, 1840."[48]

In addition to that, Litch claimed further "evidence:"

> "But have we any evidence, beside the fact of the arrival of Rifat Bey at Alexandria with the ultimatum on the 11th of August, that Ottoman supremacy ied, or was dead, that day? ... 'Yesterday,' the 11th of August, the Sultan applied, in his own capital, to the ambassadors of four *Christian nations,* to know the measures which were to be taken in reference to a circumstance vitally affecting his empire; and was only told that 'provision had been made,' but he could not know what it was; and that he need give himself no alarm *'about any contingency which might* AFTERWARDS ARISE!!' From that time, then, *they,* and not *he,* would manage that.
>
> "Where was the Sultan's independence that day? GONE. Who had the supremacy of the Ottoman empire in their hands? *The great powers.*
>
> *"According to previous calculation, therefore,* [199] OTTOMAN SUPREMACY *did depart on the* ELEVENTH OF AUGUST *into the hands of the great Christian powers of Europe."*[49]

The "previous calculation" (*Signs of the Times,* February, 1, 1841) was in reference to the voluntary surrender of Turkish supremacy in Constantinople to the Christian powers on August 11, 1840, thus constituting Turkey's fall from power. Litch thus claimed two distinct events for the fulfillment of the sixth trumpet. At least two prominent Second Advent writers of the time accepted and promoted his second claim. Uriah Smith, in *Daniel and the Revelation,* wrote, "The sultan dispatched Rifat Bey on a government steamer to Alexandria, to communicate the ultimatum to the pasha. It was put into his hands, and by him taken in charge, *on the eleventh day of August,* 1840!"[50] A. T. Jones, in his *The Great Nations of To-Day,* wrote, "According to this statement, the ultimatum was officially put into the hands of Mehemet Ali on the ELEVENTH DAY OF AUGUST, 1840."[51] Thus the widely-received view at the time was Fitch's claim that the "fulfillment" of the prophecy was in the "ultimatum" that was officially "put into the hands" of Mehemet Ali on the eleventh day of August, 1840.

Now we'll read the originals they quoted from, and the discrepancies will become obvious.

There are two definitive, claimed events that require a thorough and honest investigation. After all, if it is truth, then truth can withstand investigation:

---

[48] Josiah Litch, *Prophetic Exposition; Or A Connected View Of The Testimony Of The Prophets Concerning The Kingdom Of God And The Time Of Its Establishment.* (Boston: Joshua V. Himes, 1842), 192-200.

[49] Ibid., 198-9.

[50] Uriah Smith, *Daniel and the Revelation* (Washington, DC: Review and Herald, 1897), 586.

[51] Alonzo Trévier Jones, *The Great Nations of To-Day,* (Battle Creek, Mich.: Review and Herald, 1901), 81.

1. The final declaration and claim, upon further "evidence," was now that the fall of Turkey was a voluntary surrender of Turkish supremacy in Constantinople to the Christian powers, rather than by war, and that it was "fulfilled" on August 11, 1840, rather than on August 15, 1840.
2. The final declaration and claim of fundamental "fulfillment" of the prophecy was based on the "ultimatum" that was officially "put into the hands" of Mehemet Ali on the eleventh day of August, 1840, and was acknowledged as such by the Adventist pioneers.

We shall begin by examining the primary evidence concerning the historical event identified in #1, to see if Litch's understanding was correct. The treaty that the European powers made with Turkey will answer this question sufficiently. In *Hertslet's Map of Europe by Treaties*, July 15, 1840, the object of that conference is clearly stated in the preamble to that treaty:

IN THE NAME OF THE MOST MERCIFUL GOD.

"His Highness, the Sultan, having addressed himself to their Majesties the Queen of the United Kingdom of Great Britain and Ireland, the Emperor of Austria, King of Hungary and Bohemia, the King of Prussia, and the Emperor of All the Russias, to ask their support and assistance in the difficulties in which he finds himself placed by reason of the hostile proceedings of Mehemet Ali, Pasha of Egypt, -- difficulties which threaten with danger the Integrity of the Ottoman Empire, and the Independence of the Sultan's Throne, -- Their said Majesties, moved by the sincere friendship which subsists between them and the Sultan; animated by the desire of maintaining the Integrity and Independence of the Ottoman Empire as a security for the Peace of Europe; faithful to the engagement which they contracted by the Collective Note presented to the Porte by their respective Government representatives at Constantinople, on the 27th of July, 1839; -- and desirous, moreover, to prevent the effusion of blood which would be occasioned by a continuance of the hostilities which have recently broken out in Syria between the authorities of the Pasha of Egypt and the subjects of the Sultan; their said Majesties and His Highness the Sultan have resolved, for the aforesaid purposes, to conclude together a Convention and they have therefore named as their Plenipotentiaries, that us to say.....

[53] "*(Translation). The undersigned have this morning received instructions from their respective Governments, in virtue of which they have the honor to inform the Sublime Porte that the five Great Powers have come to an understanding on the Eastern Question, and to prevail upon her to suspend all definite determination without their cooperation.

"Constantinople, 27th July 1839.

"Baron de Sturmer

"Bonsonby.

"A. Bouteneff.

"Baron Roussin

"Comte de Koenigsmarch."[52]

When the Sultan allowed his ambassadors to sign that document in his behalf, he clearly, by that act, signed away Turkish independence. From the signing of that document till the present time, that power has been maintained solely by the forbearance of the great nations in order to preserve a balance of the powers. That treaty, however, with its annexed stipulations, was, in fact, a pledge to support and maintain the Turkish Empire against the Egyptian monarch Mohammed Ali. Therefore, it cannot be said that Turkey fell. Rather, there was a deliberate, cooperative preservation of Turkey, for mutually-beneficial political ends. The claim, therefore, that the fall of Turkey came about through a voluntary surrender of Turkish supremacy to the Christian powers on August 11, 1840, is outright false.

That treaty was officially, legally signed into effect on the 27th of July, 1839, so far as Turkish independence was concerned in that particular confrontation. The Sultanate was not abolished until November 1, 1922, and by 1923 leadership of Turkey was transformed into a western-style democracy which remains to this day. When the Sultan dispatched Rifat Bey on a government steamer to Alexandria with the "ultimatum" to the pasha of Egypt, he was simply carrying out the demands of the four powers to whom he had already submitted; he had no more voice in the matter. As we continue on very shortly with the same primary document, we will show that to be the very case.

The reader will also see and understand precisely who dictated to Mehemet Ali the two ten-day periods of time given him, and the conditions and terms that commenced their initial countdown. Also, terms were clearly defined for Mehemet Ali to return the captured Turkish naval fleet to the battered and defeated Sultan. It will be seen that the Sultan's envoy, Rifat Bey, is simply the agent used to place into the hands of Mehemet Ali the demands of the four powers, and nothing more. With the treaty of July 15, 1840, France was no longer part of the governing body of five European powers; Turkish oversight was left to the four remaining signees of the treaty. **Appendix VI**[53]

We now continue with the treaty of the four European powers of July 15, 1840, with the added, annexed stipulations to be placed upon the Egyptian Mehemet Ali:

> "...And desirous moreover, to prevent the effusion of the hostilities which have recently broke out in Syria between the Authorities of the Pasha of Egypt and the subjects of the Sultan; their said Majesties and His Highness the Sultan have resolved, for the aforesaid purposes to conclude together a Convention, and they therefore named as their Plenipotentiaries, that is to say:
>
> "Her Majesty, the Queen of the United Kingdom of Great Britain and Ireland, the Right Honorable Henry John, Viscount Palmerston, Baron Temple, a Peer of Ireland, a member of Her Brittanic Majesty's Most Honorable Privy Council, Knight Grand Cross of the Most Honorable Order of Bath, a Member of Parliament, and the Principle Secretary of State for Foreign Affairs:

---

[52] Edward Hertslet, *The map of Europe by treaty; showing the various political and territorial changes which have taken place since the general peace of 1814* (London: Butterworths, 1875-91), 1009.

[53] For an understanding of how France separated herself from the four powers we direct the reader to *The Morning Chronicle*, Oct. 3, 1840. See **APPENDIX VI,** pg. 220. "On July 3, 1840, without the knowledge of the French ambassador, was signed the convention of London, by which the four Powers, Russia, Austria, Prussia, and England, undertook to protect the Sultan against Mehemet Ali" [whose cause against the Sultan was being championed by France]. W. Alison Phillips, *Modern Europe 1815-1899* (London: Rivingtons, 1932), 228.

"His Majesty King of Prussia, the Sieur Henry Williams, Baron de Bulow, his Chamberlain, Actual Privy Councillor, Envoy Extraordinary and Minister Plenipotentiary of Her Brittanic Majesty, etc.,

"His Majesty the Emperor of Austria, King of Hungary and Bohemia, the Sieur Philip, Baron de Neumann, his Aulick Councillor and his Plenipotentiary to her Brittanic Majesty, etc.;

"His Majesty, Emperor of all the Russians, the Sieur Philip, Baron de Brunnow, his Privy Counciller, etc.;

"And His Majesty the Most Noble, Most Powerful, and Most Magnificent Sultan Abdul-Medjid, Emperor of the Ottomans, Chekib Effendi, decorated with the Eichan Iftihar of the first class, Beyhkdgi of the Imperial Divan, Honorary Councillor of the Department of Foreign affairs, His Ambassador Extraordinary to her Brittanic Majesty; -

"Who, having reciprocally communicated to each other their Full Powers, found to be in good and due form, have agreed upon and signed the following articles:

"<u>Arrangement in favor of Mehemet Ali.</u>

"His Highness the Sultan, having come to an agreement with their Majesties the Queen of the United Kingdom of Great Britain and Ireland, the Emperor of Austria, King of Hungary and Bohemia, the King of Prussia, and the Emperor of all the Russians, as to the conditions of the arrangement which it is the intention of His Highness to grant to Mehemet Ali, conditions which are specified in the separate Act hereunto annexed, their Majesties engage to act in perfect accord and to unit their efforts in order to determine Mehemet Ali to conform to that arrangement; each of the High Contracting Parties reserving to itself to cooperate for that purpose, according to the means of action which each may have at his disposal.

"Measures to be adopted in case of refusal by Mehemet Ali. Naval Assistance by Great Britain to Turkey.

"Art. II

"If the Pasha of Egypt should refuse to accept the above measure, which will be communicated to him by the Sultan, with the concurrence of their aforesaid Majesties engaged to take at the request of the Sultan, measures concerted and settled between them in order to carry that arrangement into effect. In the meanwhile, the Sultan having requested his said allies to unite, and to assist him to cut off the communications by sea between Egypt and Syria, and to prevent the transport of troops, horses, arms, and warlike stores of all kinds from one province to another, their Majesties the Queen of the United Kingdom of Great Britain and Ireland, and the Emperor of Austria, the King of Hungary and Bohemia, engage to go immediately, to that effect the necessary orders to their Naval Commanders in the Mediterranean. Their said Majesties further engage that the Naval Commanders of their squadrons shall, according to means at their command, afford in the name of the Alliance, all the support and assistance in their power to those subjects of the Sultan who may manifest their fidelity and allegiance to their Sovereign.

"Defense of Constantinople by Allied Powers against Mehemet Ali.

"Art. III

"If Mehemet Ali, after having refused to submit to the conditions of the arrangements above mentioned, shall direct his land or sea forces against

Constantinople, the High Contracting Parties which on the express demand of the Sultan, addressed to the representatives at Constantinople, agree in such case to comply with the request of the Sovereign, and to prevent any advance on His Throne by means of cooperation agreed upon by mutual consent, for the purpose of placing the two straits of the Bosphorus and Dardanelles, as well as the capital of the Ottoman Empire, in security against all aggression.

"Allied Forces to withdraw at Request of Sultan.

"It is further agreed that the forces which, in virtue of such concert may be sent as aforesaid, shall there remain employed as long as their presence shall be required by the Sultan; and when His Highness shall deem their presence no longer necessary, the said forces shall simultaneously withdraw, and shall return to the Black Sea and to the Mediterranean respectively.

"ANNEX – Separate Act to the Convention of 15th July, 1840.

"Conditions imposed on Mehemet Ali. Withdrawal of Egyptian Troops from Arabia, Candia, etc.

"The Sultan, however, in making these offers, attaches thereto the condition that Mehemet Ali shall accept them within the space of ten days after the communication thereof shall have been made to him at Alexandria by an agent of His Highness; and that Mehemet Ali shall at the same time place in the hands of that agent the necessary instructions to the Commanders of his sea and land forces to withdraw immediately from Arabia, and from all the Holy Cities which are therein from all other parts of the Ottoman Empire which are not comprised within the limits of Egypt, and within those of the Pashalic of Acre, as above defined.

"Time within which Mehemet Ali is to accept arrangement.

"2. If within the space of ten days, fixed as above, Mehemet Ali should not accept the above mentioned arrangement, the Sultan will then withdraw the offer of the life administration of the Pashalic of Acre; but His Highness will still consent to grant to Mehemet Ali, for himself and for his descendants in the direct line, the administration of the Pashalic of Egypt, provided such offer be accepted within the space of the ten days next following, that is to say, within a period of twenty days, to be reckoned from the day on which the communication shall have been made to him; and provided that in this case also, he places in the hands of the agent of the Sultan, the necessary instructions to his military and naval commanders to withdraw immediately within the limits, and into the ports of the Pashalic of Egypt.

"Tributes to be Paid to the Sultan.

"3. The annual Tribute to be paid to the Sultan by Mehemet Ali, shall be proportioned to the greater or less amount of territory of which the latter may obtain the administration, according as he accepts the first or the second alternative.

"Mehemet Ali to deliver up the Turkish Fleet

"4. It is moreover, expressly understood that, in the first as in the second alternative, Mehemet Ali (before the expiration of the specified period of 10 or of 20 days), shall be bound to deliver up the Turkish Fleet, with the whole of its crews and equipments, into the hands of the Turkish agent who shall be charged to receive the same. The commanders of the allied squadrons shall be present at such delivery....

"Offers to be withdrawn if not accepted within 20 days.

"7. If, at the expiration of the period of 20 days after the communication shall have been made (according to the stipulation of Sec. 2) to him, Mehemet Ali shall not accede to the proposed arrangement and shall not accept the hereditary Pashalic of Egypt, the Sultan will consider himself at liberty to withdraw that offer, and to follow, in consequence, such ulterior course as his own interests and the counsels of his Allies may suggest to him.

"Separate Act to form part of the Convention of 15th of July 1840.

"8. The present Separate Act shall have the same force and validity as if it were inserted, word for word, in the Convention of this date....

"Done in London, the 15th day of July, in the year of Our Lord, 1840.

"(L.S.) Palmerston
"(L.S.) Neumann
"(L.S.) Bulow
"(L.S.) Brunnow
"(L.S.) Chekib."[54]

In light of the facts from the primary historical source, it is crystal clear that the claim that Turkey's acceptance of intervention by and dependence upon four European powers on August 11, 1840, equaled the end of the Turkish Empire is unwarranted and, again, utterly false.

What follows next is simply an illustration of European intervention in Turkish affairs between 1827 and 1856. The reader will see that it seems difficult to make 1840 stand out as conspicuously as one would like when marking the termination of a prophetic period. To Josiah Litch, the convention of the Powers in 1840 and their intervention to maintain the Sultan seemed decisive, as he expected the result would be the speedy fall of Turkey. But looking at it in relation to events before and after, it does not stand out so prominently in history.

For years before and years after the treaty of July 15, 1840, the combination of the Powers intervened in Turkish affairs, sometimes in favor of the Sultan, with his consent, and sometimes against him without consent. For example:

> 1827 – "In July, 1827, England, France, and Russia signed a treaty of London, by which they bound themselves to compel the Turk, by force, if it should be needful, to acknowledge the freedom of Greece."[55] The powers sunk the entire Turkish fleet in their handling of the matter, and of this interference in Turkey's affairs, the famous Metternich said: "For Europe the event of October 20 began a new era."
>
> 1829 – Treaty between Russia and Turkey. "Wellington declared that the Turkish Power in Europe no longer existed, and that this being so, it was absurd to talk of bolstering it up. In any case, since the Russian occupation of the principalities made Turkey to all intents and purposes a province of Russia, the integrity of the Ottoman Empire was no longer of supreme importance to England."[56]
>
> 1833 – "On July 8, 1833, was signed the famous treaty of Unkiar Skellisi, which, under the form of an offensive and defensive alliance between Russia and the Ottoman Empire, virtually in the words of Count Nesselrode himself, legalized for the future the armed intervention of Russia in Turkish affairs.... In France and England

[54] Ibid., 1009.
[55] Edward Augustus Freeman, *The Ottoman Power in Europe; its Growth, and its Decline* (London: Macmillan and Co., 1877), 183.
[56] W. Alison Phillips, *Modern Europe 1815-1899* (London: Rivingtons, 1932), 165.

the news of the conclusion of this treaty roused immense excitement. Palmerston declared that it placed Turkey under Russian vassalage, and that, as far as England was concerned, it [Turkey] had no existence."[57]

1841 – "Mohammed Ali, by the treaty of 1841, was confined to his Egyptian possessions, under the suzerainty of the Sultan, the integrity and independence of whose empire was now placed formally under the guarantee of the Great Powers. The treaty of 1841 was a new and vital departure: Turkey was for the first time placed in a state of tutelage."[58]

1856 – (after the Crimean War) "The war was ended by the treaty of Paris in 1856. The terms of that treaty are well worth studying. By its seventh article, the powers which signed it, France, Austria, Great Britain, Prussia, and Sardinia, declared that the Sublime Porte, -- that is, the Turk, was admitted to partake in the advantages of public law and the European concert.... To admit the Turk was to give an European recognition to a power which is not and never can be European.

In the same spirit the powers further engaged to respect the 'independence and territorial integrity of the Ottoman Empire.'"[59]

We shall resume our investigation of primary historical documents, this time to determine if Litch's second claim was true or false. Our question this time is, "Was the ultimatum that was in the form of a diplomatic 'document' or 'note' officially 'put into the hands' of Mehemet Ali on the eleventh day of August, 1840?"

We begin this search in another document acquired from the archives of the General Conference of Seventh-day Adventists in Silver Spring, MD. It was from an inquiry by LeRoy Edwin Froom in his quest for an answer to the same question we have posed:

"In our D. & R. page 586, Elder Uriah Smith writes as if it were an established historic fact what he states, and it is as follows:

"The Sultan dispatched Rifat Bey on a government steamer to Alexandria to communicate the Ultimatum to the pasha. It was put into his (the Pasha's hands) and by him (pasha) taken in charge on the eleventh day of August, 1840."

"When Elder A. T. Jones was in his prime, he wrote very emphatically in 'The Great Nations of Today,' page 80-81, saying, 'The Ultimatum was put into the hands of Mehemet Ali on August 11, 1840,' and in support of his statement, he seems to quote from the *London Morning Chronicle* of September 18, 1840.

"Elder Conradi, in his work on the 9th chapter of Revelation, seems to be more discreet in making statements. He quotes from the Hamburger Correspondent of September 8, 1840, saying 'Rifat Bey arrived at Alexandria on August 11, 1840, with the ultimatum of the Porte,' but is silent as to the deliverance of it to the Pasha.

"Where got Elder Smith his positive information from? I do not know.

"Where got Elder A. T. Jones his information? I do know. In correspondence with Prof. Magan in 1909 over the Eastern Question. I asked him [Magan] in one of my letters if A. T. Jones had copied from the papers themselves of 1840. Those things

---

[57] Ibid., 216

[58] Stanley Lane-Poole, *The Story of Turkey* (New York: G.P. Putnam's Sons, 1888). NA.

[59] Edward Augustus Freeman, *The Ottoman power in Europe; its growth, and its decline* (London: Macmillan and Co., 1877), 195-6.

which he had given on the August 11th, 1840, question in 'The Great Nations of Today.'

"The following is Brother Jones' answer to my question.

"Omaha, Nebraska, Nov. 12, 1909.

"'Your letter reached me here yesterday. Those quotations – Moniteur Othoman, and London Morning Chronicle, I got from the original pamphlet on the 'Seven Trumpets' published by our people away back, and I think it was practically a reprint of the one used in the 1844 movement on that subject, and that one of '44 was written, I think by Josiah Litch, at the time of the fulfillment of the prophecy in 1840: And the quotations were taken evidently from the papers themselves, just as we would take a news item from a paper today. For this reason I am sure that the quotations never appeared in any book of history nor in any other connection than that of the pamphlet on the seven trumpets as a reprint of the original one of 1840-44. The only way to verify the item would be, of course, reference to the papers themselves in London, and when I was there I did not do it. I wish that I had.' (Signed) A. T. Jones."[60]

LeRoy Froom visited the Congressional Library in Washington, D.C., where he found many good newspaper articles shedding light on the events that transpired on and around August 11, 1840. However, he was unsuccessful in obtaining the newspaper article that was claimed by J. Litch, U. Smith and A. T. Jones to prove the August 11, 1840, prophetic event. This is what Froom said:

> "The London *Morning Chronicle* from September 17 to October 3, 1840, is missing. No answer can be given at the Congressional Library why it are missing."[61]

The missing newspaper article was originally printed in the London *Morning Chronicle* on Friday, September 18, 1840, in column 1 on page 4. That newspaper has long since stopped being printed; however, I have been fortunate enough to have found and obtained a copy of the original in full, along with many other such documents. Therefore, we can find the answer we seek from the very same sources used by Josiah Litch and the Millerites in their claim that the ultimatum, in the form of a diplomatic "document" or "note," was officially "put into the hands" of Mehemet Ali on August 11, 1840. The historical truth can now be ascertained. It is long past time to lay this controversial issue to rest permanently, and the following documentation will do just that. *The Times* and *The Morning Chronicle*, both of London, were the primary sources used to validate the claims by Josiah Litch and the Millerites. The reader may now read the pertinent articles without interruption; an analysis will follow:

The Times
September 4, 1840

"The arrival of Rifat Bey and Mr. Alison in the Bair-Tahir steamer from Constantinople on the 11th inst. with the Ultimatum of the four powers produced a great sensation here. The Pasha was absent at Damietta (it is believed on purpose to

---

[60] LeRoy Froom, Box 6805, Archives, Statistics, and Research, General Conference of Seventh-day Adventists, Silver Spring, MD.
[61] Ibid.

be out of the way at the moment when all eyes would naturally be turned on his, to read the fate of Egypt in their expression) and speculation was left to indulge itself at leisure: for all other occupation amongst the commercial portion of the inhabitants was virtually at an end."[62]

The Times
September 5, 1840

"I wrote to you yesterday by the Levant steamer a very long letter, (this writing is from a French correspondent) in which I recounted the events now passing in our city. I acquainted you with the manner in which the Pasha received the alleged envoy of the Porte. Rifat Bey, who is in reality the envoy of the four powers, coalesced against us."[63]

The Times
September 4, 1840

"He (Mehemet Ali) appears to have made up his mind which part he will take, but seems to think it beneath his dignity to be in any degree of haste to announce it, and says smilingly to inquiring friends, 'Let us first see what their proposition is. We shall hear it all on Monday.' This afternoon, [Saturday, August 15, 1840] Rifat Bey was admitted to a complimentary interview on obtaining free prat que after his brief purification, but the formal declaration of the four great powers will not be delivered until tomorrow."[64] ["Tomorrow" would be Sunday, August 16, 1840.]

The Times
September 7, 1840

"A Turkish steamer has arrived in the City from Constantinople with a Turkish officer, a member of the Council, and several attaches of the four allied powers, bringing the Ultimatum of the Porte and these powers....

"His Highness, the Pasha, was absent, and returned here yesterday morning, when he was received under salutes from the fleet in the bay. ["Yesterday morning" is August 15th.] Other communications state positively that a blockade is soon expected to take place.

"On the morning of the 16th inst. the Ultimatum was communicated to the Pasha and 20 days are given him to decide thereon."[65]

The Morning Chronicle
September 7, 1840

---

[62] *The Times*, London, September 4, 1840, page 4, col. 6. Private Correspondence, Alexandria, August 16.

[63] *The Times,* London, Saturday, September 5, 1840. Alexandria, August 17, 1840.

[64] *The Times*, London, Friday, September 4, 1840, page 5, col. 1. Alexandria, August 15, 1840.

[65] *The Times*, London, Monday, September 7, 1840, p. 3, col. 3. Alexandria, August 16, 1840.

"At length, 'The Eastern Question' seems to have reached a crisis. On the morning of the 11th a steamer of the Sultan arrived here from Constantinople, having on board Rifat Bey, on a special mission to present to the Pasha the ultimatum of the Porte, with the convention signed by the four powers. Although the envoy was not out of quarantine, and of course his communication not made until yesterday ["until yesterday" = August 16], yet the object of his mission soon became very generally known here, nor would it be easy to give you an idea of the anxiety and excitement which it created....

"When the envoy of the Sultan has presented the Ultimatum, he waits for ten days, that is, to the 26th for the answer of the pasha. The consuls of the four nations communicating to the pasha the convention signed at London will urge upon him the acceptance of the proposed terms. If rejected at the end of ten days, the second proposition will be made, and if that be rejected at the end of ten days, the four consuls will strike their flags and leave Alexandria....

"It was late on the evening of the 14th when the Pasha returned from an excursion he had been making up the Nile. When informed that a British ship had anchored off the palace, he took immediate precautions, ordering the gunners to remain at the batteries through the night. In the morning, a transport was dispatched with ammunition for Syria. Indeed, everything indicates an intention on the part of the Pasha to meet force by force."[66]

A comparative analysis of these newspaper excerpts and Josiah Litch's several predictions for the date of the alleged fall of Turkey now follows:

1. July 27, 1839, was an important date in regards to "Turkish independence" or, rather, "Turkish dependence" upon the powers of Europe. In fact, this was recognized the world over, as we just read in one of our previous correspondences from the treaty of the European powers:

The Times

September 5, 1840

"I acquainted you with the manner in which the Pasha received the alleged envoy of the Porte. Rifat Bey, who is in reality the envoy of the four powers, coalesced against us."[67]

2. On August 5th, 1840, Rifat Bey and Mr. Alison were sent to the government steamer Bair-Tahir from Constantinople to Alexandria, Egypt, to deliver the ultimatum to Mehemet Ali. They arrived on August 11, and were put in quarantine.

3. The Pasha was purposely absent and returned late on the 14th, which was Friday.

---

[66] *The Morning Chronicle*, London, Monday, September 7, 1840, pg. 1, col. 5-6. Alexandria, Egypt: August 17, 1840.
[67] The Times, London, Saturday, September 5, 1840. Alexandria, August 17, 1840.

4. Rifat Bey had an audience with the Pasha on August 15, which was Saturday, during which it was arranged that the next day, August 16, which was Sunday, Rifat Bey, in company with the representatives of the four great powers (England, Russia, Austria, and Prussia), the ultimatum should be delivered to the Pasha. Perhaps word of this first audience with the Pasha on Aug. 15 is why Josiah Litch shifted his prediction in the *Signs of the Times*, November 1, 1840, from the 11th to the 15th of August, 1840.

5. The ultimatum was delivered on that very day of August 16, 1840, which was Sunday. It was delivered on that day and no other, according to *The Times*, London, September 7, 1840, and also according to *The Morning Chronicle*, London, September 7, 1840. A confirmation of that fact is that the first of the two ten-day periods allotted to Mehemet Ali by the four European powers ended on the 26th of August, 1840, which will shortly be proved. Therefore, that diplomatic "document" or "note" was officially "put into the hands" of Mehemet Ali on Sunday, the sixteenth day of August, 1840, and no other.

This should prove conclusive, but wait! We have more. We now supply the reader with the minutes of the British government's *Parliamentary Papers*, which contain an account of those diplomatic meetings. These *Parliamentary Papers* extracts will change nothing; they will simply confirm and prove beyond a doubt the integrity and correctness of the reporters' daily accounts. They will further establish the inviolability of the five facts in this case, as just stated.

> "PARLIAMENTARY PAPERS, VOL. 29, PART 2.
> "No. 116.
> "Colonel Hodges to Viscount Parlmerston. - - (Received September 9).
>
> (Extract)   Alexandria, August 17, 1840.
> "On the 11th instant, Rifat Bey, bearer of the demands of the Sublime Porte, reached Alexandria. The general object of his mission soon began to be known in the city, and as the French and Russian Consuls-General had within a few days officially cautioned the merchants and residents of their respective nations, I felt that the time was now arrived to follow that example. I therefore addressed to Mr. Consul Larking the enclosed dispatch of the 11th instant, which produced the three subsequent public letters of the 12th, 14th, and 15th of August, all of which I have the honor to submit to your perusal.
>
> "Inclosure 1 in Number 116.
> "Colonel Hodges to Mr. Consul Larking.
>
> (Circular)   Alexandria, August 11, 1840.
> "Sir,
>
> "THE resolutions which have been taken by four of the Great European Powers for the pacification of the East, the arrival this morning of a special Envoy from the Sublime Porte, and the inflexible demeanour assumed by Mehemet Ali, have inspired some doubts as to the continuance of friendly relations with the Pasha.
>
> "Inclosure 1 in Number 117.
> "Colonel Hodges to Viscount Ponsonby
>
> (Extract)   Alexandria, August 16, 1840.
> "On the 11th of August, Rifat Bey reached this port, and was subjected to six days' quarantine, which expire this morning. He has been lodged very

commodiously in the Pasha's sea baths. Both in conjunction with my Colleagues, and alone, I have had with his Excellency several protracted and confidential interviews. We are all gratified by the very judicious choice of the Sublime Porte, whose Envoy displays those rare qualities which render him perfectly equal to the difficult mission with which he is entrusted.

"Inclosure 2 in Number 117.

"Colonel Hodges to Viscount Ponsoby.

(Extract)   Alexandria, August 16, 1840.

[6] "ON the arrival of Rifat Bey in Alexandria, Mehemet Ali was absent from thence on a tour of the Delta.

"The Pasha returned to this city on the afternoon of the 14th instant. The same evening he was visited by the French Consul-General.

"Early this morning, Rifat Bey was liberated from quarantine, and at half-past eight o'clock, A.M., he had his first audience of the Pasha. This was private, as had been arranged between Rifat Bey and the Consuls-General of the Four Powers.

"It appears that the reception of the Sultan's Envoy was anything but gracious or favorable; but the results of that interview are fully related by Rifat Bey himself, in Minutes which I have now the honor to inclose.

"Discouraged by his want of success, Rifat Bey at first proposed an immediate return to Constantinople; but, in conjunction with my Colleagues, I represented to him the propriety of awaiting the expiration of the first and second periods of ten days specified in the Convention, and at the termination of which it will be proper to make new and formal summonses of compliance. With these suggestions Rifat Bey has fully concurred, to console him for his recent check.

"Inclosure 3 in No. 117 (Translation)

"Report of the Interview between Rifat Bey and Mehemet Ali.

"THIS day, Sunday, at 2 o'clock, Turkish time, His Excellency, Rifat Bey proceeded to Mehemet Ali, at his express invitation, accompanied by the individuals attached to his person, and the result of the Interview which took place between them is contained in the following lines:

"No. 130.

"Colonel Hodges to Viscount Palmerston – (Received September 9)

"My Lord,

"I HAVE the honor to enclose, for the information of your Lordship, the minutes of an interview which took place this morning between Mehemet Ali and his Excellency Rifat Bey, the special Envoy from the Sublime Porte, who was accompanied by the Consuls-General of the Four Powers parties to the Convention of the 15th of July.

"I have, &c.,

(Signed)   G. Lloyd Hodges.

"Inclosure in Number 130.

"Minutes of an interview on the 26th of August, between Mehemet Ali and Rifat Bey, accompanied by the Consuls-General of the Four Powers, on the expiration of the first term of ten days.

"No. 199

<u>"Colonel Hodges to Viscount Palmerston. – (Received October 6.)</u>

[7] Alexandria, September 6, 1840.

"My Lord,

"YESTERDAY morning his Excellency Rifat Bey, together with the Consuls-General of the Four Powers parties to the Convention of the 15th of July, waited on Mehemet Ali in order to receive his final reply to the demands of the Sublime Porte. The Pasha, being confined to his room by a painful indisposition, gave his official answer through the medium of his Minister, Sami Bey.

"The details of our interview are contained in the Minutes I have the honor to inclose, and of which the original was yesterday forwarded to his Excellency Rifat Bey, and the consequent want of his signature prevent my forwarding to your Lordship a duplicate instead of a copy.

"I have, &c.,

(Signed) G. Lloyd Hodges.

"Inclosure in No. 190 (Translation)

"<u>Minutes of the interview which took place on the 5th of September, between Sami Bey and Rifat Bey, accompanied by the Consuls-General of the Four Powers.</u>

"PARLIAMENTARY PAPERS, VOLUME 29, PART I.

"No. 616.

(Translation)

"SEPARATE ACT

"<u>Annexed to the Convention concluded at London on the 15th of July, 1840, between the Courts of Great Britain, Austria, Prussia, and Russia, on the one part, and the Sublime Ottoman Porte, on the other.</u>

"HIS Highness the Sultan intends to grant, and to cause to be notified to Mehemet Ali, the conditions of the arrangement hereinafter detailed: --

"2.

"If within the space of ten days, fixed above, Mehemet Ali should not accept the above-mentioned arrangement, the Sultan will then withdraw the offer of the life administration of the Pashalic of Acre; but His Highness will still consent to grant Mehemet Ali, for himself and for his descendants in the direct line, the administration of the Pashalic of Egypt, provided such offer be accepted within the space of the ten days next following; that is to say, within a period of twenty days to be reckoned from the day on which the communication shall have been made to him; and provided that in this case also, he places in the hands of the agent of the Sultan, the necessary instructions to his military and naval Commanders, to withdraw immediately within the limit, and into the ports of the Pashalic of Egypt."[68]

The reader now has, for the first time, an unbiased, factual account of the stream of pertinent events from the primary sources. Now, however, given the conflict between the dates of these official documents and Fitch's chosen and oft-repeated date of prophetic fulfillment, the most logical question the reader might ask next is, "Is there anything in *The Morning Chronicle* of September 18, 1840, that could be said to prove the August 11, 1840, date, as claimed by Litch, Smith, Jones and

---

[68] British Government *Parliamentary Papers*, 1840.

others?" After all, the accounts on both sides are taken from one of the same previously-read newspapers, *The Morning Chronicle* of September 7, 1840. Can there be such a contradiction of events just eleven days earlier from the same newspaper, as well as from their very own correspondent? The answer will become obvious as one reads the claimed documentation in its entirety for himself. Only in this way can we be thorough and honest in our quest for truth. Readers will find the full article below:

The Morning Chronicle

September 18, 1840

TURKEY

CONSTANTINOPLE, Aug. 27.

[From our own correspondent.]

"By the French steamer of the 24th we have advices from Egypt to the 16th, but they show no alteration in the resolution of the Pacha. Confiding in the valour of his Arab army, and in the strength of the fortifications which defend his capital, he seems determined to abide by the last alternative; and as recourse to this is, therefore, now inevitable, all hope may be considered at an end of a termination of the affair without bloodshed. Immediately on the arrival of the Cyclops steamer with the news of the convention with the four Powers, Mehemet Ali, it is stated, had quitted Alexandria to make a short tour through Lower Egypt: the object of his absenting himself at such a moment being partly to avoid conferences with the European consuls, but principally to endeavour by his own presence to rouse the fanaticism of the Bedouin tribes, and facilitate the raising of his new levies. During the interval of this absence, the Turkish government steamer which had reached Alexandria on the 11th, with the envoy, Rifaat Bey, on board, had been by his orders placed in quarantine, and she [sic] was not released from it till the 16th. Previous, however, to the poet's leaving, viz., on the very day on which he had been admitted to pratique, the above-named functionary had had an audience of the Pacha, and had communicated to him the commands of the Sultan with respect to the evacuation of the Syrian provinces, appointing another audience for the following day, when in the presence of the consuls of the European powers, he would receive from him his definitive answer, and inform him of the alternative of his refusing to obey, giving him the ten days which have been allotted him by the convention to decide on the course he shall think fit to adopt. But, though this period must still elapse before his reply can be officially received, it may be said, in fact, to be already known, for, nothing daunted by the presence of the Bellerophon, which, with four other vessels, whose names are not given, is stated to have anchored off the port on the 14th, he had at once expressed to Rifaat Bey his resolution of confiding in the success of his army; and the preparations he is making for a determined resistance are a sufficient earnest of his intention to keep to it. Allowing, therefore, these ten days to expire, and another ten for the second proposal, which he will hardly accept after refusing the first one, we may look forward to the 6th proximo as the period when hostilities will be positively commenced, and a few hours will doubtless suffice for the complete overthrow of the Arab empire. According to a letter in the *Echo de l'Orient,* three regiments of the Yermen army have already arrived at Alexandria, and had received orders to march to El Arich, the first town on the Syrian coast, probably intended as a *corps de reserve,* in the event of the defeat of Ibrahim Pacha. The remainder of the troops daily expected were to form a camp at Damanhour, into which also would be thrown a corps of Bedouins of two thousand strong, under the command of Ahmet Pacha and Ibrahim Kutchuk Pacha. But the arm on which Mehemet Ali appears chiefly to rely, is the fanaticism of the population of the Asiatic provinces, which his numerous agents are most busy in exciting – holding them up as the defenders of Islamism, which the Giaours, they give out, are endeavouring to subvert. The recent disturbances in Asia Minor, to which I alluded in a former letter, and numerous outbreaks of a more trivial nature which have occurred subsequently, are known to have been fomented by the agents of the Pacha; and the Porte, in order to counteract this, has deemed it necessary to publish a manifesto, laying before its subjects a statement of affair from the commencement of the quarrel up to the present period, and proving to them, by the clearest arguments, that the Pacha himself is the enemy of their religion, and that the object he is aiming at is to dethrone the Sultan, and warning them, under the severest punishment, against receiving and circulating the doctrines he is preaching to them. This document has been publicly read in the mosques of the capital on several days during the last week, and has been also transmitted, for the same purpose, to the governors of the provinces of Asia Minor. I doubt of its effect being such as is desired. Where the sway of the Pacha has been already felt, the means he has adopted will avail him little; but where the tyranny of his government is yet unknown--namely, in the provinces which are still under the dominion of the Porte, and where general discontent is known to exist in consequence of the reforms which have been latterly introduced-- an appeal to the fanaticism of the Mussulman population will, I fear, be listened to but too eagerly.

"The communication to the Porte from the French ambassador, to which I alluded in my last letter, has given rise, it would appear, to a most serious misunderstanding, and has formed the subject of discussion during the whole week between the four ambassadors and the Reis Effendi, delivered by the Dragoman in a harsh tone, perhaps more so than it was intended it should have been. It had, it would seem, been misinterpreted by the Pacha into a declaration of war on the part of France in the event of the convention being executed by the Porte, and was transmitted by him as such to the ambassadors of the Powers. Against this construction which had been put upon his words, M. Pontois thought fit to protest, putting into writing his former communication, and accompanying it at the same time by an official note, the language of which was most violent. To this the Porte returned no answer, and M. Pontois, in consequence, has become quite furious, denouncing Reschid Pacha to his colleagues in office as the most determined enemy to his country and religion, and he is now endeavouring by every means in his power to displace both him and Ahmet Pacha. This absurd conduct of the French ambassador has made him the object of general ridicule, and the more so, of course, as it can now be no longer doubted that he will not be supported in it by his own government. Had fighting been the intention of the French government, its line of policy would have been obviously a different one, and better would it have been for the dignity of France had she at once decided on so doing, and avowed openly her motives and reasons for supporting a despot like

Mehemet Ali. Her shuffling diplomacy throughout the whole question, endeavouring by intrigue and the most underhand means, to achieve an object she was ashamed to avow, pretending withal to the noblest motives, has not only ended in the completest failure, but will bring on her the scorn of the whole of Europe. We have no news of the movements of Ibrahim, but it is supposed he remains in his former position, being prevented from advancing by the want of supplies, and the general disorganization of the whole of his army. The Porte in the meanwhile is fast preparing, and will be ready to meet him with a formidable movement. In addition to the camp which I alluded to at Koniah, another is being formed in the neighbourhood of the capital, which will chiefly be composed of Albanian troops. The troops, it is here reported, are to be placed under the command of General Jochmus, who arrived on Monday with despatches from England, having been sent out for this special service. If this report be correct, the only remark that can possibly be made is that a fitter individual could not have been chosen. General Jochmus held command in Greece throughout the period of the Greek revolution, and is perfectly acquainted with the Albanian character, and he also distinguished himself in the war in Spain.

"The trial of the ex-vizier, Khosreff Pacha, on the first charges which had been brought against him, for defalcations in his public accounts, was brought to a termination on Sunday, and he is condemned to be exiled for three years. He is still to be tried on another indictment, and that of a character far more serious, viz., that of plotting for the overthrow of the government, but it is not known when the trial will commence.   B."[69]

As one may clearly discern, there is nothing in this newspaper article, whether by implication or fact, that counters the official, eye-witness information we readers (and those living at that time) have previously viewed from the original sources. We also submit the entire article of *The Morning Chronicle* of September 7, 1840, in our **Appendix VII**.[70] It will become obvious that there is no variance to instigate confusion and nothing to support and validate the claim of Josiah Litch and the others.

There is one more area that calls for clarification. Josiah Litch, Uriah Smith and A. T. Jones all referenced an article of The Morning Chronicle, September 3, 1840, as further proof that the Sultan lost Turkey's independence on August 11, 1840. Let us then remind ourselves of that initial claim made by those three men as we read that particular newspaper account. The last two paragraphs, with emphasis added, are central to the issue at hand, and are here presented in full context. Josiah Litch wrote:

"But have we any evidence, beside the fact of the arrival of Rifat Bey at Alexandria with the ultimatum on the 11th of August, that Ottoman supremacy died, or was dead, that day? Read the following, from the same writer quoted above, dated 'Constantinople, August 12, 1840:' –

"I can add but little to my last letter, on the subject of the plans of the *four powers*; and I believe the details I then gave you comprise everything that is yet decided on. The portion of the Pacha, as I then stated, is not to extend beyond the line of Acre,

---

[69]*The Morning Chronicle*, London, September 18, 1840, pg. 4, col. 1.
[70] See *The Morning Chronicle*, London, September 7, 1840; **APPENDIX VII**, pg. 221.

and does not include either Arabia or Candia. Egypt alone is to be hereditary in his family, and the province of Acre to be considered as a pachalic, to be governed by his son during his lifetime, but afterward to depend on the will of the Porte; and even this latter is only to be granted him on the condition of his accepting these terms, and delivering up the Ottoman fleet within ten days. In the event of his not doing so, this pachalic is to be cut off. Egypt is then to be offered him, [198] with another ten days to deliberate on it, before actual force is employed against him.

"The manner, however, of applying the force, should he refuse to comply with these terms, -- whether a simple blockade is to be bombarded, and his armies attacked in the Syrian provinces, -- is the point which still remains to be learned; nor does a note delivered yesterday by the four ambassadors, in answer to a question put to them by the Porte, as to the plan to be adopted in such an event, throw the *least light* on this subject. It simply states that provision has been made, and there is no necessity for the Divan alarming itself about any contingency that might afterwards arise.

"Let us now analyze this testimony:

"1. The letter is dated 'Constantinople, August 12.' [The remaining paragraphs of this quote are to serve our purpose.]

"2. 'Yesterday,' the 11th of August, the Sultan applied, in his own capital, to the ambassadors of four *Christian nations,* to know the measures which were to be taken in reference to a circumstance vitally affecting his empire; and was only told that 'provision had been made,' but he could not know what it was; and that he need give himself no alarm '*about any contingency which might* AFTERWARDS ARISE!!' From that time, then, *they,* and not *he,* would manage that.

"Where was the Sultan's independence that day? GONE. Who had the supremacy of the Ottoman empire in their hands? *The great powers.*

"According to previous calculation, therefore, [199] OTTOMAN SUPREMACY *did depart on the* ELEVENTH OF AUGUST *into the hands of the great Christian powers of Europe."*[71]

As we have already witnessed in official documentation, however, the Sultan's independence was *already* "GONE." Who had the supremacy of the Ottoman Empire in their hands? *The great powers. According to previous-displayed documents and facts, therefore,* OTTOMAN SUPREMACY *did depart on the* TWENTY-SEVENTH OF JULY 1839 *into the hands of the great Christian powers of Europe.*

This universally-acknowledged event of July 27, 1839, with all its ramifications, did not resonate properly with the Millerites as it did with the rest of the world. They were confident of Litch's interpretation and continued to adamantly express it in a number of ways. For example:

---

[71] Josiah Litch, *Prophetic Exposition; Or A Connected View Of The Testimony Of The Prophets Concerning The Kingdom Of God And The Time Of Its Establishment.* (Boston: Joshua V. Himes, 1842), 197-199.

THE MIDNIGHT CRY

November 25, 1842

TURKISH EMPIRE

" Bible distinctly points out many signs which must be fulfilled in the last days; yet they will be of such a nature that they can be overlooked, or explained away, for, people will still say, 'Where is the promise of his coming! For, since the fathers fell asleep, *all things continue as they were*, from the beginning of creation.'

"One would suppose the sign relating to the Turkish Empire was so plain, that he who runs must read, that the sixth trumpet had ceased its sounding, and, of course, we are living 'in the days of the voice of the seventh angel.' That the sixth trumpet relates to the Turkish Power, most of our learned commentators agree. That its independence has departed is most clearly proved by the Eastern correspondence of the 'New York Observer,' published in August 1841. Their correspondent uses the following expressive language, probably having no more suspicion that he was sustaining our views of the near coming of Christ, than that he was building up Mahometanism: 'The Turkish Empire is becoming decomposed, and is but A MERE CORPSE!'

"Now let us suppose a case, and ask a question.

"Imagine an ambitious politician at the south-west part of this union. He draws around him the heterogeneous French, Spanish, and English population of Louisiana and Florida, and becomes their leader in rebellion against the General Government; Our navy is manned and sent against him, but he captures it, and sets our armies at defiance. Our President is reduced to such extremity that he is compelled to accept the intervention of friendly powers. They, by their ambassadors at Washington, agree upon terms to be offered to the bold rebel. They tell him, if he will give up the fleet he has captured, and withdraw his troops from the rest of the Union, they will give him Louisiana, to be held by him and his family forever, and Florida to be his during life. The President agrees to these terms, with the further humiliating proviso that, if they are not accepted by the rebel, the friendly powers may take the matter into their own hands. After the messenger has left Washington, the President sends to the ambassadors of the friendly powers to know what is to be done, if the successful rebel refuses even this offer. The ambassadors answer,- 'WE WILL TAKE CARE OF THAT!' Would not everyone feel that the independence of this country had departed? What if we were afterwards permitted to keep up the forms of government! So are some slaves permitted to keep up the forms of freedom!

"We believe the Sixth trumpet has ceased its sounding; and for those who are not prepared for the last blast of the LAST TRUMPET, it is a fearful thought. You cannot say, '*All things continue as they were.*' The fate of the Turkish Empire proves that assertion false. The time was, when all Europe could not dispossess the Turks of the 'Holy Sepulchre.' Now, all Europe cannot keep the Turkish Empire from crumbling to pieces, for it has fulfilled its commission, and *it has fallen*! Thus God is speaking to us by his providence. O, hear his voice. PREPARE TO MEET THY GOD."[72]

---

[72] *The Midnight Cry*, November 25, 1842. Also referenced and quoted in *The Signs of the Times,* May 31, 1843.

We now submit the entire article of *The Morning Chronicle* of September 3, 1840, that has been claimed by Litch and the pioneers to prove that Turkish "independence" ceased. August 11, 1840. In this way the reader will have a complete and unbiased account of <u>all</u> the relative facts from all the resources. We now can lay this issue to rest:

The Morning Chronicle

September 3, 1840

TURKEY

CONSTANTINOPLE, Aug. 12.

[From our own correspondent.]

"I can add but a little to my last letter on the subject of the plans of the Four Powers; and I believe that the details I then gave you comprise everything that is yet decided on. The portion of the Pacha, as I then stated, is not to extend beyond the line of Acre, and does not include either Arabia or Candia. Egypt alone is to be hereditary in his family, and the province of Acre to be considered as a pachalik, to be governed by his son during his lifetime, but afterwards to depend on the will of the Porte; and even this latter is only to be granted to him on the condition of his accepting these terms and delivering up the Ottoman fleet within the period of ten days. In the event of his not doing so, this pachalik is to be cut off. Egypt alone is to be then offered, with another ten days for him to deliberate on it before actual force be employed against him. The manner, however, of applying the force, should he refuse to comply with these terms – whether a simple blockade is to be established on the coast, or whether his capital is to be bombarded and his armies attacked in the Syrian provinces – is the point which still remains to be learned; nor does a note delivered yesterday by the four ambassadors, in answer to a question put to them by the Porte, as to the plan to be adopted in such an event, throw the least light on this subject. It simply states that provision had been made, and there was no necessity for the Divan alarming itself about any contingency that might afterwards arise. But the Porte, notwithstanding, seems preparing for a struggle; and the bustle and activity which have prevailed here since affairs have taken their present turn have been such as to excite universal astonishment. Eight thousand troops have already left to join the camp to be formed at Kutiah. Upwards of forty vessels have been chartered by the government to convey troops and stores to the Syrian coast; and two first-rates and three frigates, the sad remains of the Sultan's fleet, are to sail immediately in the same direction, to be under the command of Captain Walker. Two other vessels also, just launched, are to be got ready with all dispatch. With regard to the movements of our own fleet, no intelligence has been yet received; but, according to letters by the Smyrna post, an express had reached the Austrian admiral, ordering him to sail for the Syrian coast, and follow movements of Admiral Stopford; and from this we may conclude he had already left. In addition to the employment of its marine force, Austria furnishes fifteen thousand men, who are also to proceed to the coast of Syria, and will augment her numbers in case of need; and Russia is to furnish an army in the event of Ibrahim's advancing on the capital. A coalition so formidable as this Mehemet Ali cannot resist; but he seems determined to do his utmost, and hold out to the last moment. On the first intelligence of the signing of the protocol, he had dispatched a courier to Kourshil Pacha, commanding him immediately to abandon the Hedjias and return to Egypt by forced marches; and he had also sent one to Ibrahim Pacha, ordering him to advance without delay. The ability of the latter to comply with his instructions may, however, I am of opinion, be fairly doubted. He is already entangled in the Syrian revolt, and the disaffection among his troops was gaining ground; and with so large a force to be landed in his rear, by which, of course, he would be pursued and harassed, he would hardly venture on a forward movement, where he knows he must fight at every instant. Blood, notwithstanding, will be doubtless shed before affairs be brought to a conclusion; and the loss may still possibly be great for Turkey; or, at all events, she may lose her fleet by Mehemet Ali's fulfilling his threat of burning it if attempts be made to take it. It is the result, however, we must only look to; and if the object in view be once obtained, the loss we have suffered must not be considered. The safety of Turkey is the stake played for; and unless we are willing to incur a risk, we can never hope to win the game.

"To add to the difficulties she is already involved in to meet the contingencies of a fresh war, and ere the disturbances in the capital are hardly quieted, another affair has now occurred to call for exertion on the part of the Porte, viz., a serious revolt in the Tocat provinces. The cause assigned for this outbreak is the general discontent of the Turks of the interior at the new measures lately introduced, which place them on a footing with the Rayah subjects; and, determined to resist them to the utmost of their power, they had risen *on masse*, strangled the governor, and committed excesses of every kind. The accounts received of the spreading of disaffection have been considered by the government to be so alarming that the Austrian steamer was instantly chartered and dispatched yesterday to Sampsoun with 1,500 Albanian troops, and another steamer with the same number will leave to-night for that port. This promptness and energy on the part of the government, unparalleled in former instances, will doubtless be followed by the desired result; and, in addition to the quelling of the present disturbance, the more solid advantage will likewise be obtained of inspiring the people with a wholesome terror and teaching them for the future to respect the laws.

"We have letters from Tabreez to the 20th ult., which left the Shah at Hamadan, where he was collecting an imposing force, but nothing was known of his future movement. Affairs, however, throughout the country were assuming, it is stated, a threatening aspect, and, according to the opinion generally entertained, a long period would not elapse ere Persia became the scene of great events. A shock of an earthquake has been felt at Tabreez, which had seriously damaged several buildings, and, according to the accounts received there, it had been felt severely at other places. Several villages were completely destroyed, and even part of Mount Ararat had been thrown down, overwhelming and crushing the village at its base.

"Constantinople, since Friday last, has been a continued scene of public rejoicing in honour of the marriage of the sister of the Sultan. Festivities, however, of a similar kind have been so often described on former occasions, that I shall not attempt to detail them here. This being the day when the dower is presented, a grand dinner is given by his highness, to which all the ambassadors have received invitations. The table was to be laid for 200. The marriage will be celebrated to-morrow morning, and, with illuminations at night and a display of fireworks, the happy affair will be brought to a close.   B."[73]

It has now become evident that here, as well, there is no variance to instigate and nothing to acknowledge that claim of Josiah Litch and the others. This concludes one segment of our study.

We will close chapter 2 by wrapping up a few loose ends. We start first by quoting from the last paragraph of Josiah Litch's *Prophetic Exposition* as he lamented the lack of interest shown by the multitude in his prophetic prediction:

> "The present calculation was before the world two years and more before the time of fulfilment; and the attention of the whole community was turned toward it. There are few persons, in New England at least, whose minds were not arrested and turned to the 11th of August; and vast multitudes were ready to say, ay, did say, If this event takes place according to the calculation, at the time specified, we will believe the doctrine of the *advent near. But how is it with them now? Why, just as it was with the old Jews in the days of Christ; when he was every day performing the most stupendous miracles in their sight, they said to him, "Master, we would see a sign of thee." So now: men desire a sign from heaven.* But let them be assured, they can never have a more convincing one than this; -- the last great prophecy with which a prophetic period is connected, except the concluding period, when Christ will come, has been filled up in the exact time, and has brought us to the very verge of eternity."[74]

In the following article in 1844, Litch again expressed his disappointment concerning the public's disinterest in prophetic fulfillment:

The Western Midnight Cry
January 20, 1844

> "In 1838, Josiah Litch, an Episcopal Methodist Preacher in Massachusetts, published a work entitled, "The Probability of the Second Coming of Christ, about A.D. 1843, shown by our comparison of Prophecy with History, up to this present time, and an explanation of those prophecies which are yet to be fulfilled." He Commenced his preface by saying "The writer would here acknowledge himself indebted to Mr. William Miller's valuable lecture for the leading ideas of his book." In that work, it was clearly shown that the fifth and sixth of the seven trumpets relate to the Ottoman power, and that the period of Mahomedan ascendency over the Eastern Capital or Greek division of the Roman Empire would end in August, 1840. *The events fully confirmed the exposition, but instead of waking up the world, they*

---

[73] *The Morning Chronicle*, London, September 3, 1840, pg. 4, col. 2-3.
[74] Josiah Litch, *Prophetic Exposition; Or A Connected View Of The Testimony Of The Prophets Concerning The Kingdom Of God And The Time Of Its Establishment* (Boston: Joshua V. Himes, 1842), 200. [Emphasis mine]

were overlooked or denied. But many were aroused to examine that system of truth to which God had so manifestly set his seal."[75]

In contrast to Litch's disappointment in the public reaction, though, we read J. N. Loughborough's statement:

"This striking fulfilment of the prophecy [on August 11, 1840] had a tremendous effect upon the public mind."[76]

Considering how we have just read the same public material that was available to all at that time, it is remarkable that two parties emerged, both claiming the same reference point yet differing markedly in their understanding of events and their significance. Clearly, one of those parties was in error. When I read that statement by J. N. Loughborough that "the alleged fulfillment of the prophecy [of Aug. 11, 1840] had a tremendous effect upon the public mind," I could not help but wonder how the general public could rationalize the difference between what they could read for themselves and what they heard being proclaimed. Remember, Miller's terms that we saw early on that he used to describe the "final dissolution" or the "final overthrow" of the Turkish Empire leaves the reader with no doubt that Miller was awaiting the absolute end of Turkey, never again to play a role in history. The following documents will help to tell that story:

THE SIGNS OF THE TIMES
February 1, 1843

"The prediction of the downfall of Turkey is spoken of as another failure. 'Again they say the Turkish power was to be broken in the summer of A.D. 1840, and for the result they refer to the interference of the Allied Powers, at that time, in the political affairs of Turkey. But Turkish independence no more ceased then, than French independence ceased, when the same Allied Powers did more violence to France, invading her capital, and giving her one monarch in the place of another.'

"The entire subversion of that government was never expected at that time, but only 'a voluntary surrender of Mohamedan supremacy.' This it is believed has been proved to have been fulfilled. The Turkish Sultan now only reigns by the sufferance of the Christian powers of Europe, and not as an independent Mahomedan prince. Mahomedanism can no longer carry terror to the hearts of any in Christendom; and it is no more contrary to the fulfillment of that calculation, that the Turkish sultan should remain upon his throne by the consent of Europe, that it was for Deacoze, the Greek monarch, to continue in the same manner on his throne, by permission of Amureth, for four years after he had voluntarily relinquished his supremacy. The reference to the French revolution is just in point. The government of Napoleon was opposed to the legal heir of the French throne. When therefore the Allied powers defeated him, and placed the legal heir on the throne, French supremacy was not gone, but the supremacy of Jacabinism ceased in France."[77]

---

[75] *The Western Midnight Cry*, January 20, 1844. [Emphasis mine]
[76] J. N. Loughborough, *The Great Second Advent Movement Its Rise and Progress* (Washington, D.C.: Review and Herald, 1905), 132.
[77] *Signs of the Times*, February 1, 1843.

Again we quote:

"One person deeply impressed by Litch's arguments was the abolitionist Angeline Grimke Weld. Early in 1843 she wrote to her husband that she had been studying the fifth and sixth trumpets. 'It does seem to me,' she wrote, 'the fulfilling of the period of an hour, a day, a month, and a year – 391 years and 15 days from the rise to the fall of the Ottoman Empire – is the most startling and convincing evidence that the end of all things is at hand, of anything I have seen.' Less startled was the Millerite critic Reverend O. E. Daggett, who wrote: '…They say the Turkish power was to be broken in the summer of A.D. 1840, and for the result they refer to the interference of the Allied Powers, at that time, in the political affairs of Turkey.' But Turkey did not 'fall' in 1840, argued Daggett, any more than France permanently lost its independence when 'the same Allied Powers' deposed Napoleon. James Hazen, a Massachusetts clergyman who denounced Millerism as *A False Alarm,* noted that Miller's followers 'triumphantly' pointed to Turkey's fall, August 11, 1840. But the facts were, he said, that European intervention had kept Turkey from falling. The argument that in accepting European aid Turkey fell was 'ridiculous,' Hazen wrote. 'Do these men know no better than to believe this story themselves?'"[78]

Then in the year 1892 J. N. Loughborough declared Litch was establishing the year/day principal of prophetic time, based on the fall of the Ottoman Empire on August 11, 1840:

"The passing of the powers of the Turkish Sultan into the hands of the allied powers of Europe on the 11th day of August, 1840, was an event that served greatly to establish the fact that in symbolic prophecy a day represents a literal year. In the year 1838, Josiah Litch, of Philadelphia, published an exposition of the three woe trumpets of Revelation 9, basing his calculation of the time given under the fifth and sixth trumpets, on the ground of a *day* for a *year.* He ventured to assert, on the strength of his faith in the 'year-day' principle, that the Ottoman empire would lose its independence on Aug. 11, 1840."[79]

In 1905 he wrote again:

"In 1838 Dr. Josiah Litch, of Philadelphia, Pa., having embraced the truth set forth by William Miller, united in the work of giving greater publicity to the message. He prepared articles for the public print on the subject of the seven trumpets of the Revelation. He took the unqualified position that the sixth trumpet would cease to sound and the Ottoman power fall on the 11th day of August, 1840, and that that would demonstrate to the world that a *day* in symbolic prophecy represents a *year* of literal time…. The publication of Dr. Litch's lecture made a general stir, and many

[78] Ronald L. Numbers and Jonathan M. Butler, *The Disappointed Millerism and Millenarianism in the Nineteenth Century.* See Chapter 5, Eric Anderson, *The Millerite Use of Prophecy* (Knoxville: University of Tennessee Press, 1993), 87.

[79] J. N. Loughborough, *The Rise and Progress of the Seventh-day Adventists with Tokens of God's Hand in the Movement and A Brief Sketch of the Advent Cause From 1831 to 1844* (Battle Creek, Michigan: General Conference Association of the Seventh-day Adventists, 1892), 38.

thousands were thus called to watch for the termination of the difficulties that had sprung up between Mehemet Ali, the pasha of Egypt, and the Turkish sultan. Hundreds said, 'If this affair terminates as the doctor has asserted, it will establish the *'year-day'* principle of interpreting symbolic time, and we will be Adventists.'"[80]

Turning to the writings of Josiah Litch, we will let him speak for himself as to whether he was trying to establish "the *'year-day'* principle of interpreting symbolic time," as Loughborough claimed he was:

> "But still there is no positive evidence that the first period was exactly to a day, fulfilled; nor yet that the second period began, to a day, where the first closed. If they began and ended so, the above calculation will be correct. If they did not, then there will be a variation in the conclusion; but the evidence is clear that there cannot be a year's variation from the calculation; we must wait patiently for the issue.
>
> "...But yet, whenever it is fulfilled, whether in 1840, or at a future period, it will open the way for the scenes of the last day. Let no man, therefore, triumph, even if there should be an error of a few months in our calculation on this prophesy.   L.
> "EVENTS TO SUCCEED THE SECOND WOE.
>
> "...It is impossible for me to tell what will come in the month of August. If the foregoing calculations are correct, however, and the Ottoman power falls, we shall be brought to a point where there is no certainty that the day of grace will be continued for one hour...."[81]

That presents quite a stretch. Let us always remember our divine instruction:

> "We shall be attacked on every point; we shall be tried to the utmost. We do not want to hold our faith simply because it was handed down to us by <u>our fathers</u>. Such a faith <u>will not stand the terrible test that is before us</u>."[82]

---

[80] J. N. Loughborough, *The Great Second Advent Movement Its Rise and Progress* (Washington, D.C.: Review and Herald, 1905), 129-130.
[81] *Signs of the Times*, Boston, August 1, 1840.
[82] Ellen G. White, *Review and Herald* (Battle Creek, MI), April 29, 1884.

3

Examining the Evidence: July 27, 1299?

One challenge in the course of this study was to evaluate the accuracy of the date of July 27, 1299, which was claimed by Josiah Litch and others to be the beginning of the prophetic time periods of the fifth and sixth trumpets of Revelation. Anyone who studies Islamic primary sources can fully appreciate the words of Herbert Gibbons as one who speaks from experience:

> "The risk that I run of incurring criticism from Oriental philologists on the ground of nomenclature is very great. I ask their indulgence. Will they not take into consideration the fact that there is no accepted standard among English-speaking scholars for the transliteration of Turkish and Slavic names? Wherever possible, I have adopted the spelling in general usage in the Near East, and in English standard lexicons and encyclopedias. When a general usage cannot be determined, I have frequently been at a loss.
>
> "There was the effort to be as consistent in spelling as sources and authorities would permit. But where [6] consistency was lacking in originals, a consistent transliteration sometimes presented difficulties with which I was incompetent to cope. Even a philologist, with a system, would be puzzled when he found his sources conflicting with each other in spelling, and – as is often the case - with themselves. And if a philologist thinks that he can establish his system by transliterating the *spoken* word, let him travel from Constantinople to Cairo overland, and he will have a bewildering collection of variants before he reaches his journey's end. I was not long in Turkey before I learned that *Osman* and *Othman* were both correct. It depended merely upon whether you were in Constantinople or Konia! After you had decided to accept the pronunciation of the capital, you were told that Konia is the Tours of Turkey."[83]

For example, Bapheum or Bapheus from Pachymeres' account that is central to our investigation has also been called and spelled as Kujunhissar, Koyunhisar, Koyunhisari. Today it is called Koyun-Hisar, all meaning one and the same.

Despite such challenges, our next study begins with Georgius [George] Pachymeres, a Byzantine Greek historian and philosopher (AD 1242–1310). Pachymeres settled in Constantinople, studied law and entered the church; he subsequently became chief advocate of the church and chief justice of the imperial court. His literary activity was considerable, his most important work being a Byzantine history in thirteen books, which has become the primary contemporary source among historians for that era. He is recognized the world over by Islamic and Western historians as the most credible

---

[83] Herbert Adams Gibbons, *The Foundation of The Ottoman Empire: A History of the Osmanlis up to the Death of Bayezid I (1300-1403)* (New York: Century Co., 1916), 5-6.

primary source for the events leading up to the battle of Bapheum (Bapheus) near Nicomedia, and the origins of the Ottoman Empire in general:

> "As a contemporary observer Pachymeres is, in general, our most reliable source for 'Osmān's activities, in particular for the battle of Bapheus.[84] In the introduction to his history Pachymeres makes it clear that his account is based either on his own observations or the statements of those who were the eye-witness of the events. Nevertheless, Pachymeres should be used critically, comparing his information with Ottoman traditions." [85]

Georgius Pachymeres wrote his multi-volume history in Old Greek. In the year 1668 Petrus Possinus translated the Old Greek into Old Latin. Two columns now appeared on each page, along with Possinus' chronological charts in his *Possini Observationum*, Liber III, 804.[86] Here is Pachymeres' statement, translated into Latin, that briefly recounted the attack that began the battle at Bapheum:

> "Mensis siguidem Iulii die vicefima septime circa Bapheum (locus hic prope inclytam Nicomedian) Atman cum suis multorum millium numerum explantibus improvise apparens & subito irreuns. - sed melius fuerit rem aliquanto repetitam altius a suis retro ducere principiis."[87]

> Translation: "On the 27th day of the month of July, in the neighborhood of Bapheum (this place is near the renowned Nicomedia), Atman with his men totaling the number of many thousands, unexpectedly appearing and making a sudden attack – but it would be better to recount this whole matter from its beginnings."

While Pachymeres is our most reliable source for the battle at Bapheum, he is our only source for identifying the exact date for Osman's [Othman's] invasion of Bapheum on July 27. However, unbeknownst to some, while he gave us the day, he never gave us the year! That fact was the prime cause for the debates concerning the "year" for the date of July 27 given by Pachymeres for the Ottoman Turkish invasion of Bapheum in Byzantine territory. Those debates among the international academic community have now largely ceased, due to previously-unknown Islamic sources and meticulous research among historians, who have come to a consensus that we will soon begin to examine. As it is, William Miller was indeed the first (1831) to tie together the two claimed

---

[84] George Pachymeres' account on 'Osmān Ghāzī's activities has been examined by various specialists, including G. Caro, "Zür Chronologie der drei Letzten Bücher des Pachymeres," BZ 6 (1897) 116 ff.; G. G. Amakis, *Early Ottomans*, Athens, 1947, 71 ff, in particular note 153; Tinnefeld, "Pachymeres und Philes als Zeugen für ein frühes Untemehmen gegen die Osmanen", BZ. 64(1971), 46-54; E. Zachariadou, "Pachymeres on the 'Amourioi' of Kastamonu," *Byzantine and Modern Greek Studies* (1971), 57-70; Professor Zachariadou most kindly clarified for me several points in the Greek text. I am also indebted to Timothy O. Baldwin for his translation for me of the whole section on 'Osmān into English.

[85] Halil İnalcik, *Essays in Ottoman History* (Istanbul: Eren Yavincilik, 1998), 56.

[86] Georgius Pachymeres, *Corpus Scriptorum Historiae Byzantinae* (Bonnae, Impensis Ed. Weberi 1835), Volumen Alterum, [II]. Pages 847-853 will be our interest.

[87] Ibid., 327.

prophetic time periods of the fifth and sixth trumpets of Revelation. He interpreted them successively, without interruption, straight through to the year 1839.[88]

> "It was given them, after the rise of the Ottoman empire, to torment or harass and weaken men (the Roman empire in the east) five months. If these are prophetic months as is probable, it would be one hundred and fifty years. But when did that empire rise? Mr. Miller has fixed on A.D. 1298. Others, among whom is Gibbon in his Decline and Fall of the Roman Empire, 1299. He says – Othman first [154] invaded the territory of Nicomedia on the 27th of July, 1299. He also remarks on the singular accuracy of the date, a circumstance not often found in the history of those times. He says – 'The singular accuracy with which this event, is given, seems to indicate some foresight of the rapid growth of the monster.'
> "If we date the origin of this empire in 1299, the hundred and fifty years would end 1449."[89]

Our requirements in historical research are specific and very straightforward: authenticity and documentation derived from primary sources. Necessary, too, is a clear concept of the questions needing definitive answers. In this case, the questions are these:

1. Did Osman (Othman) "first" invade the territory of Bapheum near Nicomedia on the 27th of July, 1299?

2. What is the validity of the "singular accuracy" of the claimed date of Gibbon of July 27, 1299?

3. Was the 27th of July, 1299, the origin of the Ottoman Empire?

Recapping our previous findings, we saw that Josiah Litch's prediction rested entirely on a single date in the writings of a cultured despiser of religion, Edward Gibbon. The reader must understand that William Miller's and Josiah Litch's interpretation for the fifth and sixth trumpets of Revelation was never established upon any Scripture whatsoever. Ellen White counseled the church on the faulty foundation upon which they were building, but to no avail:

> "God intends that improvement shall be the lifework of all His followers and that it shall be guided and controlled by correct experience. The true man is one who is willing to sacrifice his own interest for the good of others and who exercises himself in binding up the brokenhearted. The true object of life has scarcely begun to be understood by many, and that which is real and substantial in their life is sacrificed because of cherished errors.... Gibbon the skeptic, and many others whom God endowed with giant minds, and whom the world called great men, rallied under the banner of Satan and used the gifts of God for the perversion of truth and the

---

[88] William Miller, *Evidence from Scripture and History of the Second Coming of Christ, about the year 1843*; exhibited in a course of lectures. (Boston, 1842), 112, 121.
[89] Josiah Litch, *The Probability of the Second Coming of Christ About A.D. 1843* (Boston: David H. Ela, 1838), 153-4.

destruction of the souls of men. Great intellect, when made a minister of vice, is a curse to the possessor and to all who come within the circle of its influence."[90]

In an article in the *Review and Herald,* January 8, 1880, Ellen White again wrote, this time to a wider audience, concerning the danger of placing confidence in the written works of the world's great men. Unfortunately, the problem persists to this day. But do not believe that after she wrote that Gibbon "rallied under the banner of Satan," she then, in *Great Controversy,* 334-5, endorsed Litch's prediction, whose foundation rested entirely on Gibbon's date of July 27, 1299.

In fact, the error of Edward Gibbon of fixing July 27, 1299, for the commencement of the claimed prophetic time periods of the fifth and sixth trumpets of Revelation has been well-known among the international academic community and by our own brethren. Objections by Amadon in *Ministry* magazines of June and July, 1944, in regard to the Ottoman "Muharram" (calendar), the discrepancies surrounding the year of the Ottoman "Hegira," and more will all be addressed. The original authorities followed the lunar chronology, as will be presented. Others later followed the solar chronology, which does present a variation in time. However, the reader will see for himself that neither school of chronology nor the primary historical (European or Islamic) sources that include the annals and chronological tables will be seen to cement the desired outcome and position of Josiah Litch. In the year 1919 the then-president of the General Conference of the Seventh-day Adventist Church, A. G. Daniells, called together from all over the world a group of Adventist theologians, historians and teachers to contend with the many theological and historical discrepancies found in our then-published books and periodicals of the church, as its members were constantly receiving light and growing in their understanding. Many who attended those meetings returned home discouraged and distraught after coming face-to-face with the many inconsistencies in their faith, yet leaving devoid of definitive answers. This book will endeavor to supply those answers from primary sources for the sincere searcher of truth. We begin by pulling back the curtain of time, by first examining the minutes of the 1919 Bible Conference called by Elder Daniells:

1919 Bible Conference Minutes

[31] "...Nelson's encyclopedia gives the date of the independent power of the Ottoman Empire as 1301.

"Creasy says Von Hammer divided the history of the Ottomans into five divisions. In regard to the first period he makes the following quotation, 'The first period consists of a hundred and fifty years of rapid growth, from the assumption of independent sovereignty by Othman to the consolidation of the European and Asiatic conquests of his house by the taking of Constantinople.' – Gibbon's Rome, page 236, Vol. 6.

"The first battle between the Ottomans and the Greeks took place 1301. Edward Gibbon makes the following statement: 'It was on the twenty-seventh of July, in the year 1299 of the Christian era, that Othman first invaded the territory of Nicomedia.' – (H. A. Gibbons, page 34 [is now going to be quoted]) He quotes Pachymeres as his authority. H. A. Gibbons, in quoting the same author, puts the date of the same battle in 1301. His statement follows: 'In 1301, twelve years after Osman began to form his state, he fought his first battle, and came into direct contact with the Byzantine

---

[90] Ellen White, *Testimonies for the Church* (Nampa, ID: Pacific Press, 1948), 4:519-520.

Empire. At Baphacon, near Nicomedia, the Heterarch Muzalon, with two thousand men, attempted to check a raid the Osmanlis were making into the fertile valley whose products contributed so greatly to the well-being of Nicomedia. It was mid-summer, just before the gathering of the harvests. In a pitched battle, the unarmoured horsemen of Osman charged so speedily and so impetuously that they broke through the heavy line of their opponents, [32] and the Greek commander's retreat was covered only by the opportune arrival of Slavic mercenaries. The Osmanlis were too few in number to follow up this victory.' – H.A. Gibbons, page 34.

"To explain the reason of this discrepancy between the two historians the following letter [by a Greek scholar] is cited:

5518 Dorchester Ave., Chicago, March 15, 1919.
State Library of Nebraska, Lincoln,

" 'Gentlemen:

" 'The Librarian of the University of Chicago has referred to me the attached letter. The following is the result of the investigation:

" 'Pachymeres (De Andronico Palaeologo, Bk. IV, Chap. 35) recounts the defeat of the Romans fighting for the Greek Emperor Andronicus by the "Persians" xx i.e. the Ottomans near Nicomedia and dated it July 27. The year is not given, as the system of dating used by us was not yet introduced into Greece from the Western (Roman) empire. The chronology employed by Gibbon and other recent writers on the period is based on a Latin work, Chronologus, by Petrus Possinu [sic], a Jesuit scholar writing at Rome about 1660. He constructed a chronological table for the events chronicled by Pachymeres, using as evidence eclipses of the sun or moon described by the historian and dated by astronomers, Arabian and Ottoman records, which were dated from the Hegira, or documents written by the Latins dated by the Christian system.

" 'The date of the event in question is inferred from the following circumstances: Possimus [sic] was able to establish by a Latin document that Andronicus formed an alliance with the Roman general Ronzerius in the last months of 1302. Surmising that he was driven to this by a series of reverses, one of the last of which was the defeat by the [32a] "persians' (Ottomans) under Atman on July 27, Possinus placed this event in 1302. H. A. Gibbons in his 1916 edition of the "Foundation of the Ottoman Empire" evidently preferred to put it back to 1301. The earlier editions (works) give 1299, the year in which Possinus put the assembling by Atman of the marauders who later won the battle referred to. The authority of Possinus thus points rather to 1301 than to 1299 for the battle near Nicomedia (?).

" 'Edward Gibbon in writing the work seems to have thought it more probable that the battle immediately followed the collection of the force than that it was the immediate occasion of the alliance between Andonious and Ronzerius. I should be inclined to agree with the 1916 edition and place the battle in 1301 or even in 1302. Hoping this will satisfy your inquirer, I am

Yours truly,
John W. Taylor
Dept. of Greek, University of Chicago.

" 'By the way of summary the following quotations are subjoined. "One of them, Othman, proclaimed himself independent at the end of the thirteenth century, and took the title of Sultan, or padishah." – Catholic Ency. Vol. XV, Sub. "Turkish."

"Osman captured three castles in the last year of the seventh century of the Hegira, and the last year of the thirteenth century of the Christian century. This victory was the blow that put a final end to the tottering Seljukian Empire, and at the same time established Osman as the ruler of his people. The Osman family date their independent rulership from this year." – Von Hammer, page 74. (Ger. Ed.). . . .

[46] "PRESCOTT: …Of Revelation 9, in harmony with the view that has been held by Protestantism for centuries, is that this is a symbol of the Saracens, the rise and work of the Saracens, but on the basis of the paper this morning, and any other discussion of the same thought, we take the time that in the prophecy belongs to the Saracens and give it to the Ottomans. Now it is of little value to me to try to establish any date with reference to the Ottoman empire, when I am dealing with a symbol applied to the Saracen power. It appears to me an inconsistency to take a symbol and say this belong to the Saracens that had their rise in Arabia, Mohammed was their leader, and that they applied the instruction that they should not hurt the grass of the earth, nor any green thing, nor any tree, but only such men as had not the seal of God on their foreheads. Then we attempt to take that fifth month period from the period of the rise and work of the Saracens, and carry it forward to the very end of the thirteenth century, centuries after the Saracens had ceased to be an aggressive power at all. So I don't see that I can get much out of the matter if is presented in that way. Now if we are to apply the time for the fifth trumpet to the Ottoman empire, let's apply the symbol to the Ottoman empire. But so long as we apply the symbol to the Saracens, how can we carry the period describing their work five or six centuries after they ceased to be an aggressive power? Until that is out of the way, any paper that attempts to establish dates with regard to the Ottoman empire doesn't help me any about the matter."

[47] "WAKEHAM: I have not been able to see how we could interpose a great interregnum of six hundred years between the fourth and fifth verses of chapter 9, when there is nothing in the prophecy to indicate that. It seems to me that we are presenting a false exegesis, interposing a great hiatus of six hundred years between one verse and the next, when there is absolutely nothing there to indicate it. The two reasons usually given are absolutely without historical confirmation. I have not been able to find any history that will substantiate the statement made so much, that there was no king over the Mohammadens until the time of Othman. Gibbon says, 'By the end of the first century of the Hejira, the Saracen Caliphs were the most absolute and powerful monarchs on the face of the globe.' Now with that statement and others of similar character I don't see how anyone can maintain there was no king over the Mohammadens until the end of the thirteenth century. The second reason is that the Mohammaden world was never united under one head until the time of Othman. When as a matter of fact the only time it was under one head was under the Saracen Caliphs. Freeman's history has for the heading of his first chapter, 'The Undivided Caliphy' in the seventh and eighth chapters [sic: centuries]."

"PRESCOTT: Perhaps I could explain how this came around. In looking up the difficulty, I found this, that previous to 1844 in the exposition of this prophecy both symbols, the locust symbol and the later symbol were given to the Ottoman Empire, and that there was no effort to separate them or show that anything happened at the close of this 150 years, or at the beginning [48] of the hour, day, month, and year period. The two were added together and made 541 years and five days, and reckoned from July 27, 1299, right straight on. Well now, that was inconsistent in itself, because it gave the time to the symbol interpreting both symbols of one power, and gave both periods of time to one power. When Thoughts on Revelation was written a separation was made of the first symbol, taking it to represent the Saracens, yet the time was still all given to the Ottoman power, and that is where we find ourselves. I think we should separate the time as we have done the symbols and give the time to the power that we interpret as fulfilling the symbol, therefore give it the five months or 150 years to the Saracens during their period of actual aggressive power as tormentors.

"That application of the period to the symbol gets away from two difficulties. First, it gets us away from what appears to be a very strange inconsistency of applying a symbol to some power, and the time period of that to another power. And second it gets away from the necessity of establishing a date that has been discredited. Lay aside everything else and ask yourself, Now how you are going to establish a definite day for the beginning of this period. The paper this morning I suppose was seeking for evidence for 1299. Now grant any weight to the historical evidence submitted that you please, yet you haven't established a day. We must find a definite day to date from if we are to take a prophecy and interpret it as meaning so many years and so many days. It must have a day to commence it, and it must have a day to end it, otherwise we don't have any proper interpretation or application of the prophecy.

[49] "Now the day July 27 1299 is absolutely discredited. I had the original Greek history out of the Congressional library for quite a long time, and went over the whole matter. It is a history in Greek with a parallel column translated into Latin, and accompanied by a chronological table, and the author put that event that Gibbon refers to as occurring in 1302. Von Hammer puts it in 1301. Somebody else in 1300, I believe. From my standpoint it doesn't make any difference which it is, and there is no occasion to attempt to prove which it is, because just so long as we interpret the symbols as applying to the Saracens, we certainly must give the time to the Saracens and not to the Ottoman power, and what was presented this morning was simply to show in a general way the beginning of the Ottoman power here at the end of the 13th century. But the same authority said that from these small beginnings rose a power that was established in 1453. Now we don't date our interpretation of the prophecy of the Roman power from 754 B.C., and yet Rome had its beginning in 754. Now all I ask for is that we shall be consistent with ourselves so that when we stand up before an audience or appear in print we don't expose ourselves any longer to that shocking inconsistency of applying the symbols to two powers, and then turn right around and give the time that belongs right in that prophecy and date it five centuries at least after the power has ceased to be aggressive as a tormentory.

"Before 1844 in William Miller's lectures he gives both symbols to the Ottoman power. He adds the periods together, makes 514 [sic] 541 years and 15 days date from July 27, 1299 and follows it straight through. Now when you go further you say we will start from July 27, 1299 and we come to 1449. What happened [50] then? We must have something on a day. What happened July 27, 1449, that both marked the ending of one period and the beginning of another, because you must not begin the next day. That is, when we are trying to arrive at August 11, 1840 you can't say this period ends July 27, 1449, and the next began July 28. You have got to make them lap one day or else you are thrown out when you get to the end. That question must be answered. What marked the close of the 150 years on July 27, 1449? What event on that day marked the beginning of the next period? What marked the close of the next period? Until that is out of the way I don't see that we shall be helped very much by any papers seeking to establish a date for something relating to the Ottoman Empire."[91]

My primary purpose for visiting the archives of the General Conference of Seventh-day Adventists in Silver Spring, Maryland, was to locate and read the document presented by Brothers Spicer, Benson, and Prescott to the General Conference Committee in council. I hoped also to learn of the committee's response to their presentations. The reference that led me to the General Conference Archives appeared in the 1919 Bible Conference minutes as follows:

"PRESCOTT: According to the best light I can get, and I am not alone – I suppose it is more or less known here that this whole matter came up several years ago, and the Review and Herald Board appointed a committee to study the question. This committee was composed of F. M. Wilcox, Chairman, W. A. Spicer, M. E. Kern, C. S. Longacre, C. L. Benson, S. M. Butler, and myself. We took up this question, went into it quite thoroughly, and that committee, which I think you will regard as not a very extreme or wild committee, came to the conclusion that we could not apply this 150 years beginning July 27, 1299, for the double reason, first, it didn't belong to that power, and second, the date itself could not be established. Then there were further things brought in, so that all the committee came to the conclusion that there was not sufficient evidence to establish the [51] date August 11, 1840. Therefore it was recommended that since it was too large a question for us, it be presented to the General Conference Committee in Council. The board adopted the recommendation presented. Brother Spicer was to present one phase, Brother Benson another, and I was to present a third phase. We prepared our matter and presented it at the Spring Council, and our papers, working together, set forth these suggestions, not as established orthodoxy, but as suggestions from the Committee for consideration."[92]

Although we did not find their document addressed to the General Conference Committee in council, I did find an array of pertinent material by all three men addressing this very issue of the dates of July 27, 1299, through August 11, 1840. Their writings appear to be their research and suggestions presented to the General Conference Committee for consideration. I said "we" did not find the desired document, in order to gratefully acknowledge the brethren at the General Conference Archives for all their kind and courteous help. No one knew why the document could not be found. Whether it was there at one time or not, or lost or destroyed, they could not say, for they had never seen it themselves, although they told me they had made a very serious search for it

---

[91] Transcript of the 1919 Bible Conference of the General Conference of Seventh-day Adventists, July 17, 1919 (Silver Spring, MD), 31- 50.
[92] Ibid., 50-1.

when I contacted them and asked to see it. I was very forthright in my purpose and objectives, and they accepted what I proposed to do, giving me unrestricted access to anything in the vault, with permission to publish anything I collected for my forthcoming book. Their only request was that all my photocopies of the original documents not be distributed on my website or otherwise, to which I fully agreed. They were entirely supportive of my sole objective, and likewise wanted the people to have nothing but the truth. For that, they have my respect and I commend them to you as well. I am also happy to tell you that the Biblical Research Institute (BRI) of the General Conference is now looking into the trumpets of Revelation from a Biblical viewpoint.

I purchased the necessary primary Islamic sources from Turkey for this book you now hold in your hand. They are among the hundreds of books and documents that I have scrutinized over the last number of years in a quest for the truth. In so doing I have found that many credible Islamic historians take very serious issues with some of the claimed facts and conclusions of Edward Gibbon and Herbert A. Gibbons. However, I am happy to tell you that I have not found any respected Islamic or Western historians that take any issues with the Hegira chronology that was connected to the battle of Bapheus (in its clarified contextual context). In fact, we will now see from the latest academic scholarship among the international community and of my own personal study of the primary sources why there is a mutual agreement among historians for the dating of the battle of Bapheus. Its validity will be soon displayed before all, since this is our primary concern at this juncture.

The reader can now appreciate the efforts made over the years to get definitive dating and defensible interpretation of Revelation 9. Adventism in particular, and the world in general, need reliable facts and honest conclusions. We fully reject the erroneous claim being put forth by some that the commencement of the 5th and 6th trumpets of Revelation took place on July 27, 1299, or that the fifth and sixth trumpets of Revelation have to do with Islam or the Ottoman Empire. Nevertheless, since those claims have been accepted by many as accurate, we will endeavor to end the misconceptions through irrefutable documentation. Truth is long overdue in this matter, and will withstand investigation. We will want, then, to look for the best arguments put forth for the dating of the battle of Bapheus on July 27, 1299, which has been interpreted to be the initial act establishing the Ottoman power. Two articles in *Ministry* magazine of June and July of 1944 by Grace Edith Amadon, a research worker at Takoma Park, Maryland, are the best defense I have seen on behalf of Josiah Litch's position for the year 1299. Due to copyright infringement and space, we encourage the reader to view those two entire *Ministry* articles of June and July, 1944, here: https://www.ministrymagazine.org/archive/.

We shall begin with fundamental extracts from those articles by Amadon in order to allow the opposition to present their case. We will then outline our objections. Then together we will unearth the truth and lay this issue to eternal rest.

Ministry Magazine

June, 1944

[18] "A Landmark of History – July 27, 1299

[Amadon stated]: "The historical date to be investigated in this study has to do with the first substantial clash between the Ottoman (Osmanli) Turks and the troops of the Byzantine Empire; that is, the first encroachment of Othman, or Osman, and his tribe upon the Oriental border of medieval Europe and its fortified castles. The limited sources extant agree that the invasion began with the Ottoman assault on Bapheum (Turkish: *Kujun-Hissar*), a sheep castle, whose protective moat was filled with water from the river Sangarius, flowing not far from Nicomedia.'"[93]

We do not disagree with Amadon that, in her day, there was limited documentation available to western historians who were not familiar with Islamic language and manuscripts. (Since World War I, more old Islamic manuscripts have been discovered.) Those who could understand them grasped the ramifications and clarity that finally came pertaining to Pachymeres' account on the attack on Bapheum:

> "It is a Seldjukid source *Musāmarat al-Akhbār* by Aksarāyī (ed. O. Turan, 1944) that brought clarification to Pachymeres' account."[94]

I have been in conversation with Turkish authorities. They referred me to a new translation of this book, including updates, that is based on Osman Turan's initial work (Those who wish to confirm this Islamic primary source and more, see the reference below.[95]) A major and unanimous complaint voiced among the academic Islamic historians is the fact that Edward Gibbon and H. A. Gibbons could use only those manuscripts that were translated into Western languages; they were therefore incapable of including in their research the many primary Islamic manuscripts. Because of this, they say, Westerners have grossly misrepresented Islamic history in many ways. From the primary Islamic sources I have surveyed, this statement is not without merit. For example:

> "Turkish libraries today possess the richest and most valuable collection of Islamic manuscripts in the world. This priceless collection consists of approximately 160,000 manuscripts in Arabic, 70,000 in Turkish and 13,000 in Persian, making a total of 250,000, which rises to 600,000 if one includes majmu'as. These figures do not take account of the thousands of pamphlets and reports in the archives and manuscripts in private collections.
>
> "Approximately 146,000 volumes of the total of 250,000 manuscripts kept in Turkish libraries are in Istanbul. According to the aforementioned figures Istanbul is the repository of the largest Islamic manuscripts collection in the world. Although we do not have systematic catalogues, it is possible to say that only 6-7% of those manuscripts kept in Turkey are written in Persian. However, these manuscripts are extremely important in terms of their age, originality and artistic value. Ancient and valuable copies of many manuscripts regarding Iranian language, literature, history and culture are kept in Turkish libraries."[96]

---

[93] Grace E. Amadon, "A Landmark of History," *Ministry,* June 1944, 18.

[94] Halil İnalcik, *Essays in Ottoman History* (Istanbul: Eren Yayincilik, 1998), 57 (footnotes).

[95] Kerîmuddin Mahmud-i Aksarayî, ed., and Mursel Ozturk, trans., *Musâmeretu'l-Ahbâr* (Ankara: Turk Tarih Kurumu Basimevi, 2000), 224-239. (ISBN 975-16-1221-7) This has been translated from Arabic characters into English characters, but it has not been translated or made available in the English language.

[96] Osman G. Özgudenl, Yrd. Doç. Dr. M.Ü. Türkiyat Arastırmaları Enstitüsü (Istanbul); Istanbul Kütüphanelerinde Bulunan Farsça Yazmaların Öyküsü: Bir Giris [The Story of Persian Manuscripts in Istanbul Libraries: An Introduction] PDF, 2.

For an English translation and for confirmation of some of these Islamic complaints of Gibbons and others, see M. Fuad Koprulu.[97] Amadon now begins to make her case:

> "Othman did not invade the territory of his Turkish neighbors; and out of all these terrors of nomadism which were impinged upon medieval civilization, *his tribe only* increased to such a state that for four centuries it continued an empire in Southeastern Europe. The prophecy of the fifth and sixth trumpets appears to be based upon this historical fact. To this tribal invasion of Christian territory, history has assigned a beginning date;[98] and to the length of time that the Ottoman invaders were to continue their "torment" and ultimate Moslem rule in Christendom, prophecy has assigned an exact period of time. (Rev. 9:5, 15.) In addition, history has also recorded the collapse of this independent Turkish state in Europe, and Turkey became but a mere line of demarcation between the Near East and its European border.[99] It remains to point out (1) the unquestionable historical sources with respect to the Turkish invasion; and (2) to demonstrate the true date for this invasion, which admittedly has marked the beginning of the Turkish era under the trumpets.[100]

> "It is not within the province of this study to discuss the interpretation of the symbols obviously applied by the prophecy in Revelation 9 to the events of contemporary history. The exactness of the fulfillment of the prediction was declared by the Millerites themselves, and has been definitely stressed by the Spirit of prophecy. This fact lends encouragement to the investigation of the underlying chronology."[101]

We just read that "the prophecy of the fifth and sixth trumpets <u>appears</u> to be based upon this historical fact." However, "ifs," "buts," "maybes" and "supposes" should hold no place for Seventh-day Adventists. Amadon also told us "history has assigned a beginning date," <u>not Scripture</u>. Note, though, that Edward Gibbon is her sole source for the July 27, 1299, date. Amadon, like almost all others before and after her, sidestepped Scripture and the work of identification of the symbols of Revelation 8 and 9. Instead, she placed her foundation on the traditions of the fathers, "the Millerites themselves." Amadon also supplies us with a list of 124 other scholars and historians cited for her proof that can be found on pages 24-25 of this *Ministry* article. And, of course, we already addressed in the introduction the misread statement by Ellen White in *The Great Controversy*, pages 334-5, and in chapters 1 and 2, the exposed misunderstandings and errors of the Millerites themselves.

Amadon further declared:

> "The Millerites do not mention any review of either Gibbon's or Von Hammer's authorities, or of the thirteenth-century source – Gorgius Pachymeres – who appears

---

[97] M. Fuad Koprulu (trans. by Gary Leiser), *The Origins of the Ottoman Empire* (Albany, New York: State University Press, 1992).

[98] Edward Gibbon, *The Decline and Fall of the Ottoman Empire*, 2nd ed., vol. VII (Notes by J. B. Bury; London: 1902), 24.

[99] *Signs of the Times* (Boston), Nov. 15, 1840, 128-129, citing "War Party" in *Bell's Messenger*, Aug. 22, 1840.

[100] L. E. Froom, *Tabulation of Historical School of Expositors on Time Periods of Fifth and Sixth Trumpets*. The nineteenth-century section of this tabulation mentions a score of expositors who terminated the period around 1840. See p. 24 of this issue of *Ministry*.

[101] Amadon, *Ministry*, June 1944, 18.

to be the one contemporary historian contributing the exact date for Othman's invasion.[102] However, these early Adventists had in hand Keith's two-volume work in which Von Hammer's criticism was mentioned, and from these volumes were making numerous selections for their publications. Moreover, in a current *Signs of the Times*, a writer refers to a possible "1300 or 1301 date" for the attack of Othman.[103] They must therefore have been fully cognizant of the criticism against Gibbon.

"It is of outstanding significance that the Millerites rejected the 1301 date of Von Hammer for Othman's first attack upon the Byzantine border, and deliberately founded their prophetic argument upon the 1299 date proposed by Edward Gibbon. Apparently they do not state why their choice was made, nor discuss error in the 1301 date. The course of events in the Near East ultimately defended their decision."[104]

Amadon is misleading here. Gibbon was, at this point in time, believed by the Western world at large to be almost infallible for his literary attainments. For some time he was not questioned. The sole reason Mr. Wall suggested the possible dating of the year "1300 or 1301" for the attack of Osman (Othman) referenced in *The Signs of the Times* of Sept. 1, 1840, is that the Millerites knew that nothing had happened as they predicted for August 11, 1840, since it came and went without a relevant historical marker. They were simply looking for answers for their embarrassment!

Amadon wrote:

"Von Hammer Errs in Turkish Calendar

"It is not necessary to employ the Turkish calendar in reconstructing the chronology of Pachymeres. We introduce it here merely to aid in pointing out the error in the 1301 date.

"The Turkish year was a calculation based upon observation of the moon only, and it was not tied to the solar seasons. Its beginning recedes through the various months of the year, going back to the starting point about every thirty-two years, inasmuch as each year ran short of the solar about ten or eleven days. The calendar is called that of *Muharram*, which is the name of the first month. The year is designated as *A.H.*, signifying *in the year of the Hegira,* that is, from the flight of Mohammed. Much difference of opinion has existed as to the point of time from which the Hegira years should be reckoned, and this has led to a variation in dates in Turkish chronology. There are numerous standard Hegira tables, all of which agree in their reckoning. *Webster's Dictionary* gives a simple method for computing the corresponding Julian year for any given year of the Hegira. At the time of Othman's attack, and for several subsequent years, the *Calendar of Muharram* began the year in the fall."[105]

By this writing, Amadon thought to have dismantled the credibility of Von Hammer's 1301 date. Continuing on, she stated:

---

[102] Pachymeres, op. cit., Vol. Alt., pp. 327, 830.

[103] *Signs of the Times,* Sept. 1, 1840, p. 87, col. 3.

[104] Amadon, *Ministry*, June 1944, 19.

[105] Cf. Calendar of Muharram in *Encyclopedia Britannica* under "calendar."

"Von Hammer was an Orientalist of repute, but he was not always a careful computer, for he did not prove his dates when it was in his power to do so. In his outline he follows the Turkish chronologer Hadschi Chalfa, who died in the year 1658, and hence is not a *source* authority."[106]

I have been through enough primary sources (European and Islamic) to know where Hadschi Chalfa's credibility stands in the estimation of the international academic community. If I were to tell someone like Halil İnalcik or Von Hammer or any Islamic or European historian that Hadschi Chalfa is not a *"source"* authority, I would be accounted naive and willfully ignorant. Can Amadon's private verdict be justified? We shall let a reputable, unbiased source answer this one:

ENCYCLOPÆDIA AMERICANA

"Hadschi Chalfa"

[382] "One of their oldest and most esteemed annalists is Saad-ed-din, who, after having been the instructor and tutor of two sultans, died in the office of mufti at Constantinople, in 1599. His chronicle is entitled *Tadsch-et-tawarich* (that is, the Crown of Annals), and extends from the origin of the Turks to the death of Selim I, in 1520, and is regarded by the Turks as a classical work. It has been translated by Leunclavius into Latin, by Bratutti into Italian, and by Podesta into German and Latin. In the works of Naima, Raschid and Tchelebisade, the annals of the Turkish empire, from 1592 to 1727, are continued in unbroken succession. Hadschi Chalfa, surnamed Tchelebisade, who died at Constantinople, 1657, was distinguished for his historical and literary attainments. Under the title of *Open Books,* and *Knowledge of Science*, he composed a work of a cyclopaedic and bibliographical character, in which the names of all the branches of science cultivated by the Arabians, Persians and Turks, are given, and the titles of all the works written in these three languages, from the 1st to the 1050th year of the Hegira (A.D. 1640). This work served as the foundation of the Encyclopaedic View of Oriental Science (by Joseph von Hammer, Leipsic, 1804), to which is prefixed an autobiography of Hadschi Chalfa. Besides this biographical work, and several other writings of Hadschi Chalfa, his chronological tables, beginning with Adam, and continuing to 1640, deserve to be particularly mentioned. The Latin translation of these, by Reiske, is still to be found in manuscript in the royal library at Copenhagen. In poetry, also, the Arabians and Persians are their models. Their poems are chiefly of a mystical or moral cast, or devoted to love. We need only mention the romantic poem of the Turk Molla Khosrew, *Chosroes and Shercen.* Some Turkish eclogues are contained in Hammer's *Morgenländisches Kleeblatt* (Eastern Trefoil, Vienna, 1819). Riddles, logogryphs, chronograms, and similar poetical trifles, are very popular among them. All their poetical productions are [383] in rhyme. Their prosody and the technical part of their poetry are the same as those of the Arabians and Persians. *Mosnevi* is a long poem, in which each distich has its peculiar rhyme; *gazelles* and *cassides* are odes or songs with a single rhyme; the *rubaji* (tetrastichon) is mostly epigrammatic; the *kitaa* has 4-8 strophes with various rhymes, and is applicable to all subjects. Accounts of Turkish poets, and

---

[106] Amadon, *Ministry*, June 1944, 19.

specimens of their poetry, are contained in *Lalifi*, or Biographical Sketches of eminent Turkish Poets, together with an Anthology drawn from their works; translated from the Turkish of Monka Abdul Latifi and Aschik Hassan Tschelebi, by Thomas Chabert (Zürich, 1808). The *Divan* of Baki, the principal lyric poet of Turkey, who died in 1600, has been translated into German, entire, by Joseph von Hammer (Vienna, 1825)."[107]

Despite Amadon's stated rejection of Chalfa as a highly-regarded and highly-qualified "source," she reversed herself later and acknowledged Hadschi Chalfa as a "*source*" authority. The following statements taken from the July 1944 *Ministry* magazine display this well:

"It has also been demonstrated that the Von Hammer date of 1301 for the same event came about from his erroneous use of the Hegira calendar, and that his date actually corresponds to the year 1302, when the Greek Muzalo was finally overcome. The record in the *Cronologia* of Hadschi Chalfa appears to bear out this conclusion."[108]

"Both Pachymeres and Possinus are in agreement with Hadschi Chalfa that the *final* defeat of Muzalo – not his first attack – was in 1302."[109]

Amadon continued with her case:

"Petrus Possinus, the chronologer and analyst of the Pachymerian volumes, and one with whom Von Hammer checks, also employs the Turkish calendar in his *Synopsis*.[110] But he is commonly correct in his Julian dates, for he proves them. However, there are historians for this period who err in their use of the Turkish calendar, as Cantemir has pointed out.[111] We shall cite two statements from Possinus in order to show that he himself had in hand a correct Turkish table:
a. "In the year of the Hegira 700 [A.H.], whose beginning was the 16th day of September, in the year 1300 of the vulgar Christian era." Etc.[112]
b. "The first day of that year of the Hegira 702 [A.H.] was the 26th of the month of August in the year of 1302 of our era."[113]
"These two statements and their accompanying dates are in precise agreement with the standard Turkish calendar for our period. The section of the Turkish table to which they belong is here repeated:

Calendar of Muharran[114]

---

[107] *Encyclopedia Americana* (Philadelphia: Blanchard and Lea, 1851), 382-383.
[108] Amadon, *Ministry*, July 1944, 5.
[109] Georgius Pachymeres, *Corpus Scriptorum Historiae Byzantinae* (Bonn ed.: 1835), Vol. Alt., p. 851. (Petri Possini, *Observationum*) Found in Amadon, *Ministry* magazine, July 1944, 12.
[110] A synopsis by Possinus is found at the end of each volume of Pachymeres' Byzantine history.
[111] Demetrius Cantemir, *History of the Growth and Decay of the Othman Empire*, Sec. I (London: 1734), preface. Herbert Gibbons says, "It is typically Ottoman to be vague about names as well as about dates." – Op. cit., 270.
[112] Pachymeres, op. cit., Vol. Alt., 823. (Petri Possini, *Observationum*.)
[113] Ibid.

Hegira   Julian Months   Months

[a] 700 A.H. = 1300 (ix to xii) + 1301 (i to viii)

701 A.H. = 1301 (ix to xii) + 1302 (i to viii)

[b] 702 A.H. = 1302 (viii to xii) + 1303 (i to vii)

"The foregoing section of a standard Hegira table agrees with the statements of Possinus, but not with those of Von Hammer, who, following Hadschi Chalfa, chose for the July battle of Bapheum the year 701 A.H.,[115] and equated it with the Julian year 1301. He necessarily admits that the attack on Bapheum occurred in the summer harvest,[116] but he overlooked the fact that in 701 A.H., the corresponding Julian year 1301 does not include the month of July, but begins with September."[117]

Amadon is right that Petrus Possinus is commonly correct in his Julian dates, for he does prove them, but it is now time to speak regarding Amadon's criticism of Von Hammer's chronological reckoning of the Hegira calendar. Amadon stated:

"Baron von Hammer, whose names carries with it the highest authority in oriental literature and researches, has lately corrected this *singular* error of Gibbon's; and refers to the very authority of Pachymere [*sic*], appealed to by Gibbon, in proof that 1301 is the true date. He refers also to other authorities, such as Had[s]chi Chalfa's Chronology. – *Geschichte des osmanischen Reiches, durch von Hammer, vol. I, p. 68, et not. P. 577.*"[118]

Translated from the German, let us first read, in their full context, pages 67 and 68 of Von Hammer's account:

Conquest of Dimsuf, Marmara, and Kujunhissar after the previous success.

"The invasion Köpruhissar inspired Osman's lust for the conquest of other neighboring castles in the vicinity of Nicaea, such as *Dimsuf, Kujunhissar*, and *Marmara*. He was further spurred by the poor circumstance of the garrisons and the flooding of the Sangaris [Sakarya]. Before the reign of the first of the Palaiologans, the commanders of the Greek border outposts were strengthened in their defense of the same through a substantial subsidy, gifts of land, and the surrender of battle spoils. When Michael Palaiologos, after the re-conquering of Constantinople from the Franks, and following the disastrous advice of Chadenos, collected the funds from the border officials and then vexed them with yet further constraints, the foreign

---

[114] Edward Mahler, *Wüstenfeld-Mahler' sche Vergleichungs-Tabellen der mohammedanischen und christlichen Zeitrechnung* (Leipzig:1926), Zweite Auflage, 19, 20; Gregorio Abul-Pharajio, *Historia Compendiosa Dynastiarum* (Oxoniae: 1663), In Supplemento. Tr. ab Edvardo Pocockio. (This latter is the Turkish calendar used by Possinus.)

[115] Von Hammer, op. cit., 67.

[116] Id., 68.

[117] Amadon, *Ministry*, June 1944, 19.

[118] Alexander Keith, *Signs of the Times* (Edinburgh: 1833), Vol. I, p. 334. Found in Amadon, *Ministry*, June 1944, 19.

mercenaries lost the desire to keep defending the strongholds that had been entrusted to them.[119] On top of this, since the Sangaris river had recently altered its course, with the help of a number of natural waterways, many of them left their castles, which had been robbed of one of their natural defenses; the river did eventually return to its usual bed, after flooding the region for a month, but in returning it so filled its bed with slime that the shallower parts of the river could no longer be traversed.[120] As a result, *Ali Ümürbek*, the ruler of Kastamonu, one of the ten princes who had shares in the Seljuk realm, was enticed to break the peace that had been made with the Greek emperor, and this lure was even stronger for *Osman*.[121] At *Kujunhissar* [today called *Koyun-Hisar*] (the Bapheus of Pachymeres), in the vicinity of Nicomedia, there came a meeting between Osman and Muzalo, the Heteriarch (that is, the commander) of the Byzantine guards, [Marginal reading: 701/1301] and the downfall of the Greeks was so disastrous that they [68] left the field free for Osman's troops, and this just at harvest time. † {27. July} Osman then had to mourn the loss of his nephew Aitoghdi ††, the son of Gundusalp, who had fallen in the battle of *Kujunhissar* and was buried near this castle, where they raised a monument, a site that is reputed to produce miraculous healings for horses,[122] like the grave of the Scotsman Oswald, the victor over the Britons at Caedwalla;[123] when brought to the same, horses whose sides have been wounded by spears can be healed. The Turks spread out until they reached the walls of Nicaea, the great height and fortification of which dashed any hopes of siege or takeover. To keep the occupiers in a state of fear and intimidation, Osman ordered the construction of another castle on the near side of the Jenischehr, which he named after the brave and similarly earnest Tharghan…."[124]

Then Amadon also referenced Von Hammer's note for page 68 on page 577, but she should have finished quoting the small paragraph to which she referred. Here is what it says, translated from the German:

"Gibbon hypothesizes [conjectures or assumes] the year 1299 without confirmation. According to Hadschi Chalfa's chronology, tables, and other Ottoman sources, the date is 1301; according to Pachymeres's chronology, given by Possinus,

---

[119] Pachymeres I. Ch. 1 – 6, edited by Possinus at the beginning of the 2nd volume, p. 610, and according to the same Gibbon, Ch. LXIV, quarto edition VI. B. p. 311. Note.
[120] Pachymeres II, Vol. IV, Book 24. Cap. Edition from Rome, 229.
[121] Pachymeres II, Vol. IV, Book 24. C., 230.
[122] Neschri folio. 38; Seadeddin folio 13.
[123] Humes, *History of England*, chapter I, according to Beda L. III, ch. 9.
[124] Seadeddin folio 12. Found in Joseph von Hammer, *Geschichte des osmanischen Reiches, durch* (*History of the Ottoman Empire*) (Pest, in C. A. Hartleben's Press, 1827), p. 67-68. [We learn from Inalcik: In *The Anonymous Chronicle* (Tevarih-i Al-i Osman), it is mentioned that, first of all, Kopruihisar was taken before the siege of Nicaea. Kopruihisar was taken with *yagma*, "pillaging," that is, by force with the result of plunder. Kopruihisar is at the junction point of the main roads coming to Nicaea from Bilecik in the south and from Yenisehir in the west. This fortress is the starting point of the Kizilhisar-Derbend valley leading to Nicaea. Osman went through this valley to Nicaea. Anyway, it was necessary for Osman to take Kopruhisar first for his campaign to Nicaea.]

it is 1302, which accords perfectly with Hadschi Chalfa's statement, because d. J. d. Hegira 701 does not end until August 1302."[125]

It is true that Edward Gibbon "assumed the year 1299 without confirmation," and so does everyone else who follows his lead. Amadon's accusation of Von Hammer for miscalculations may well now be seen in its true light, as completely false! To be fair, as we have seen from page 19 of *Ministry* magazine, Amadon can and has rightly calculated the beginning of the two following years correctly:

a. "In the year of the Hegira 700 [A.H.], whose beginning was the 16th day of September, in the year 1300 of the vulgar Christian era." Etc.[126]

b. "The first day of that year of the Hegira 702 [A.H.] was the 26th of the month of August in the year of 1302 of our era."[127]

If she would have done the same and rightly calculated for the Hegira 701 [A.H.], her mistake would have been placed in bold relief for all to see! This fact is further cemented by the following admission, correctly stated by Amadon:

"There is no Turkish calendar that makes the year 701 A.H. coincide with that part of the Christian year 1301 that embraces the month of July."[128]

To remove any further confusion on the dating of the beginning of the Islamic Hegira year with the Western (Julian) calendar year, we submit this small but accurate chart that designates the Month, Day, and Year:

698 A.H. – (Julian) Oct. 9, 1298
699 A.H. – (Julian) Sept. 28, 1299
700 A.H. – (Julian) Sept. 16, 1300
701 A.H. – (Julian) Sept. 5, 1301
702 A.H. – (Julian) Aug. 26, 1302

This means that the year 701 A.H. began in September of 1301. July 27 would naturally not come around until the next year of the Julian calendar year of 1302. This would also hold true for the 698/1298 Hegira year because the year 698 A.H. began in October of 1298 and July 27 would again not fall into place until the summer of the Julian calendar year of 1299. This is the method used by all historians concerning 701/1301 when they do not qualify a Julian calendar date, contrary to what Amadon claims.[129] That is because it is generally understood that the reader knows how to compute the Hegira calendar of Muharram.

Amadon is correct that the day and month of July 27 fall into the Julian calendar year of 1302. In fact, Pachymeres, Possinus, Hadschi Chalfa, Edouard de Muralt, Halil Inalcik and, of course, Joseph von Hammer, as we have just witnessed, as well as others, all place the month, day, year, and "event" of July 27 in the year 1302. All along the question should have been, "Which of the two

---

[125] Joseph von Hammer, *Geschichte des osmanischen Reiches* (Pest, 1827), I Band, p. 577. [Emphasis mine]
[126] Pachymeres, op. cit., Vol. Alt., 823. (Petri Possini, *Observationum.*)
[127] Amadon, *Ministry*, June 1944, 19.
[128] Ibid. [Emphasis in the original]
[129] Amadon, *Ministry*, July 1944, 12.

dates can be found and sustained from the primary historical sources for the claimed event of 698/1298 or 701/1301?"

Before we address some of Amadon's remaining remarks in the June *Ministry* article of 1944, and before we bring this to a conclusion, we need to first tackle some issues she raised in the July article:

Ministry Magazine

July, 1944

"In the first part of this historical series, it was shown that Von Hammer erred in his use of the Turkish calendar. . . . Both Pachymeres and Possinus are in agreement with Hadschi Chalfa that the *final* defeat of Muzalo – not his first attack – was in 1302.[130]

We have just witnessed that Von Hammer did not err, and that Amadon's claims to that end-were utterly false. Amadon next claimed the "final" defeat of the Byzantine commander Muzalo took place on July 27, 1302, not during his first attack. As we will see, Amadon placed the first substantial clash or attack on Byzantine soil at Bapheus (Bapheum) on July 27, 1299, and claimed the support of Possinus in his narrative of Pachymeres. Let's see if Amadon's assessments can withstand investigation:

"The historical date to be investigated in this study has to do with the first substantial clash between the Ottoman (Osmanli) Turks and the troops of the Byzantine Empire; that is, the first encroachment of Othman, or Osman, and his tribe upon the Oriental border of medieval Europe and its fortified castles. The limited sources extant agree that the invasion began with the Ottoman assault on Bapheum (Turkish, *Kujun-Hissar*), a sheep castle, whose protective moat was filled with water from the river Sangarius, flowing not far from Nicomedia."[131]

"Hence the sudden announcement of the defeat of Muzalo as the worst defeat of the [13] war must have come in the year 1302, probably in the summer when the Turks were customarily raiding the harvests.[132] At this time not only Othman but other leaders also were in command of the attacking barbarians. Pachymeres now proceeds to describe the initial assault on the Byzantine border three years before, when Othman first met Muzalo in the fields around Nicomedia, where he was pillaging food for his army. *This is the event that dates the beginning of the Turkish prophecy.*

"Othman's Attack on Bapheum, Bk. IV, ch. 25)

"The attack on the castle of Bapheum in 1299, when Othman first met Muzalo, represents the actual beginning of the Turkish invasion of the empire. Pachymeres calls it the 'beginning of enormous evils,' and one in which 'during the space of a few

---

[130] Georgius Pachymeres, *Corpus Scriptorum Historiae Byzantinae* (Bonn ed., 1835), Vol. Alt., 851. (Petri Possini, *Observationum.*) Found in Amadon, *Ministry*, July, 1944, 12.

[131] Amadon, *Ministry*, June 1944, 18.

[132] Ibid., p. 851. Here Possinus places the final defeat of Muzalo in 1302; but he apparently refers also to the first attack, which on page 830 he definitely dates in 1299. The irregularity in the narrative makes the analysis difficult.

months all the territory around Nicaea and Brusa was plundered and pillaged.'[133] The narrative begins:

> "*Mensis siquidem Julii die vicesima septima circa Bapheum (locus hic prope inclytam Nicomediam), Atman cum suis multorum millium numerum explentibus improvise apparens et subito irruens – sed melius fuerit rem aliquanto repetitam altius a suis retro ducere principiis.*"[134]

> "TRANSLATION: Without doubt,[135] on the twenty-seventh day of the month of July around Bapheum (this place was the well-known Nicomedia), Othman, with his army full of many thousands in number, unexpectedly appearing, and suddenly attacking – but it would be better to prolong the account, and repeat it somewhat further back from the beginning.

> "Othman *suddenly* and *unexpectedly* appears for the attack –"[136]

Then on page 13 Amadon presented a chart of Pachymeres' narrative through the years 1299, 1300 and 1301, outlining by synchronisms and astronomical events, rather than using the chronological chart by Possinus of Pachymeres' narrative through the years 1298, 1299, 1300, 1301 and 1302 that would have corrected her errors, just as Von Hammer said of Edward Gibbon.

Amadon stated:

> "...The Millerites based their deductions upon the historical statement of Edward Gibbon that on July 27, A.D. 1299, 'Othman first invaded the territory of Nicomedia.'[137] Gibbon stresses the date as one of 'singular accuracy.' About half a century later Joseph von Hammer challenged Gibbon's 1299 date, claiming that the year 1301 was correct for the invasion of Othman, and saying that a study limited merely to the Byzantine writers would have corrected his errors."[138]

As to the authority of Joseph von Hammer's history, the following quotation from the preface to the *History of the Ottoman Turks,* by Sir Edward S. Creasy, will be pertinent:

> "Von Hammer's history of the Ottoman Empire will always be the standard European book on this subject. That history was the result of the labors of thirty years, during which von Hammer explored, in addition to the authorities which his predecessors had made use of, the numerous works of the Turkish and other Oriental writers of the Ottoman history, and the other rich sources of intelligence which are to be found in the archives of Venice, Austria, and the other states that have been [4] involved in relations of hostility or amity with the Sublime Porte. Von Hammer's long residence in the East and his familiarity with the institutions, habits, as well as with the literature of the Turks, give an additional attractiveness and value to his

---

[133] Ibid., 337.

[134] Ibid.

[135] The word *siquidem* in medieval Latin signifies "without doubt." J. H. Baxter and Charles Johnson, *Medieval Latin Word-List* (London: Oxford University Press, 1934), 390.

[136] Amadon, *Ministry*, July 1944, 12-13.

[137] Gibbons, op. cit., 265.

[138] Joseph von Hammer, *Geschichte des osmanischen Reiches* (Pest, 1827), I Band, Preface XXIII. Found in Amadon, *Ministry*, June 1944, 18.

volumes. His learning is as accurate as it is varied, his honesty and candour are unquestioned, and his history is certainly one of the productions of the first half of our century."[139]

Here is what Joseph von Hammer actually said about Edward Gibbon, translated from the German:

"Who should believe that Cantemir and Petis de la Croix, though both were Orientalists, garble the actual Oriental names to the point of unrecognizability, and that particularly the former left behind a heap of philological errors which make clear his complete lack of basic knowledge of the Arabic, Persian, and Turkish languages. And finally, who should believe that even Gibbon,[140] the only classical author to write about the first period of Ottoman history, who unites a comprehensive knowledge of the sources with the greatest historical critique, and the greatest artfulness of style with the most important conclusions, still allowed certain oversights and errors to take place, all of which could have been prevented by a simple study of the Byzantines!"[141]

We shall view this source momentarily. Amadon states:

"Hence neither Von Hammer nor those who have followed his lead have any authority for the year 1301 as the date of the Ottoman invasion…. Von Hammer himself employs the July 27 date of Pachymeres, although he takes his *year 1301* from Hadschi Chalfa. We are therefore faced with the problem of proving the year to which Pachymeres' July 27 date belongs."[142]

We shall soon see to which year the 27th of July truly belongs. Moving ahead, we observe the foundational points of Amadon as she presented them:

"…By the aid of the fierce plunderers from Paphlagonia under Amurius, Othman achieved his pillage of Bapheum on July 27, 1299, just as Pachymeres implies, and Possinus insists in his analysis. The Latin translator says:
"Othman increased in power when a very strong force of the fiercest warriors from Paphlagonia had been joined to his army, and, in a battle near Nicomedia, the metropolis of Bithynia, he subdued Muzalo, the Roman leader who had attempted to resist, which [city] he, as lord of the field, then held as a city besieged. Pachymeres plainly reports that these things happened around Bapheum near Nicomedia on the twenty-seventh day of the month of July: from a series of things in the *Synopsis*, we truly affirm in like manner that this was the year 1299 of the Christian Era."[143]

---

[139] Sir Edward S. Creasy, *History of the Ottoman Turks* (London: Richard Bentley, 1854), preface, vi-vii.
[140] Gibbon's *History of the Decline and Fall of the Roman Empire*. London, 1788. 6 Quarto Volumes.
[141] Joseph von Hammer, *Geschichte des osmanischen Reiches, durch* (History of the Ottoman Empire) (Pest, in C. A. Hartleben's Press, 1827), xxiii.
[142] Amadon, *Ministry*, June 1944, 19.
[143] Pachymeres, op. cit., Vol. Alt., 830. (Petri Possini, *Observationum.*)

"The character of the year 1299 and the circumstances connected with the first raid of Othman precisely agree, while with them the year 1301 does not agree....

"It is obvious that some historians have confused the two battle scenes with Muzalo – the initial attack at Bapheum, and his final rout in Mesothinia, which the Turks appear to include in their *Caramania*.[144] An understanding use of the year of the Hegira and its correct application to the Julian year would have harmonized these important records of medieval Turkish history. Let us note the contrasting features between the two military scenes with Muzalo:

"1. In the raid on Bapheum in 1299 the Alans were brave and fell in the fight, 'offering their own bodies as a protection to the fleeing Romans.'[145] In the Turkish battles of 1302 the Alans were not dependable, and asked for a three months' rest in the midst of the fight, and got it. This discouraged the remainder of the listless troops, and in the end Michael was defeated and fled to Pergamum with the remnant of his army, while the Alans went toward home, pillaging and plundering the Greek villages en route.[146]

"2. In the 1299 attack on Bapheum, Muzalo was 'the lone guard of the border.'[147] He was not permanently captured by Othman. After the 1302 battle [15] of Magnesia, it was announced that Muzalo also was completely defeated and overthrown. Pachymeres' narrative mentions the three barbarian leaders who were in the field at this time, besides 'others,' too! In this year, therefore, the Persians were attacking in several sections, while in 1299, the army of Othman was the only offensive.

"3. The first attack on the empire was in Bithynia, of which Nicomedia was the metropolis. The final defeat of Muzalo in 1302 was in Mesothinia, which was farther inland than Bithynia and was also called *Mesonesium* by Pachymeres.[148] This territory appears to be the same as the Turkish *Caramania* of Hadschi Chalfa.

"In this analysis and review of Pachymerian history, in harmony with the analysis of the same by Possinus, it has been shown that July 27, 1299, was the date of the first Ottoman assault on Byzantine territory. It has also been demonstrated that the Von Hammer date of 1301 for the same event came about from his erroneous use of the Hegira calendar, and that his date actually corresponds to the year 1302, when the Greek Muzalo was finally overcome. The record in the *Cronologia* of Hadschi Chalfa appears to bear out this conclusion. The date July 27, 1299, therefore, consistently marks the beginning of the 150-year 'torment' in Revelation 9."[149]

Let's begin our analysis by differentiating between what is fact and what has been assumed. The reader must be reminded that prior to the Crusader campaign in 1097, the Turkish invaders had established the Anatolian Seljukid Sultanate in Nicaea (Iznik) in 1087. Skirmishes of the Turkmen (Turcoman) and Seljukids against the Byzantine lords (tekfurs) in their area continued throughout

---

[144] Hazi Halifé Mustafá, op. cit., 110.
[145] Pachymeres, op. cit., Vol. Alt., 334.
[146] Ibid., 319-321.
[147] Ibid., 333.
[148] Ibid., 460.
[149] Amadon, *Ministry*, July 1944, 14-15.

the years and among different localities. However, our concern does not come into focus until the first contact between the imperial army and Osman at Bapheus.

The historian Halil İnalcik, professor at Bilkent University, Turkey, is recognized the world over yet today (although deceased in 2006) as the man at the pinnacle of his field for his scholarship, uncompromising integrity, and clarity regarding the facts of Ottoman history. Professor İnalcik published more than 200 scholarly articles and numerous books. It is a pleasure to share this man's life work and toil in helping the international academic community bring closure to the many outstanding issues surrounding the history of Islam and the origins of the Ottoman Empire. The beauty of truth is that nothing is forced; it just falls into place as Halil Inalcik goes through the primary sources, showing how Pachymeres and Islamic sources complement one another:

> "In the Anonymous [Tevarih-i Al-i Osman] Chronicle it does not mention the first reconnaissance force of about one hundred men *(Pachymeres)* sent by Osman against Bapheus castle blocking the road. Actually, these two independent sources give information complementing each other. Both sources unite on the point that the Emperor sent his army to save Nicaea under siege. The Anonymous Chronicle provides complementing details about the Nicaea siege and the city."[150]

Did Osman (Othman) "first" invade the territory of Bapheum near Nicomedia on the 27th of July, 1299, as Gibbon and Amadon claim? We shall hear from Halil Inalcik first:

> "The Byzantines had determined the line of fortresses on the Sakarya River as the final defense line protecting Nicaea and Constantinopolis. Osman Gazi took the complete control of the Dorylaion defense line by first of all conquering Karacahisar in 1288 *(figs.1,2)*. Karacahisar was under a Tekvur who used to pay [60] tribute to the Seljukid Sultan; but acting against Osman, he had lost the Sultan's protection (Asikpasazade, 6. *Bab)*. After the capture of Bilecik *(Belokomis)* in 1299, Osman attempted in 1302 to seize Nicaea, which caused the battle of Bapheus. The collapse of the second line with his conquests of Lefke, Mekece, Akhisar and Geyve *(1304)*, Nicaea *(iznik)* was cut off on all sides. The Turkish raiders, just as in the reign of Suleymansah (1075-1086), were seen at the shores of the Bosphorus as early as 1304-1305. In the following paragraphs we will examine the siege of Nicaea by Osman, the battle of Bapheus *(Koyunhisar)* in 1302, and the campaigns in 1304 and 1305 to capture the fortresses on the Sakarya River to complete the blockade of Nicaea.... The conquest of the Bilecik-Yenisehir region in 1299 signifies a definite development stage in Osman's career. Between 1300-1302, soon after this conquest, Osman attempted to directly conquer Nicaea and Prussa *(Bursa)*. Unable to conquer, he held them under blockade by building forts around them. Only at this stage, Osman's activities caused serious concern in the Byzantine capital. Pachymeres, the historian close to the palace, mentioned Osman as a threat at that time.
> "Like the other beys conquering Western Anatolian territories from the Byzantines, towards 1299, Osman Gazi undoubtedly took under his control an extensive region beyond the Seljukid borders from Karacahisar to Bilecik-Yenisehir and appeared to be in the position of a bey ruling over many cities and fortresses. Subsequently,

---

[150] Isil Akbaygil, Halil Inalcik, Oktay Aslanapa, eds., *Iznik Throughout History* (Istanbul: Ofset Yapimevi, Yahya Kemal Mahallesi Sair Sokak, 2003), 65. ISBN: 975-458-431-1.

Osman dealt no more with the local Byzantine tekfurs, who were subject to paying tribute to the Seljukid Sultan, but started gaza activities directly against the forces of the Byzantine Empire." [151]

Osman's first attack was Karacahisar in the year 1288. The attack of Bilecik *(Belokomis)* in 699/1299 is consequently somewhat south of Bapheus *(Koyunhisar)*. Halil Inalcik gave no reference as to the source of his information, but I recognized the source right away as none other than Pachymeres. In fact, it is the same source and page numbers that Amadon claimed fulfilled the "first" battle at Bapheum, July 27, 1299. For convenience's sake, we repeat this pertinent, earlier-quoted excerpt from Amadon:

> "Hence the sudden announcement of the defeat of Muzalo as the worst defeat of the [13] war must have come in the year 1302, probably in the summer when the Turks were customarily raiding the harvests.[152] At this time not only Othman but other leaders also were in command of the attacking barbarians. Pachymeres now proceeds to describe the initial assault on the Byzantine border three years before, when Othman first met Muzalo in the fields around Nicomedia, where he was pillaging food for his army. *This is the event that dates the beginning of the Turkish prophecy.*
>
> "Othman's Attack on Bapheum Bk. IV, ch. 25)
>
> "The attack on the castle of Bapheum in 1299, when Othman first met Muzalo, represents the actual beginning of the Turkish invasion of the empire. Pachymeres calls it the 'beginning of enormous evils,' and one in which 'during the space of a few months all the territory around Nicaea and Brusa was plundered and pillaged.'"[153]
> The narrative begins:
>
> *"Mensis siquidem Julii die vicesima septima circa Bapheum (locus hic prope inclytam Nicomediam), Atman cum suis multorum millium numerum explentibus improvise apparens et subito irruens – sed melius fuerit rem aliquanto repetitam altius a suis retro ducere principiis. "*[154]
>
> "TRANSLATION: Without doubt,[155] on the twenty-seventh day of the month of July around Bapheum (this place was the well-known Nicomedia), Othman, with his army full of many thousands in number, unexpectedly appearing, and suddenly attacking – but it would be better to prolong the account, and repeat it somewhat further back from the beginning.
>
> "Othman *suddenly* and *unexpectedly* appears for the attack –"[156]

Here is a more accurate and unbiased translation of Pachymeres:

---

[151] Ibid., 59-61.

[152] Pachymeres, op. cit., Vol. Alt., p. 851. Here Possinus places the final defeat of Muzalo in 1302, but he apparently refers also to the first attack, which on page 830 he definitely dates in 1299. The irregularity in the narrative makes the analysis difficult. Found in Amadon, *Ministry*, July 1944, 13.

[153] Id., 337.

[154] Ibid., 327. [Misquoted footnote of 337 should have been 327.]

[155] The word *siquidem* in medieval Latin signifies "without doubt." J. H. Baxter and Charles Johnson, *Medieval Latin Word-List* (London: Oxford University Press, 1934), 390.

[156] Amadon, *Ministry*, July 1944, 12-13.

"On the 27th day of the month of July, in the neighborhood of Bapheum (this place is near the renowned Nicomedia), Atman with his men totaling the number of many thousands, unexpectedly appearing and making a sudden attack – but it would be better to recount this whole matter from its beginnings."[157]

In this unbiased account, it is clear that Pachymeres did not start his narrative of events with the July 27th date. He went back in time, as pages 328 and onward clearly confirm.

On her part, Amadon claimed that July 27, 1299, was the "beginning of enormous evils:"

"Pachymeres calls it the 'beginning of enormous evils,' and one in which 'during the space of a few months all the territory around Nicaea and Brusa was plundered and pillaged.'"[158]

However, Pachymeres and other historians alike placed the "beginning of enormous evils" after the battle of Bapheus on July 27, 1302, because this was truly the turning point in the war with Osman and his hordes:

"The Greek historian[159] describes with dramatic expressions in his final sections, the situation of anarchy and hopelessness between 1302-1307 into which the Byzantine Empire fell after the Bapheus defeat."[160]

"…With the Bapheus victory won in 1302 against an imperial army, thousands of gazis, who believed that the resistance of the Byzantine Empire had been broken, came in hordes from the interior of Anatolia to the Bithynia region for gaza and spoils. Pachymeres himself indicated that the news had reached the gazis in Paphlagonia *(Kastamonu region)* and that the fame of Osman Gazi had reached there. He says that now the threats came up to the gates of Istanbul and the Turks were wandering around freely in small groups on the other side of the Straits. *There* is *not a single day that passes without hearing that the enemy* is *attacking the fortresses on the coast and taking people prisoners or killing them....*"[161]

In a footnote Amadon submitted her own proof as follows:

"Here Possinus places the final defeat of Muzalo in 1302; but he apparently refers also to the first attack, which on page 830 he definitely dates in 1299. The irregularity in the narrative makes the analysis difficult."[162]

That "irregularity in the narrative" will be seen to be of her own devising. Note that Amadon specifically claimed that the "first attack" of Osman against Bapheum was on July 27, 1299:

---

[157] Georgius Pachymeres, *Corpus Scriptorum Historiae Byzantinae* (Bonn ed., 1827), Vol. Alt., 327.

[158] Pachymeres, p. 337. Found in Amadon, *Ministry,* July 1944, p. 13.

[159] Pachymeres, 4:13, Chapter 35, 700.

[160] Isil Akbaygil, Halil Inalcik, Oktay Aslanapa, eds., *Iznik Throughout History* (Istanbul: Ofset Yapimevi, Yahya Kemal Mahallesi Sair Sokak, 2003), 68. ISBN: 975-458-431-1.

[161] Ibid., 74.

[162] Amadon, *Ministry*, July 1944, p. 30, footnote 27.

"This is the event that dates the beginning of the Turkish prophecy."[163]

Her proof is claimed to be on page 830 of Possinus' narrative, which we will view after submitting one more foundational statement from Amadon. We want to reader to be clear on her stated position:

> "By the aid of the fierce plunderers from Paphlagonia under Amurius, Othman achieved his pillage of Bapheum on July 27, 1299, just as Pachymeres implies, and Possinus insists in his analysis. The Latin translator says:
> "Othman increased in power when a very strong force of the fiercest warriors from Paphlagonia had been joined to his army, and, in a battle near Nicomedia, the metropolis of Bithynia, he subdued Muzalo the Roman leader who had attempted to resist, which [city] he, as lord of the field, then held as a city besieged. Pachymeres plainly reports that these things happened around Bapheum near Nicomedia on the twenty-seventh day of the month of July: from a series of things in the *Synopsis,* we truly affirm in like manner that this was the year 1299 of the Christian Era."[164]

Note that her claimed and only proof that mentions the July 27 date is to be found on page 830 of Possinus' narrative. Ironically, so is Halil İnalcik's proof of what he earlier said, that we just quoted. It will not only be seen that Amadon has superimposed her views on the text, but that she is misleading, as well. We therefore now submit Possinus' narrative as translated from the Latin from pages 829 to 830, so the reader may view it in a complete context.

> "V. From this it is evident how the annals of the Arabs agreeing with the memory of this history of mine relate what I have written out in full earlier, that Ortogrules father of Othman had died in the year of Hegira 687, which partly coincides with the year of Christ 1288, famous for the successes of war, reported concerning the Roman militia namely of the Persian frontier, which (Roman militia) indeed began clearly to weaken already at the time after Constantinople was seized from the Latins, sixteen years earlier. Since Othman the son succeeding Ortogrules even at that time held several places acquired from the Romans by force, to which he had added more and larger places later continuously by the felicity of more years for the paternal authority of Karaiaptaga, accordingly the name of Sultan, the highest prince, he did not hesitate at all to usurp, hoping it [the name] would be able to protect himself. To establish the seat of this first and as if fundamental epoch of the Ottoman Empire indeed in the order of our time, is what I will try to bring about by comparing the witness of the Arab chronologies and of our Pachymer. Pachymer says, p. 327 v. 6, that Atman [Osman] had increased in power with wealth by means of joining to himself a very strong force of very fierce warriors [830] from Paphlagonia, and the Roman leader Muzalon had in turn tried to resist him [Osman] with a battle line near the Nicomedian metropolis of Bithynia, which town the ruler of the open field held at that time as if though besieged. Pachymer relates clearly that these things happened

---

[163] Ibid., 13.
[164] Pachymeres, op. cit., Vol. Alt., 830. (Petri Possini, *Observationum.*) Found in Amadon, *Ministry,* July 1944, 14.

around Bapheus close to Nicomedia on the twenty-seventh day of the month of July: I affirm that, from the order of things in the Synopsis, this year likely [*verisimiliter*: probably, realistically; in all probability] was 1299 of Christ. For the following 1300 I would think that what had happened was what our {historian} says p. 415 v. 1, namely that certain Roman troops with the leader a certain Siurus, who was sent by the emperor to protect this province, after having been gathered by Atman had been destroyed by massacre; 'whence the victor Atman proceeding to Belocoma' (the words are Pachymer's) 'leaping into by force captures [it], and there he kills the ones hidden. He himself however is considered very rich after that, since he is in possession of the immense wealth which was locked up for this entrenchment. Naturally making use of the fortresses of that fortification which were strong in place and by design for the protection of the special money, a great treasury for himself, whence he supplied the costs of war and of the principate, he had it (the treasury) in readiness securely stored. A great part of these calamities overflowed back into Prusa, which was thus emptied of the occupation of its land (country) and forced within the borders of the walls' etc. These are the words of Pachymeres; which indicate clearly enough the change made at this time under Atman, as it were from a private citizen into foremost position. Let us hear now the Arabs. These affirm with great consensus that Atman from the toparch/province of Karaiaptaga and the simple satrap had adopted the name of Sultan or supreme ruler in the year of Hegira 699. Since the Kalends of Muharramus of this year settled on the day 28 of the Julian September in the year of Christ 1299, and the battle of Belocoma which we have remembered from Pachymer seems to have extended to the summer months, it is resigned <u>that</u> it should be understood that Atman begins to rule, without even any dissimulation by usurping openly the designation of empire, in the year of Christ 1300, and that which Pachymer intimated <u>that</u> it had been in Bithynia at the city Prusa, which a little later had been added to him in the name of a peace subject to tribute, in fact full of surrender and subjection, while he writes thus p. 597 v. 14: 'Prusa herself having fallen under great calamities bought from the Persians at a huge enumerated price the shadow of peace, in place of true peace, which they displayed to the promised thieves.' Thus he says.

"VI. Nevertheless I do not draw from him this, that I think Prusa was fully possessed even then by Atman at the time from the beginning of the kingdom, since certain ones of the Arabs recount that close at the approach of the end only of the life of Atman, certain ones only after his death by his son and successor Urchan that it was subjugated thoroughly. Since indeed he had this city girded with fortresses everywhere possessed by him and (thus had) revenue at will, however he bore with a calm mind that he had been excluded from its entrance, which, at some time or other for himself and his family, as things were then, he presumed with certain hope would be opened freely. Therefore he worked on this, to assert dominion for himself of the land and of that province, nearly of all of Bithynia, which he obtained by seizing and keeping with a very strong protection the first-rate fortresses, whence both the safety and security of great cities....”[165]

Just as Halil İnalcik declared, we have witnessed from the primary sources that in 1288, Othman (Osman), the son succeeding Ortogrules, even at that time held several places acquired from the Romans by force, to which he added more and larger places later from the Byzantine lords:

“By 700/1301 ‘Osmān had advanced far enough to press in close on the old Byzantine capital of Nicaea (Iznik). Old Ottoman traditions on his origin and on his activities before that date, show that he had come under the pressure of the Germiyan dynasty and was thus forced to work in the most forward part of the marches. It was this circumstance which made for his future success and for that of the principality which he founded. According to the same traditions, ‘Osmān’s early activity did not amount to a general and ceaseless struggle against the Byzantines. At first he tried to get on with the more powerful of the Byzantine lords (*tekfurs*) in his area. He appeared in the light of a bey of a semi-nomadic group of Turcomans in conflict with the *tekfurs* who controlled their summer and winter pastures.[166] Old sources, which are legendary in character, attribute ‘Osmān’s decision to come forward as a *ghāzī* to the influence of Shaykh Ede Bali. In fact, however, the factors which [268] impelled ‘Osmān to become a leader of *ghāzīs* were the same factors as motivated the whole activity in the marches of western Anatolia, in other words, the pressure of population and the need for expansion resulting from the movement of immigration from central Anatolia, the decay of the Byzantine frontier-defense system, and religious and social discontent in the Byzantine frontier areas, as well as the desire of Anatolian Turks to escape from Mongol oppression and to start a new life in new territory.
“‘Osmān had become master of an area stretching from Eskishehir to the plains of Iznik and Brusa (Bursa), and had organized a fairly powerful principality. When he started threatening Iznik, anxiety was for the first time felt in the Byzantine capital on his score. It was then that the Byzantine Empire began counting him among the most important beys of the marches alongside the houses of ‘Alīshīr, Aydin and Menteshe.”[167]

At first Osman tried to establish peaceful interaction with the more powerful Byzantine lords (*tekfurs*) in his area. Then in the year of the Hegira 699, since the Kalends of Muharramus of this year settled on the day 28 of the Julian September in the year of Christ 1299, the battle of Belocoma, not Bapheus, is what Possinus’ narrative clearly states took place, as Halil İnalcik also rightly declared. If the battle “seems to have extended to the summer months,” it can hardly be said to have

---

[165] Georgius Pachymeres, *Corpus Scriptorum Historiae Byzantinae* (Bonn ed., 1835), Vol. Alt., 829-830. (Petri Possini, *Observationum.*)

[166] On ‘Osmān’s tribal origin and his membership of the Kayi tribe of the Oghuz Turks, see M. F. Köprülü, ‘Osmanli imparatorluğunun etnik menşei meseleleri,’ in Belleten, 28, pp. 219-303, who defends against P. Wittek the view that ‘Osmān was the leader of a small clan of the Kayi. According to Köprülü, this tribal nucleus played a negligible part in the formation of a state which did not have a tribal character even at its inception; on this point Köprülü is in agreement with Wittek and Giese.

[167] P. M. Holt, Ann K. S. Lambton, & Bernard Lewis, *The Cambridge History of Islam,* of *The Central Islamic Lands* (Cambridge: Syndics of the Cambridge University Press, 1970), 1:267-8.

begun July 27, 1299! However, we are not told when it commenced, so while the Hegira year 699 rightly commenced on September 28, 1299, in the Julian calendar year, as Possinus correctly said, the following summer months would then extend this to the Julian year of 1300. As Inalcik has accurately reported:

> "The conquest of the Bilecik-Yenisehir region in 1299 signifies a definite development stage in Osman's career.... Osman's activities caused serious concern in the Byzantine capital. Pachyrneres, the historian close to the palace, mentioned Osman as a threat at that time."[168]

It should now be obvious that Possinus totally conjectured about July 27 and the year 1299. This is where it is believed Gibbon and everyone else after him got the July 27, 1299, date. As we previously noted, Von Hammer correctly wrote:

> "Gibbon hypothesizes [conjectures or assumes] the year 1299 without confirmation. According to Hadschi Chalfa's chronology, tables, and other Ottoman sources, the date is 1301; according to Pachymeres's chronology, given by Possinus, it is 1302, which accords perfectly with Hadschi Chalfa's statement, because d. J. d. Hegira 701 does not end until August 1302."[169]

Inalcik brings clarity to the Bapheus conflict that followed the conquest of the Bilecik-Yenisehir region in 1299:

> "According to the Ottoman tradition, by 1337 fortresses of Yalak-Ova and Koyun-Hisari formed the appanage of a Byzantine princess. The fortresses are described exactly as follows: 'the fortress in the valley (deredeki) in the [75] Yalak-Ova belonged to an infidel by the name of Yalknya (or Balknya), and on the hill there was another fort which they call Koyun-Hisari at the present time.' Yalak-Ova was the name given to the area between Yalova and Hersek or Kara-Mursel. Ottoman tradition adds that Koyun-Hisari was put under the command of Kaloyan, brother of the 'master' (sahib) of Yalak-Ova, Yalknya. Joseph von Hammer correctly identifies Bapheus with Koyun-Hisari,[170] but confuses it with another Koyun-Hisari ner Dimboz where Osman confronted the coalition of the tekvurs [the Byzantine lords (tekfurs)] of the Bursa plain. Just before the battle of Bapheus Osman had captured a man from Yalak-Hisari and learned from him that his ambush at the Yalak-Ova was not known to the enemy. The Koyun-Hisari village in the Kite cadiship had its karye (village) status in the 16th century and then was mentioned in the following survey registers as a simple mezra'a, or an abandoned village. Apparently, it was a gathering point of the sheep herds, the tax revenue of which was levied by the Koyun-emini. In this period the yuruks, mostly Akca-Koyunlu, are mentiond in the area."[171]

---

[168] Isil Akbaygil, Halil Inalcik, Oktay Aslanapa, eds., *Iznik Throughout History* (Istanbul: Ofset Yapimevi, Yahya Kemal Mahallesi Sair Sokak, 2003), 60-61. ISBN: 975-458-431-1.

[169] Joseph von Hammer, *Geschichte des osmanischen Reiches* (Pest, 1827), I Band, p. 577. (Emphasis mine.)

[170] Joseph von Hammer, *Geschichte des Osmanischen Reiches* (Pest 1835), I. 67, p. 85.

[171] Halil İnalcik, *Essays in Ottoman History* (Istanbul: Eren Yayincilik, 1998), 74-5. (Emphasis mine.)

We now return to Amadon's narrative and, momentarily, to the events of the final Koyun-Hisari-Bapheus conflict. We will now show that Amadon, like Gibbon, superimposed the battle of Bapheus onto July 27, 1299, because there is no such account from any of the "primary sources" (European or Islamic) that give the July 27th date to the year 1299. All primary sources listed by Von Hammer that quote the July 27 date unanimously declare the year to be 1302! This proof is forthcoming.

We begin with the primary of the primaries, Pachymeres. In his *Observationum,* Possini presented his chronological tables of the works of Pachymeres. Everything he wrote pertaining to Osman's military excursions against the Byzantine (*tekfurs*) and military from the year 1298 – 1302 will be presented below, translated from the Latin. Lest it be said we have been selective, we include the entire chronological tables of Possini's *Observationum* from the years 1298 – 1302 in an **Appendix:**[172]

> **"1298** – The Persians, when they are incited by the slaughter of their men who had stuck with Philanthropenus the insurgent, forsake all the Oriental regions with savage excursions."[173]

> **"1299** – Atman the satrap of the Persians, said by others to be Ottomans, the originator of the house which today rules among the Turks, becomes strong with resources, when there were joined to him numerous troops of fierce bandits from Paphlagonia."

> **"1300** –

> **"1301** – About this time Atman or Ottomanes took up the name of the kings, and after Prusa was later occupied placed there the seat of the kingdom. Then dying in the year of Hegira, according to Al Iannabius the Arabian chronologer, 726, this is in the year of Christ about 1327, he left his son Urchanes as the heir of the kingdom which was begun in the recently captured city Prusa. Pachymer gives a sign to the siege of Prusa 1.5 c.21 p.296, [that it was] also a taking by storm at 1.7 c.27.

> **"1302** – The Hetaeriarch [official of a confraternity] Muzalo the leader of the Roman troops in Bithynia, while he endeavors himself in opposition--to withstand Osman who is devastating everything, is conquered by an ignoble languor of the Roman soldiers, who were fighting with a weariness, spite, and listless despair; and by the strong effort of the Alans he scarcely conceals the rest of the scattered army within Nicomedia. This defeat happened on the 27th day of the month of July around Bapheum close to Nicomedia."[174]

Possini's *Observationum* for the year 1302 speaks for itself, but we are just beginning to prove our point. Von Hammer quoted Hadschi Chalfa's chronological tables for the Hegira year of 701, which

---

[172] See **APPENDIX VIII**, 225.

[173] Georgius Pachymeres, *Corpus Scriptorum Historiae Byzantinae* (Bonn ed., 1835), Vol. Alt., 848. (Petri Possini, *Observationum.*)

[174] Ibid., 847-851.

begins in AD 1301 Julian reckoning. We have an Italian copy of Hadschi Chalfa's chronological tables dated from the year 1697. On page 110 under the Hegira year of 701, we have this acknowledgment, translated from the Italian:

> "There happens also in the Caramania in the vicinity of Koyunhisar [Bapheus] between the Bellicose Ottoman Turkish Prince, and the Greeks a violent battle, in which these were routed, and put to flight."[175]

We also submit the French chronological tables of Edouard de Muralt. He quoted Pachymeres' account, "Pach. IV. 25. P. 327-335," and placed this event of 701 A.H. correctly under the Julian calendar of 1302. Translated from the French, we read:

> "July 27. Bapheum, that is close to Nicomedia. The Hetaereiarch [official of a confraternity] Muzalon, commanding 2000 men, is beaten by Othman and hardly safe by the Alains."[176]

This chronology is confirmed by Halil İnalcik in *The Cambridge History of Islam*:

> "In 701/1301 the Byzantine emperor dispatched against 'Osmān a force of 2,000 men under the command of the *Hetaereiarch* Muzalon charged with the task of relieving Iznik. When 'Osmān ambushed this force and destroyed it at Baphaeon, the local population was panic-stricken and started to leave, seeking shelter in the castle of Nicomedia (Izmit). In another direction 'Osmān's forward raiders advanced as far as the approaches of Bursa. In Ottoman tradition this victory is known as the victory won near Yalakova over the forces of the emperor during the siege of Iznik. It was at this time that 'Osmān is said to have been recognized by the Seljuk sultan as a bey, in other words as a person wielding political authority. After 701/1301 'Osmān's fame is reported to have spread to distant Muslim countries, and his territory was filled with wave upon wave of immigrant Turkish households."[177]

The fact of the matter is that there are no credible chronological tables that exist or sources that could withstand investigation for the battle of Koyun-Hisar (Bapheus) for the Hegira year of 698 that would fall in July of AD 1299, Julian calendar year, but there are many primary sources that positively designate 701 A.H/1302 Julian!

Let us now hear once more from the world's foremost Islamic historian, Halil İnalcik:

"Osman Gazi's Siege of Nicaea and the Battle of Bapheus (Koyunhisar) July 27, 1302

[175] Hazi Halife Mustafa [Hadschi Chalfa], *Cronologia Historica* (*An Historic Chronology*) (Venetia: Andrea Poletti, 1697), 110.

[176] Edouard de Muralt, *Essai de Chronographie Byzantine 1057 – 1453,* No. 17 (St. Petersbourg: Eggers, 1871), 480.

[177] P. M. Holt, Ann K. S. Lambton, & Bernard Lewis, *The Cambridge History of Islam,* of *The Central Islamic Lands* (Cambridge: Syndics of the Cambridge University Press, 1970), 1:266-268.

"First of all, let us determine the date of Osman's Nicaea siege and the place of the Battle of Bapheus.[178] Pachymeres indicates that in the spring of 1302, at the date when the Emperor's son Michael IX departed for Western Anatolia, *'Amourios'*, the son of the Chobanid emir of Kastamonu *(actually Emir Yavlak Arslan oglu Ali)*, Lamises and Osman were in a state of attack.[179] Also, when mentioning the attacks on the Prinkipo *(Buyukada)* island in the Marmara Sea of the Venetian pirates in the spring of 1302, he mentions that the Byzantine General Mouzalon suffered a severe defeat in Mesothynia *(Battle of Bapheus)* and all the local Byzantine people were fleeing and the defeat had created an emergency situation of defense against the Turks.[180] Here, the Byzantine historian opens a parenthesis[181] and describes former clashes with the Amourioi, that is, the Emir Cobanogullari, of Kastamonu, in the Sakarya region and sidetracks the subject.[182] After describing the old situation, then he starts to relate in detail the Battle of Bapheus[183] between Mouzalon and Osman. By keeping this chronological order under consideration, A. Failler sets 27 July 1302 as the date of the Battle of Bapheus. The Ottoman narratives also verify this. *The Anonymous Tevarih-i Al-i Osman*[184] describes the battle in detail and the old Menakibname summarized by Asikpasazade *(henceforth)* Aspz.), sets the Battle of Bapheus *(Koyunhisar)* one year prior to the Battle of Dimbos *(Dinboz, Dinanoz)*. The old Menakibname in Aspz. gives the date of AH 702 for the Battle of Dimbos *(Erdogan today)* by Osman against the united army of the Bursa Tekfur and his allies, the tekfurs of Kestel, Kite, Bidnos and Adranos.[185] The same Menakibname sets the siege of Nicaea immediately before the Battle of Dimbos. Thus, according to the Ottoman tradition, the Battle of Bapheus occurred in AH 701. AH 701 started on 6 September 1301 and finished on 28 July 1302. If it is considered (Pachymeres) that the battle occurred in July, then the Battle of Bapheus occurred towards the end of AH 701, that is, in July 1302.[186]

---

[178] See H. Inalcik, "Osman Gazi's Siege of Nicaea and the Battle of Bapheus," *The Ottoman Emirate, 1300-1389* (ed. E. Zachariadou) Rethymnon, 1991.

[179] Georges Pachymeres, *Relations Historiques*, ed. by Albert Failler. French trans. by Vitalien Laurent (Paris: Les Belles Lettres, 4, 1999), 358, note 40; P. Schreiner, Kleincbroniken. 3, pp. 217-219. Schreiner appears to have confused Osman's 1304 Sakarya campaign with the Battle of Bapheus. For the Chobanids, the emirs of Kastamonu, see Y. Yucel, "Cobanogullari Beyligi," *Anadolu Beylikleri Hakkinda Arastirmalar* (Researches on Anatolian Beylics), Ankara: TTK, 1991), 33-61.

[180] Pachymeres, Vol. 10, Ch. 24, 366-357.

[181] Pachymeres, 10, Ch.25, 358-364.

[182] H. Inalcik, "The Ottoman Empire," *The Cambridge History of Islam*, E. Holt and B. Lewis, eds. (Cambridge: Cambridge University Press, 1970), 298; E. A. Zachariadou, "Pachymeres on the 'Amourioi' of Kastamonu," *Byzantine and Modern Greek Studies* 3, 1977, 57-71.

[183] P. Schreiner, Kleincbroniken, vol. 3, 217-219. Schreiner seems to have mistaken Osman's 1304 campaign with the Battle of Bapheus (1302).

[184] *Die altosmanischen anonymen Chroniken*, ed. by F. Giese, Breslau, 1922. See in the appendix the facsimile of the izzet Koyunoglu copy of the *Tevarih*.

[185] Ahmed Asiki (Asik Pasazade), *Tevarih-i Al-i Osman*, ed. by C. N. Atsiz (Istanbul: 1947), Ch.16 and 17.

[186] Isil Akbaygil, Halil Inalcik, Oktay Aslanapa, eds., *Iznik Throughout History* (Istanbul: Ofset Yapimevi, Yahya Kemal Mahallesi Sair Sokak, 2003), 61. ISBN: 975-458-431-1. Inalcik notes, "The date of 27 July 1301, given in our previous article, *'Osman Gazi's Siege of Nicaea and the Battle of Bapheus,'* should be corrected as 27 July 1302."

"As for the Ottoman tradition on the date of the Yalak-ovasi battle, this is placed immediately before the battle of Dimboz against the *Tekvurs'* coalition in the Bursa region on the Hegira year of 702 which starts on 26 August 1302. So, the battle of Bapheus must have taken place in the previous year, in the summer of 1302."[187]

"This victory won against a Byzantine imperial army exalted Osman into a charismatic bey in the region. Pachymeres tells us that with this Victory, Osman's reputation spread all the way to the Paphlagonia *(Kastamonu)* region and the gazis ran to serve under his flag. Towards the end of the fifteenth century, the historian Nesri seems to be correct in setting this date of Osman's actual beylic. The Battle of Bapheus won the prestige of a founder bey of a dynasty to Osman and after him, his son Orhan ascended the throne of the beylic without rivals. Thus, we can accept 27 July 1302 as the definite founding date of the Ottoman dynasty and consequently, the Ottoman state."[188]

The Islamic historian of *The Origins of the Ottoman Empire* adds the following caption:

"The <u>first contact between the imperial army and Osman</u>, who threatened the area around Nicaea, occurred when the Byzantines under the command of George Muzalon fought him at Koyunhisari (Baphaeum) in 1301 (according to Muralt, 1302)."[189]

Koprulu's footnote sums up the whole matter:

"Now securely dated 1302!"[190]

Further undisputed proof is this:

The Gregorian calendar by Pope Gregory XIII replaced the Julian calendar by a papal bull signed into effect on February 24, 1582. When introduced, it immediately omitted ten days in order to realign the calendar with the spring equinox, which was tied to the celebration of Easter by the Roman Catholic Church. However, the Millerites failed to take this ten-day discrepancy into account when they fixed the date for the termination of the 6th trumpet on August 11, 1840.

---

[187] Halil İnalcik, *Essays in Ottoman History* (Istanbul: Eren Yayincilik, 1998), 78. [We have made the correction by the author as he directs: "The date of 27 July 1301, given in our previous article, '*Osman Gazi's Siege of Nicaea and the Battle of Bapheus*,' should be corrected as 27 July 1302." Authorized from this source: Isil Akbaygil, Halil Inalcik, Oktay Aslanapa, eds., *Iznik Throughout History* (Istanbul: Ofset Yapimevi, Yahya Kemal Mahallesi Sair Sokak, 2003), 61. ISBN: 975-458-431-1.

[188] Isil Akbaygil, Halil Inalcik, Oktay Aslanapa, eds., *Iznik Throughout History* (Istanbul: Ofset Yapimevi, Yahya Kemal Mahallesi Sair Sokak, 2003), 68. ISBN: 975-458-431-1.

[189] "Now securely dated 1302. There is no proof that the battle that Ottoman sources give as Koyunhisari was the same as that at Baphaeum (Bapheus)." See Inalcik, *The Rise of Ottoman Historiography*, in Lewis and Holt, eds., *Historians of the Middle East*, 152-53. Found in M. Fuad Koprulu, ed.; trans. Gary Leiser, *The Origins of the Ottoman Empire* (Albany, New York: State University of New York Press, 1992), 109.

[190] Ibid., 133.

In other words, we would now have to add 3 years to July 27, 1299, or to August 11, 1840, if you please. This would automatically move July 27, 1449, to July 27, 1452. That would bring us to August 11, 1843, and we have yet to add the ten-day discrepancy not accounted for by Josiah Litch. That, in turn, would then move us ahead a total of ten days on all three accounts, bringing us now to August 21, 1843, for the claimed fulfillment of the 541 years and 15 day/year prophecy. What happened on August 21, 1843? Nothing! The same thing that happened on August 11, 1840!

Amadon stated:

> "It was doubtless such an analysis that convinced Gibbon of the 'singular accuracy,'as he expresses it, of the July 27, 1299, date. The detailed outline of Pachymeres' Volume II, Book IV, in which the July 27 date occurs, reveals further proofs that it belongs to the year 1299, and not to Von Hammer's year 1301."[191]

> "Hence neither Von Hammer nor those who have followed his lead have any authority for the year 1301 as the date of the Ottoman invasion."[192]

Which conclusions merit belief, reader? You have read the evidence for yourself, and it is now for you to decide what you will believe.

---

[191] Amadon, *Ministry*, June 1944, 20.
[192] Ibid., 19.

4

Examining the Evidence: July 27, 1449?

Our focus in this chapter will be the validity of the historical date and event that has been claimed to fulfill the close of the so-called 5 month- or 150-year prophecy of the fifth trumpet of Revelation 9:5, 10 on July 27, 1449. We will temporally set aside the three-year, ten-day discrepancy that we witnessed at the end of chapter 3 so we can stay focused on the actual claimed events, if they will withstand investigation! These two prophetic periods of the fifth and sixth trumpets are claimed to run successively and concern the same entity, the Ottoman Empire (not the Saracens, as claimed by Uriah Smith), as predicted by Josiah Litch. There should be, therefore, some historical event that closes the 150-year prophecy on July 27, 1449, and on the same day by the same entity another historical event must commence the remaining 391 years and 15 days belonging to the sixth trumpet. These two claimed prophetic historical events must take place on July 27, 1449, and no other day, in order to land at the end on Aug. 11, 1840. As with the arguments of Amadon for the validity of July 27, 1299, set forth in chapter 3, this chapter will reveal again the totally untenable foundation the suppositions about July 27, 1449, stands upon. First, we will see just exactly what Josiah Litch predicted about the five-month or 150-year prophecy from his own published works, which may be read in full in the appendix. We begin with a portion taken from his 1838 works:

The Probability of the Second Coming of Christ about A.D. 1843

"This scene changes in the fifth verse, and power is given them to torment, but not to kill the men who had not the seal of God in their foreheads, for five months. To kill, is to conquer, in figurative language; and to torment, is to harass by sudden excursions and assaults. Five prophetic months are one hundred and fifty years there being thirty [152] days in a Jewish month. This change in the power of the locusts, when it was given them to torment men for five months, is noticed in the tenth and eleventh verses. …It was given them after the rise of the Ottoman empire, to torment or harass and weaken men (the Roman empire in the east) five months. If these are prophetic months as is probable, it would be one hundred and fifty years. But when did that empire rise? Mr. Miller has fixed on A.D. 1298. Others, among whom is Gibbon, in his Decline and Fall of the Roman Empire, 1299. He says – Othman first [154] invaded the territory of Nicomedia on the 27th of July, 1299. He also remarks on the singular accuracy of the date, a circumstance not often found in the history of those times. He says – 'The singular accuracy with which this event, is given, seems to indicate some foresight of the rapid growth of the monster.'

"If we date the origin of this empire in 1299, the hundred and fifty years would end 1449. During that length of time, the eastern empire of Rome was harassed beyond measure by the Ottoman power, but was not subjected entirely to it. The year 1448, Amurath the Turkish sultan, besieged Coria, one of the strongest cities in the Roman empire. The end of the five months would come the next year. We should naturally look for some great defeat of the Christian emperor's army. But was it so? So far from it, that after a long summer's siege and a great loss of men, the fall coming on and rains setting in, the Turks raised the siege and retired. The empire was now left in peace. One would be almost inclined to think the word of prophecy must now fail.

"But the time came, and the word of God was confirmed by the event. 'John Paleologus emperor of Constantinople, was dead, and his brother, Constantine Deacozes, would not venture to ascend the throne without the permission of Amurath, the Turkish sultan. He sent ambassadors to ask his consent before he presumed to call himself [155] sovereign. This happened A.D. 1449. This shameful proceeding seemed to presage the approaching downfall of the empire. Ducas, the historian, counts John Paleologus for the last Greek emperor, without doubt, because he did not consider as such, a prince who had not dared to reign without the permission of his enemy.' *Hawkins' Otto. Emp.* p. 113. Gibbon, an infidel, is so struck with the singular accuracy of the record of the origin of this empire, that he attributes it to some foresight in the historian, of the rapid growth of the monster. But would it not become Christians better, to attribute it to the superintending providence of that Being who had set a bound for that and other empires, which they may not pass? who had *given* them power to harass and torment the empire of Constantinople five months; and to kill or subject it to their own sway, an hour, a day, a month, and a year; the whole being five hundred and forty-one years and fifteen days.

"....But when will this power be overthrown? According to the calculations already made, that the five months ended 1449, the hour, fifteen days, the day, one year, the month, thirty years, and the year, three hundred and sixty years; in all, three hundred and ninety-one years and fifteen days, will end in A.D. 1840, some time in the month of August. The prophecy is the most remarkable and definite, (even descending to the days) of any in the Bible, relating to these great events. It is as singular as the record [158] of the time when the empire rose. The facts are now before the reader, and he must make what disposition of them he thinks best. The sixth woe yet continues, and will till the great river Euphrates is dried up, and the seventh trumpet sounds."[193]

We now wish to critique Josiah Litch's written directive from the *Signs*:

Signs of the Times
August 1, 1840

"The sounding of the fifth apocalyptic trumpet Rev. 9,1, and the accompanying event, is believed to represent the rise of Mahomedanism, and a host of warlike armies, by which that religion was propagated. These armies were for several centuries led on by the chieftains of the several clans into which they were divided: but in the one of the 13th century the different factions of Mahomedans were gathered under one leader or king, and formed one general government which has continued to the present time; I mean the Ottoman or Turkish empire. From the time of this

---

[193] Josiah Litch, *The Probability of the Second Coming of Christ About A.D. 1843*, (Boston: David H. Ela, 1838), 151-155.

organization under one leader, and he both a temporal and ecclesiastical ruler, (for he was both king and angel, or minister, of the bottomless pit) they were commissioned to torment men for five prophetic months, or 150 years. They were to be restrained from killing, politically, those who were the subjects of their oppressions; but they had power to torment them five months. The five months were to close up the period of the fifth trumpet. I think it is very generally agreed that the Greek empire was the people whom they were to torment, and ultimately politically to put to death.

"When then did the five month of Turkish torment on the Greeks commence? Not until they had a king over them, or were gathered under one government. The Ottoman government was established about A.D. 1298 or 9. And. according to Gibbon, Ottoman first entered the territory of Nicomedia, and commenced his attack on the Greeks on July 27th, 1299. The time, 150 years would bring us to 1449, when the fifth trumpet, would end, and the sixth begin to sound....

"Accordingly, from 1299 to 1449, the Turks were continually tormenting the Greeks by petty incursions and wars, yet without conquering them. But in 1449 a circumstance took place which strikingly fulfilled the prophecy of the sounding of the sixth angel.

"The Greek emperor died in that year and left his throne to his brother. But although it was a time of peace in the empire, before that brother dared ascend the throne of Constantinople and reign, he sent his ambassadors to Anereth, the Turkish sultan, and requested and obtained his permission to reign; and was then proclaimed emperor of Greece. Thus voluntarily did he acknowledge that his independence was gone and that the Greek empire only existed by permission of its deadly foe. The Turkish nations were therefore loosed by divine command....

"But still there is no positive evidence that the first period was exactly to a day, fulfilled; nor yet that the second period began, to a day, where the first closed. If they began and ended so, the above calculation will be correct. If they did not then there will be a variation in the conclusion; but the evidence is clear that there cannot be a year's variation from the calculation; we must wait patiently for the issue."[194]

Now from Josiah Litch's 1842 works that we viewed previously, titled:

Prophetic Exposition; or a Connected View of the Testimony of the Prophets Concerning the Kingdom of God and the Time of Its Establishment

"Verse 5: *"And to them it was given that they should not kill them, but that they should be tormented five months; and their torment was as the torment of a scorpion when he striketh a man."*

"Their constant incursions into the Roman territory, and frequent assaults on Constantinople itself, were an unceasing torment throughout the empire, which yet they were not able effectually to subdue, notwithstanding the long period, afterwards more directly alluded to, during which they continued, by unremitting attacks, grievously to afflict an idolatrous church, of which the pope was the head. Their

---

[194] Josiah Litch, *Signs of the Times*, Boston, August 1, 1840, 70.

charge was to torment, and then to hurt, but not to kill, or utterly destroy. The marvel was that they did not. To repeat the words of Gibbon – 'The calm historian of the present hour must study to explain by what [174] means the church and state were *saved* from this *impending, and, as it should seem, from this inevitable danger.* In this inquiry I shall unfold the events that rescued our ancestors of Britain, and our neighbors of Gaul, from the civil and religious yoke of the Koran; that protected the majesty of Rome, and *delayed* the servitude of Constantinople; that invigorated the defence of the Christians, and scattered among their enemies the seeds of division and decay.' Ninety pages of illustration follow, to which we refer the readers of Gibbon.

"...THE TORMENT OF THE GREEKS ONE HUNDRED AND FIFTY YEARS.

"Verse 10: 'Their power was to hurt men five months.'

"1. The question arises, What men were they to hurt five months? Undoubtedly, the same they were afterwards to slay; (see verse 15.) "The third part of men," or third of the Roman empire – the Greek division of it.

"...The calculation which follows founded on this starting-point, was made and published in [181] "CHRIST'S SECOND COMING," &c., by the author, in 1838.

" '*And their power was to torment men five months.*' Thus far their commission extended, to torment, by constant depredations, but not politically to kill them. '*Five months;*' that is, one hundred and fifty years. Commencing July 27th, 1299, the one hundred and fifty years reach to 1449. During that whole period the Turks were engaged in an almost perpetual war with the Greek empire, but yet without conquering it. They seized upon and held several of the Greek provinces, but still Greek independence was maintained in Constantinople. But in 1449, the termination of the one hundred and fifty years, a change came. Before presenting the history of that change, however, we will look at verses 12-15.

"THE OTTOMAN SUPREMACY IN CONSTANTINOPLE THREE HUNDRED AND NINETY-ONE YEARS AND FIFTEEN DAYS.

"...In the year 1449, John Paleologus, the Greek emperor, died, but left no children to inherit his throne, and Constantine Deacozes succeeded to it. But he would not venture to ascend the throne without the consent of Amurath, the Turkish Sultan. He therefore sent ambassadors to ask his consent, and obtained it, before he presumed to call himself sovereign.

"This shameful proceeding seemed to presage the approaching downfall of the empire. Ducas, the historian, counts John Paleologus for the last Greek emperor, without doubt, because he did not consider as such a prince who had not dared to reign without the permission of his enemy."

"Let this historical fact be carefully examined in connection with the prediction above. This was not a violent assault made on the Greeks, by which their empire was overthrown and their independence taken away, but simply a voluntary surrender of that independence into the [183] hands of the Turks, by saying, 'I cannot reign unless you permit.'"[195]

---

[195] Josiah Litch, *Prophetic Exposition; Or A Connected View Of The Testimony Of The Prophets Concerning The Kingdom Of God And The Time Of Its Establishment* (Boston: Joshua V. Himes, 1842), 173-183.

Here is what we have learned from Josiah Litch concerning his understanding of the prophetic period of the fifth trumpet of Revelation 9:5 and 10, and what can be expected regarding each point.

1. "Five prophetic months are one hundred and fifty years." If and when applicable, that calculation of five prophetic months of a Bible prophecy would hold true.

2. "There being thirty days in a Jewish month." There being thirty days in a *prophetic* month.

3. The end of the five months or the one hundred and fifty years of the fifth trumpet was 1449. However, no month, day or Scripture was ever supplied then or yet today for its claimed fulfillment that it would have to fall on July 27, 1449, and no other day. This assumption will be proven to be false!

4. The commencement date for the fifth trumpet of Revelation 9:5, 10 was the 27th of July, 1299. This date was based entirely upon the "word" of the historian Edward Gibbon. Never once were the Scriptures called upon or referenced. Its claimed fulfillment was when Osman first invaded the territory of Nicomedia [Baspheus] on the 27th of July, 1299, which date we saw in chapter 3 to be utterly insupportable.

5. The Ottoman Empire or Turkey was the entity of prophetic interest in both the fifth and sixth trumpets. The two trumpets were added together and made 541 years and 15 days, and reckoned from July 27, 1299, straight on to August 11, 1840. The confusion today of the Saracens is simply this: The Saracens were introduced and claimed to be the entity for the fifth trumpet by Uriah Smith, but never by Josiah Litch. This was obviously done by Uriah Smith in his *Daniel and the Revelation*, to help fill in the apparent discrepancies of Josiah Litch's 150-year Ottoman prophecy. Nevertheless, Uriah Smith totally overlooked the fact that the Saracens had ceased to be an aggressive power nearly five centuries earlier, making that application untenable. This discrepancy is made plain so the reader will not be deceived into thinking the Saracens were ever part of Josiah Litch's prophetic discourse. Again, all of this will be proven to be untrue!

6. The commencement of the sixth trumpet of Revelation 9 had to be July 27, 1449, and no other day, in order to end on August 11, 1840. Once again, though, never was any Scripture cited or historical event presented for its claimed fulfillment, even to this very day. This also will be proven to be completely without merit!

7. Josiah Litch declared that when the Greek emperor died in the year 1449 and left his throne to his brother, it was then that the approaching downfall of the empire was at hand, ultimately coming by a voluntary surrender of her independence into the hands of the Turks, by the brother's saying, "I cannot reign unless you permit." Or "John Paleologus, the last Greek emperor dared not to reign without the permission of his enemy", the Turkish Sultan. In other words, the Greek emperor became a vassal to the Ottoman Empire in 1449 and not before. Prophetically speaking, this event would have had to take place on July 27, 1449, because no other event is specified! And this will be proven to be groundless, as well!

We will now begin to see how those statements of so-called fact by Josiah Litch withstand the test of investigation. We refer again to the minutes of the 1919 Bible Conference of July 17th. The brethren in attendance distinctly addressed some of the issues enumerated above:

1919 Bible Conference Minutes

[46] "PRESCOTT: It is simply this. That is, that our interpretation of the fifth trumpet of Revelation 9, in harmony with the view that has been held by Protestantism for centuries, is that this is a symbol of the Saracens, the rise and work of the Saracens, but on the basis of the paper this morning, and any other discussion of the same thought, we take the time that in the prophecy belongs to the Saracens and give it to the Ottomans. Now it is of little value to me to try to establish any date with reference to the Ottoman Empire, when I am dealing with a symbol applied to the Saracen power. It appears to me an inconsistency to take a symbol and saying this belong to the Saracens that had their rise in Arabia, Mohammed was their leader, and that they applied the instruction that they should not hurt the grass of the earth, nor any green thing, nor any tree, but only such men as had not the seal of God on their foreheads. Then we attempt to take that fifth month period from the period of the rise and work of the Saracens, and carry it forward to the very end of the thirteenth century, centuries after the Saracens had ceased to be an aggressive power at all. So I don't see that I can get much out of the matter if is presented in that way. Now if we are to apply the time for the fifth trumpet to the Ottoman Empire, let's apply the symbol to the Ottoman Empire. But so long as we apply the symbol to the Saracens, how can we carry the period describing their work five or six centuries after they ceased to be an aggressive power? Until that is out of the way, any paper that attempts to establish dates with regard to the Ottoman Empire doesn't help me any about the matter.

[47] "WAKEHAM: I have not been able to see how we could interpose a great interregnum of six hundred years between the fourth and fifth verses of chapter 9, when there is nothing in the prophecy to indicate that. It seems to me that we are presenting a false exegesis, interposing a great hiatus of six hundred years between one verse and the next, when there is absolutely nothing there to indicate it. The two reasons usually given are absolutely without historical confirmation. I have not been able to find any history that will substantiate the statement made so much, that there was no king over the Mohammadens until the time of Othman. Gibbon says, 'By the end of the first century of the Hejira, the Saracen Caliphs were the most absolute and powerful monarchs on the face of the globe.' Now with that statement and others of similar character I don't see how anyone can maintain there was no king over the Mohammadens until the end of the thirteenth century. The second reason is that the Mohammaden world was never united under one head until the time of Othman. When as a matter of fact the only time it was under one head was under the Saracen Caliphs. Freeman's history has for the heading of his first chapter, 'The Undivided Caliphy' in the seventh and eighth chapters [centuries].

"PRESCOTT: Perhaps I could explain how this came around. In looking up the difficulty, I found this, that previous to 1844 in the exposition of this prophecy both symbols, the locust symbol and the later symbol were given to the Ottoman Empire, and that there was no effort to separate them or show that anything happened at the close of this 150 years, or at the beginning [48] of the hour, day, month, and year period. The two were added together and made 541 years and 15 days, and reckoned from July 27, 1299, right straight on. Well now, that was inconsistent in itself, because it gave the time to the symbol interpreting both symbols of one power, and gave both periods of time to one power. When Thoughts on Revelation was written a separation was made of the first symbol, taking it to represent the Saracens, yet the time was still all given to the Ottoman power, and that is where we find ourselves. I think we should separate the time as we have done the symbols and give the time to the power that we interpret as fulfilling the symbol, therefore give it the five months or 150 years to the Saracens during their period of actual aggressive power as tormentors.

"That application of the period to the symbol gets away from two difficulties. First, it gets us away from what appears to be a very strange inconsistency of applying a symbol to some power, and the time period of that to another power. And second it gets away from the necessity of establishing a date that has been discredited. Lay aside everything else and ask yourself, Now how you are going to establish a definite day for the beginning of this period? The paper this morning I suppose was seeking for evidence for 1299. Now grant any weight to the historical evidence submitted that you please, yet you haven't established a day. We must find a definite day to date from if we are to take a prophecy and interpret it as meaning so many years and so many days. It must have a day to commence it, and it must have a day to end it, otherwise we don't have any proper interpretation or application of the prophecy....

"Now all I ask for is that we shall be consistent with ourselves so that when we stand up before an audience or appear in print we don't expose ourselves any longer to that shocking inconsistency of applying the symbols to two powers, and then turn right around and give the time that belongs right in that prophecy and date it five centuries at least after the power has ceased to be aggressive as a tormentory.

"Before 1844 in William Miller's lectures he gives both symbols to the Ottoman power. He adds the periods together, makes 514 years and 15 days date from July 27, 1299 and follows it straight through. Now when you go further you say we will start from July 27, 1299, and we come to 1449. What happened [50] then? We must have something on a day. What happened July 27, 1449, that both marked the ending of one period and the beginning of another, because you must not begin the next day. That is, when we are trying to arrive at August 11, 1840 you can't say this period ends July 27, 1449, and the next began July 28. You have got to make them lap one day or else you are thrown out when you get to the end. That question must be answered. What marked the close of the 150 years on July 27, 1449? What event on that day marked the beginning of the next period? What marked the close of the next period? Until that is out of the way I don't see that we shall be helped very much by any papers seeking to establish a date for something relating to the Ottoman Empire.

"W G WIRTH: What dates do you give for the 150-year period?

"PRESCOTT: According to the best light I can get, and I am not alone – I suppose it is more or less known here that this whole matter came up several years ago, and the Review and Herald Board appointed a committee to study the question. This committee was composed of F. M. Wilcox, Chairman, W. A. Spicer, M. E. Kern, C.

S. Longacre, C. L. Benson, S. M. Butler, and myself. We took up this question, went into it quite thoroughly, and that committee, which I think you will regard as not a very extreme or wild committee, came to the conclusion that we could not apply this 150 years beginning July 27, 1299, for the double reason, first, it didn't belong to that power, and second, the date itself could not be established. Then there were further things brought in, so that all the committee came to the conclusion that there was not sufficient evidence to establish the [51] date August 11, 1840. Therefore it was recommended that since it was too large a question for us, it be presented to the General Conference Committee in Council. The board adopted the recommendation presented. Brother Spicer was to present one phase, Brother Benson another, and I was to present a third phase. We prepared our matter and presented it at the Spring Council, and our papers, working together, set forth these suggestions, not as established orthodoxy, but as suggestions from the Committee for consideration.

[52] "PRESCOTT: That the 150 years commenced in 612 A.D. when Mohammed made his first public proclamation of his message, and that it ended in 762 at Bagdad when the Saracen as a tormenting power ceased and they waned from that time on. I would like to ask, Brother Chairman, if anyone can explain to us how we shall get by what appears to be an absolute inconsistency in Biblical interpretation.

"WILKINSON: Would the assembly here like to withdraw its vote? There have several questions been raised; the question of whether the trumpet is Saracen or Turkish, the question whether it begins in 1299. Even if we can bring in some evidence, and I think we can, very strong evidence, then the question has been raised of July 27, 1449, and of August 11, 1840. For one man to take all that up and give a satisfactory presentation in one day, is a little too much, I think, and should prefer to decline, but if it is desired, I shall be very glad to throw my ideas into the melting pot along with the rest and let it stew.

"PRESCOTT: I didn't intend, Brother Wilkinson, to lay that burden on you in 45 minutes, but I would like in this hour of discussion on the paper this morning, to have someone deal with this direct point and let all the rest go now and deal with them later. Our published position, and the only one I have known to be published or spoken in this country, -- I didn't know about the other matter, and there are other questions also that are printed across the water in a different way than we do here, we are not dealing with that. But will anyone tell us how we shall consistently go on with our official, recognized position that the 5th trumpet indicates the Saracens?

[53] "DANIELLS: Let us have a symposium now of one-minute speeches from these teachers and hear their explanation.

"WIRTH: I can't be done. That is my answer. I agree with Prof. Prescott.

"DANIELLS: Then you are through.

"LACEY: I have agreed too, substantially, and I think the 150 years applies to the Saracens. I have in my notebook the dates 612 and 762.

"WAKEHAM: I taught this very thing six years ago and have held it ever since.

"SORENSON: It is a most perplexing question, I find, because we deal with the past. When it comes to the 11th of Daniel, we are dealing with unfulfilled prophecy, and we might differ, even when we use all the facts available, but when it comes to dealing with prophecy dealing with past facts, we must have the facts that took place; we are not able to invent events to fit the occasion, and that is the most perplexing thing about the whole prophetic proposition. All the dates that have been introduced are out of joint and the events proposed to fit the dates took place on some other day.

"M. C. WILCOX: I had the same difficulty for years, but I have also placed the 150 years 612 to 762. It seems to me to be very clear, and what a later date can be established without any regard to the 150 years.

"WALDORF: Before I came here, I heard of a new book issued called the history of the Huna. I haven't seen it, but that deals with the question of 1299 etc. It is a good work and worth looking up, but I don't know where to find it.

[54] "ANDERSON: It doesn't seem to me that this idea of applying it to the Saracen is so compelling after all. Why should we say it applies to the Saracens? Why shouldn't it apply to the Mohammedans? The idea seems to be that it must refer to the Saracens as distinguished from all the other Mohammedans. Why couldn't it apply to the Mohammedans as a religious movement?

"PRESCOTT: You are getting onto the same ground as our two-horned beast going off into an 'ism.'

"DANIELLS: Let's send the King of the North and the two-horned beast together up in a balloon.

"FRENCH: It seems to me the phraseology makes it very plain. It has reference to the Eastern division of the Roman Empire. There are tormentors who torment the third part of men, and then destroyers. Their power was to hurt men five months, and they had a king over them. The same ones that tormented men five months had a king over them, which is the angel of the bottomless pit, etc. Now the same ones that tormented are the ones that destroyed. Those who tormented five months had a king over them whose names was the destroyer, and it is the same power that tormented that finally destroyed. That is true of the Ottoman Turks. For 150 years they tormented Eastern Rome, and they finally destroyed the last vestige of Rome.

"INTERMISSION.

"...[59] DANIELLS: Now we can go on with the discussion of the Trumpets.

"WIRTH: I should like to recommend that Elliott's 'Horae Apocopypticae' be studied in that connection. It seems to me that Elliott proves beyond a shadow of a doubt that it refers to the Saracens.

"THOMPSON (G. B.): Is not this the only line of prophecy we have where the kingdom begins on a definite day? All other prophecies begin in a year. This July 26 is very difficult to establish.

"F. M. WILCOX: I would suggest that Brother Prescott give a brief outline of the whole ground.

"PRESCOTT: I am very sorry that all my documents that I have been filing for years over this question, which were in my box of books that I had with me in the Far East, and went astray on coming home, have not yet been received. However, I will give a brief study covering the prophecy.

"As the result of the work of that Committee appointed to study this question, we agreed to submit to the Conference for consideration these general views:

"That the Fifth Trumpet was applied to the Saracens. That the period of the five months – which was referred to twice – you will observe that. I notice in the last explanation of the five months period it was connected directly with the 11th verse.

Now it occurs in the tenth verse, of course, but you must note also it occurs in the fifth verse in the direct quotation which we apply to Abubeker, the second one in that Dynasty. So you must not take it away from that absolutely. [60] But the five months' period applies to the Saracens. That the most satisfactory time to apply it would be from the dates 612, when Mohammedan made his first public proclamation of his mission as prophet--to 562, when the Saracens by establishing Bagdad, entered upon a period of luxurious ease, in contrast with the aggressive campaigns of the previous time. That the Sixth Trumpet applied to the Ottoman Empire. That the period of time there belonged to the Ottomans. That the time for commencing that period was 1453, when they established themselves as a power by the capture of Constantinople. That was referred to by Mr. Gibbons – that from a small beginning at the end of the 13th century, it was about 150 years to the siege of Constantinople when they were fully established as a power.

"Now you then come to the period of the 6th Trumpet, which is that period, as we have read it of 'an hour and a day and a month and a year,' and which we have been accustomed to interpret as 391 years and fifteen days.

"DANIELLS: You have then that the Fifth Trumpet comes down to the 11th verse inclusive?

"PRESCOTT: Yes; that is, applying the Scripture.

"DANIELLS: So that both of these references of 5 months apply to the same power?

"PRESCOTT: Yes. Now as to the question of the 391 years and fifteen days. If we interpret it that way it brings us to the necessity of establishing the prophetic period to a day. As Brother Thompson has suggested, we have no other prophetic period that we attempt to establish to a day, and therefore there is a very serious difficulty when you are dealing with the developments [61] of history, to try to fix things to a day – apart from the question whether the fifth trumpet refers to the Saracens or the Ottomans. The difficulty of fixing any definite day in 1449 – No event that occurred that would mark the close of the tormenting period and introduces the period of killing – comes in there – and we have to double that period to make it come out to the day we suggest, which expires August 11, 1840, because we must reckon July 27th as the close of the other period and reckon as the beginning of the new period – or else you do not come out in 1840. This offers some difficulties. [61]....

"PRESCOTT: [65] Now to see some of the difficulties that we have been thrown into by this matter, not as a personal reference, to anybody, but simply that we may know. In order to have a good event to fix the close of that 150 years as we have been applying it, and to make it end July 27. 1449, the first edition of the Seer of Patmos said that Constantinople fell on the 27th of July, 1449. Of course that made a very good ending for the prophecy, but when you come to the fact of history, that it was four years later. Why it is rather bad for us to transfer it in order to have a good event to fulfill our idea of a prophecy.

"I plead for this:

"1. That we be consistent in this prophecy. That we give the time to the power that is signified by the symbol. If we are going to have the fifth trumpet belong to the Ottoman Empire, then we must change Bible Readings, Thoughts on Revelation, and I don' t know how many other things. If we say the fifth trumpet represents the

Saracens, then let's give the trumpet time to the Saracens. When we come to the sixth trumpet and we want to say it is 391 years and 15 days, then the burden is upon us to establish some historical event to mark the beginning of it. We must give some event that will mark the close of it, and when you get into that, you are in a sea of trouble." [196]

The following source is taken from the General Conference Archives; the author is the well-known historian LeRoy Edwin Froom. He also reveals some weaknesses in Adventism's long-accepted interpretation of the fifth and sixth trumpets:

BOX 6805

". . . . In 1449 he was sent for the fifth time to the court of Mourad.

"As to Von Hammer's authority as historian of this period, I read the following statement from page 6 of the preface to the history of the Ottoman Turk, by Sir Edward Creasey:

" 'Von Hammer's history of the Ottoman Empire will always be the standard European book on this subject. That history was the result of the labors of thirty years, during which Von Hammer explored, in addition to the authorities which his predecessors had made use of, the numerous works of the Turkish and other Oriental writers of the Ottoman history, and the other rich sources of intelligence which are to be found in the archives of Venice, Austria, and other states that have been [51] involved in relation of hostility or amity with the Sublime Porte. Von Hammer's long residence in the East and his familiarity with the institutions, habits, as well as with the literature of the Turks, give an additional attractiveness and value to his volumes. His learning is as accurate as it is varied: his honesty and condour [sic] are unquestioned, and his history is certainly one of the productions of the first half of our century.'

"It is not to be wondered at if we find Gibbon is not entirely accurate in every point of his presentation of my theme. He had outlined for himself that he would write the history covering the four great periods of the Roman Empire, the barbarian invasions and the development of their kingdoms. The Eastern Empire and the Mohammedian both in Saracen and Turkish development. While he may have had superior knowledge for his task, we do not believe that he was Divinely inspired in the same, and it is certain that no other writer since his time has undertaken to write on so extensive a period.

"Von Hammer had access to certain documents not available to Gibbon, and in addition, Gibbon's presentation of the subject. I will say in the language of Keith, found in the SIGNS OF THE TIMES, Volume 1, page 329.

" 'We have no quarrel with Gibbon, he flags in testimony to the truth of prophecy, only where he fails in position. I do not think it wise for us to ignore the testimony of such an authority, whatever weight he may be willing to give it, we must say that his statements of the case cannot be ignored by the careful student of history.'

---

[196] Transcript of the 1919 Bible Conference of the General Conference of Seventh-day Adventists, July 17, 1919 (Silver Spring, MD), 31- 61, 65.

"Connecting, as our custom is, the 150 years of Revelation 9:5, 10 with the period of Verse 15, it appears to me that we are not only involving the question of historical accuracy, but that of prepared exegesis of the task.

"As Brother Wakeman clearly presented yesterday, there is no good reason for connecting that time period with the incoming of the Turks, when very clearly there was a 150 years period of war and desolation under the early Caliphs, terminating in the founding of Bagdad in 762. As to the kingly powers of Mohammed and his successors [52], the Caliphs, I quote from Sir William Muir, Annals of the Early Caliphs, p. 7.

" 'With Mohammed ceased the theocratic power which as a prophet he had exercised, but the kingly function of all Islam descended to his successors. On the close of that period of the same work, page 450. Thus with the rise of the Abbasides the uniting of the Caliphate came to an end, never after either in theory or in fact was there a successor to the prophet acknowledged as such over all Islam.

" 'The name of Caliph, however it might survive in the Abbiside lineage or be assumed by less legitimate purposes, had now altogether lost its virtues and its significance. Bagdad, answering to its proud name of Dar al Salam, became for a time the capital of the world and the center of luxury and emporium of commerce and seat of learning.'

"The supremacy of the Turks over the eastern empire resulting in the killing of it politically, was established, according to Gibbon's, Chapter 67, paragraph 13, in the year 1449:

" 'The funeral of the late emperor was accelerated with singular and even suspicious haste: the claim of Demetrius to the vacant throne was justified by a trite and flimsy sophism, that he was born in the purple, the eldest son of the father's reign. But this empress-mother the senate and the soldiers, the clergy and the people were unanimous in the cause of the lawful successor: and the despot Thomas, who, ignorant of the change, accidentally returned to the capital, asserted with becoming zeal the interest of the absent brother. An ambassador, the historian Phranza, was immediately dispatched to the court of Adrianople. Amorath received him in honor and dismissed him with gifts; but the gracious approbation of the Turkish Sultan announced his supremacy and the approaching downfall of the Eastern Empire. By the hands of two illustrious deputies, the Imperial crown was placed at Sparta on the head of Constantine. In the spring he sailed from Morea, escaped the encounter of a Turkish squadron, enjoyed the acclamations of his subjects, [53] celebrated the festival of the new reign, and exhausted by his donatives, the treasure, or rather the indigence of the state.'

"Calculating the time on the scale for symbolic prophecy, the year is 360 years, and the month thirty years, and the day one year, gives us 391 years. This added to the date 1449, brings us down into the year 1840. During that year the arrangements began. In 1839 by the Convention of July 27 and was brought to the termination of July 15 [1840]."[197]

---

[197] LeRoy Edwin Froom, Box 6805, Archives of the General Conference of Seventh-day Adventists (Silver Spring, MD), 50-56.

The considerations of these several brethren of experience were factual, humble, straight-forward and honest, with no interpretation necessary. This is the spirit and attitude with which we should meet to address any issues that do not withstand investigation, rightly dividing the word of truth.

Earlier in this chapter, we listed seven understandings of Josiah Litch that were the foundation upon which he built his published interpretation of the fifth trumpet of Revelation 9:5, 10, followed by our comments proclaiming them to be erroneous beliefs. The seventh listed belief has not been discussed thus far; it concerns the date Litch assigned to the fall of the Greek empire. We will now review that prior entry and then investigate the accuracy of Litch's position:

7. Josiah Litch declared that when the Greek emperor died in the year 1449 and left his throne to his brother, it was then that the approaching downfall of the empire was at hand, ultimately coming by a voluntary surrender of her independence into the hands of the Turks, by the brother's saying, "I cannot reign unless you permit." Or "John Paleologus, the last Greek emperor dared not to reign without the permission of his enemy," the Turkish Sultan. In other words, the Greek or Byzantine emperor became a vassal to the Ottoman Empire in 1449.

So that terminology does not confuse us, we want to establish the definition of "vassal:"

> **1. Dependent landholder in feudal society:** Somebody who gave loyalty and homage to a feudal lord and received the right to occupy the lord's land and be protected by him. **2. Slave:** A bondman or slave. **3. Person or nation dependent on another:** A person, nation, or group that is dependent on or subordinate to another."[198]

Prophetically speaking, this historic fall of an empire would have had to take place on July 27, 1449, because no other event is listed for prophetic fulfillment or fits into the prophetic time frame! This understanding will be proven to be utterly false, as well.

In addressing this claim put forth by Josiah Litch, we first submit a preface from a well-respected historian as he defines his objective and that of two others. Charles William Chadwick Oman and George Finlay are two Byzantine historians who wrote in the 1800s. They have lost none of their prevalence among the international academic community. Due to the fact that they always referenced original or primary sources throughout their entire works, the literary contributions of those men have been able to withstand the test of time:

Preface

> "Fifty years ago the word 'Byzantine' was used as a synonym for all that was corrupt and decadent, and the tale of the East-Roman Empire was dismissed by modern historians as depressing and monotonous. The Great Gibbon had branded the successors of Justinian and Heraclius as a series of vicious weaklings, and for several generations no one dared to contradict him.
> "Two books have served to undeceive the English reader: the monumental work of Finlay, published in 1856, and the more modern volumes of Mr. Bury, which appeared in 1889. Since they have written, the Byzantines no longer need an

---

[198] *Encarta Dictionary* (English) (North America), "vassal."

apologist, and the great work of the East-Roman Empire in holding back the Saracen, and in keeping alive throughout the Dark Ages the lamp of learning, is beginning to be realized.

"The writer of this book has endeavoured to tell the story of Byzantium in the spirit of Finlay and Bury, not that of Gibbon. He wishes to acknowledge his debts both to the veteran of the war of Greek Independence, and to the young Dublin professor. Without their aid his task would have been very heavy; with it the difficulty was removed.

"The author does not claim to have grappled with all the chroniclers of the Eastern realm, but thinks that some acquaintance with Ammianus, Procopius, Maurice's 'Strategikon,' Leo the Deacon, Leo the Wise, Constantine Porphyrogenitus, Anna Comnena and Nicetas may justify his having undertaken the task he has essayed."[199]

For the reader to rightly understand the following submitted history, some clarification is needed. There has been some confusion as to Emperor John VI being declared to be John VII, and sometimes being referred to as John VIII. Similarly, Emperor Constantine XI, John VI's brother and the one who succeeded him, has been referenced by some as Constantine XII and even Constantine XIII, but there has been no mistake in his or any other Byzantine emperor's lineage, nor in the chronological events of their respective lives and reigns. That understanding will help keep one on track. For our purposes, we will stay with John VI and Constantine XI, from the authority of Phrantzes and Finlay. The following narrative of chronology will bring clarity to the reader.

Emperor John V Palaiologos reigned off and on and sometimes co-reigned with his son, from June 15, 1341, to February 16, 1391. He was deposed in 1376 by his son Andronikos IV and restored July 1, 1379. The son of Andronikos IV usurped the throne from his grandfather John V for five months in 1390, but with Ottoman mediation he was reconciled with John V and his uncle, Manuel II. Restored to senior emperor again on September 17, 1390, John V ruled until his death on February 16, 1391. He was succeeded by Emperor Manuel II, who reigned from February 16, 1391, to July 21, 1425. Manuel II was succeeded by his oldest son, Emperor John VI, who reigned from July 21, 1425, to October 31, 1448. John VI was succeeded by the fourth son of Manuel II; he would become the last Byzantine emperor of the East, known as Constantine XI Palaiologos. He reigned from January 6, 1449, to May 29, 1453.

Josiah Litch declared that the Greek or Byzantine emperor (John VI of the Palaiologos dynasty) died in the year 1449, leaving the throne to his brother. Was that a statement of fact? No. Consider the following as we establish the date of the death of Byzantine emperor John VI of the Palaiologos dynasty. Our source is from none other than Georgius Phrantzes, a Byzantine Greek historian born in Constantinople (1401-1478). He became secretary to Emperor Manuel II in 1432; he later became prefect and also chancellor. His most valuable chronicle was his detailed events and history of the house of the Palaiologoi from 1258 to 1476. Written in Greek, with footnotes in Latin, he said this:

"*Tricesimo primo die Octobris anni 6957...*"[200]

Tricesimo primo die Octobris is the 31st day of October. "6957" is the year in Greek equaling AD 1448. This is confirmed by Finlay and Oman:

[199] Charles William Chadwick Oman, *The Byzantine Empire* (New York-London: G.P. Putnam, 1892), preface.
[200] Georgius Phrantzes, *Corpus Scriptorum Historiae Byzantinae* (Bonnae Impensis ed. Weberi, 1838), 203.

"John even contrived to avoid taking any part of the war carried on against the sultan by his brother Constantine in Greece, and succeeded in preserving uninterrupted peace until his death in 1448."[201]

"John VI., in spite of the caution with which he avoided all action, was destined to see the empire lose its most important possession beyond the walls of [341] Constantinople. His brother Andronicus, governor of Thessalonica, traitorously sold that city to the Venetians for 50,000 zecchins. The Sultan, incensed at a transfer of Greek territory having taken place without his permission, pounced down on the place, expelled the Venetians and annexed Thessalonica to Ottoman Empire (1430).

"The chief feature of the reign of the last John Paloelogus was his attempt to win aid for the empire by enlisting sympathy in Western Europe. He determined to conform to Roman Catholicism and throw himself on the generosity of the Pope. Accordingly he took himself to Italy in 1438, with Patriarch of Constantinople and many bishops in his train. He appeared at the councils of Ferrara and Florence, and was solemnly received into the Roman Church in the Florentine Duomo, on July 6, 1439. It had apparently escaped John's notice that Eugenius IV., the pope of his own day, was a very different personage from the great pontiffs of the eleventh and twelfth centuries, who were able to depose sovereigns and send forth crusades at their good pleasure. Since the great schism the papacy had been hopelessly discredited in Christendom. Eugenius IV., was engaged in waging a defensive war against the Council of Basle, which was attempting to depose him, and had little thought or power to spend on aiding the Eastern Christians. All that John could get from him was a sum of money and a body of three hundred mercenary troops. This was a poor return for his journey and conversion.

"Only one thing of importance was accomplished by [342] the apostasy of the Emperor: the outbreak of a venomous ecclesiastical struggle at Constantinople between the conformist who had taken the oath at Florence, and the bulk of the clergy, who disowned the treaty of union. John was practically boycotted by the majority of his subjects; the Orthodox priests ceased to pray for him, and the populace refused to enter St. Sophia again, when it had been profaned by the celebration of the Roman Mass. The opinion of the majority of the Greeks was summed up in the exclamation of the Grand-Duke John Notaras- 'Better the turban of the Turk in Constantinople than the Pope's Tiara.'

"...John VI. passed away in 1448, and Sultan Murad in 1451. The one was succeeded by his brother Constantine, the last Christian sovereign of Byzantium, [343] the other by his young son Mohammed the Conqueror."[202]

To our question about the accuracy of Litch's date of 1449 for the emperor's death, we can state with certainly that Emperor John VI did not die in the year 1449. Emperor John VI reigned from July 21, 1425, to October 31, 1448; he died in that year.

Next we need to establish the date for the coronation of Emperor Constantine XI. This, too, will shed light on the correctness of Litch's date. George Finlay answers this need:

---

[201] George Finlay, *History of the Byzantine and Greek Empires: From MLVII to MCCCCLIII* [1057-1453] (Edinburgh-London: William Blackwood and Sons, 1854), 619.
[202] Charles William Chadwick Oman, *The Byzantine Empire* (New York-London: G.P. Putnam's Sons, 1892), 340-343.

"Constantine XI., the last of the Greek emperors, was residing in his despotat at Sparta when his brother John VI. died.... The ceremony of his coronation was performed at Sparta in the month of January 1449."[203]

Finlay's just-quoted primary source is from none other than Georgius Phrantzes.[204] January 6, 1449, to May 29, 1453, was the reign of the last of the Byzantine emperors, Constantine XI. This was established simply to show that the Greek empire did not fall on July 27, 1449.

Our next questions and answers will prove to be decisive:

1. Did a Byzantine emperor seek the permission of the Sultan to ascend to the throne for the first time in 1449? No!
2. Did the Byzantine emperor Constantine XI become the first vassal to the Ottoman Empire in 1449? No!
3. Did this claimed event by Josiah Litch take place on July 27, 1449, in order for the chronology of that prophecy to land on none other but, August 11, 1840? No!

The following primary sources will reveal that under the reign of Emperor John V, Constantinople became a vassal to the Ottoman Empire in AD 1370. Every emperor thereafter was largely in subjection to the Sultan. Thenceforth, it was the Sultan who would decide who would ascend to the throne of emperor. This condition fluctuated little, and history proves Constantinople paid annual tributes in varying amounts to the Turks until her final defeat on May 29, 1453. The origin and history of the subjection of the Greek to the Turk is here presented:

1370: "The Greek emperor [John V Palaiologos] visited the Court of Rome in person in the year 1369, and carried his hypocrisy so far as to join the Latin communion. He delivered to Pope Urban V. a written profession of faith, agreeable to the tenets of the Roman church, and declared verbally his conviction that the third person of the Trinity proceedeth from the Father and the Son; that it is lawful to distribute the communion in unleavened bread; that the church of Rome is the mother church; that she alone has authority to decide questions of faith, and that she has the sole right of receiving appeals on ecclesiastical matters. All this was publicly pronounced in the Church of St Peter's; yet the emperor gained little by his servility: the Pope only supplied him with two galleys, three hundred soldiers, and a few thousand ducats; and on his way back to Constantinople he was arrested for debt at Venice. His eldest son, Andronicus, who acted as regent of the empire during his absence, pretended that he was unable to raise the money required to release his father; but his second son Manuel succeeded in raising the necessary funds at Thessalonica, of which he was governor, and John returned covered with disgrace to his palace, A.D. 1370."[205]

"[Sultan] Murad had watched this attempt to oppose a barrier to the Othoman power with prudent circumspection. In the mean time, he had consolidated his

[203] George Finlay, *History of the Byzantine and Greek Empires: From MLVII To MCCCCLIII* [1057-1453] (Edinburgh-London: William Blackwood and Sons, 1854), 620.
[204] Georgius Phrantzes, *Corpus Scriptorum Historiae Byzantinae* (Bonnae, Impensis ed. Weberi, 1838), 205.
[205] Pbrantzcs, p. 53; Chalcocondylas, 26.

conquests in Thrace by subduing the Greek, Bulgarian, and Servian chiefs, who held independent districts in the chains of Haemus and Rhodope. But when the sultan saw the Greek emperor return to his capital as weak as ever and far more unpopular with his orthodox subjects, hostilities were renewed. John, unable to form a generous resolution, consented to become the vassal of the sultan as he had already consented to become a servant [580] of the Pope. He had hardly concluded his treaty with Murad when the imprudence of his son Manuel again exposed the empire to the attacks of the Othomans."[206]

"At this time the Greeks looked on the Latins with contempt as well as hatred; they despised the western Europeans as heretics, and the Turks as barbarians."[207]

1381: "Manuel the second son of John V., was crowned emperor at Constantinople, and proclaimed heir to the throne.[208]
"When John V. escaped from prison in the year 1381, he concluded a treaty with Sultan Murad, acknowledging himself a vassal and tributary of the Othoman empire."[209]

"Emperor John V obtained the support of the Sultan Murad to regain his throne, from which his own son was trying to keep him. 'In the year 1381, he concluded a treaty with the Sultan Murad, acknowledging himself again a vassal and tributary of the Ottoman Empire.'"[210]

1389:   "The rapid conquests of the Othomans had swallowed up the neighboring Seljouk principalities, and Sultan Bayezid, who possessed many seaports, no longer desired to see a neutral commercial city on the frontier of his dominions; on the contrary, he was eager to increase his power by its conquest. Philadelphia refused his summons to submit; but when the people saw the Emperor Manuel and the imperial standard in the hostile army, they perceived that the cause of Greek liberty and of the orthodox church was hopeless, and they capitulated. The terms conceded to their Greek subjects at this time by the Othoman sultans were not regarded as oppressive, for their fiscal burdens were lightened. The Emir of Aidin was forced to cede Ephesus

---

[206] George Finlay, *History of the Byzantine and Greek Empires: From MLVII to MCCCCLIII* [1057-1453] (Edinburgh-London: William Blackwood and Sons, 1854), 579-580.

[207] Ibid., George Finlay, 614.

[208] By the treaty of Turin, 8th August 1381, the Venetians engaged to destroy the fortifications of Tenedos, and included John V. (Calojani) in its provisions as an ally of the republic.-Marin, *Commercio de' Veneziani*, vi. 218. Sauli, Colonia *dei Genovesi, ii.* 260, gives a treaty of the emperors John V., Andronicus, and John the son of Andronicus, with the republic of Genoa, dated 2d November 1382, for giving effect to the treaty concluded between the emperors in the preceding year. Several curious documents relating to the cession of Tenedos to the Genoesc, and the destruction of the fortifications by the Venetians, in execution of the stipulations contained in the treaty of Turin (A.D. 1381), are published by Hammer, *Histoire de l' Empire Othoman, x.* 457, trad. de Hellert.

[209] Phrantzes, 56, ed Bonn. Chalcocondylas, 33, ed. Par. It would require a long dissertation to compare the order of events and the discordant facts narrated by Phrantzes, Ducas, and Chalcocondylas. Quoted in George Finlay, *History of the Byzantine and Greek Empires: From MLVII to MCCCCLIII* [1057-1453] (Edinburgh-London: William Blackwood and Sons, 1854), 583.

[210] George Finlay, *A History of Greece*: (Edinburgh: Blackwood, 1857), 3: 466.

to Bayezid, and the principalities of Saroukhan and Menteshe were at the same time incorporated in the Othoman empire. These new conquests were formed into a government of which Philadelphia, called by the Turks Alashehr, was constituted the capital, and Ertogrul, the son of Sultan Bayezid, was appointed governor."[211]

"The haughty conduct of the young sultan alarmed John V., who now, when it was too late, began to [586] strengthen the fortifications of Constantinople. Thirty-six years had elapsed since he had ordered the citadel constructed by Cantacuzenos at the Golden Gate to be destroyed. He now commenced repairing this stronghold, and proposed improving the defenses of the Golden Gate itself by the addition of two towers. In order to complete the work with the greatest celerity, he employed the solid marble blocks that had been used in building the Church of the Holy Apostles and other sacred edifices, which were now little better than heaps of ruin; while, to hide the plan of his fortifications, he lavished architectural decorations on the outer walls. [The Sultan] Bayezid, however, was no sooner informed of his proceedings, than he sent an order [the year 1389] to his imperial vassal to level the work he had already completed to the ground, threatening that, in case of any delay, he would render the Emperor Manuel responsible. The miserable old emperor, who feared that his son might be deprived of sight, immediately destroyed his work, and shortly after sank into the grave."[212]

1391: "The Emperor Manuel [reign of Manuel II, A.D. 1391-1425] was at Brusa when he heard of his father's death. He was generally esteemed, being neither destitute of talent nor personal courage, while his disposition was mild and conciliatory. Before [the Sultan] Bayezid was informed of the death of John V. the new emperor had made his escape, and reached Constantinople in safety; but the sultan treated him as a rebellious vassal in consequence of his secret departure. John Paleologos, the son of Andronicus, who had succeeded his father in the appanage of Selymbria, was encouraged to claim the empire in virtue of the treaty of 1381, by which the succession had been secured to his father and himself. A body of Turkish troops was instructed to ravage the Greek territory up to the very walls of Constantinople; but other matters calling for Bayezid's care, he accepted the submission of Manuel, [588] and the Greek emperor again appeared as a vassal at the Sublime Porte"[213]

1402: "On reaching Constantinople [Emperor Manuel II] he deprived his nephew John, who had ruled during his absence, of the imperial title, and banished him to

---

[211] Leunelaviua, *Annals Turcioi*, 318, places the conquest of Philadelphia in 1380. Hammer places it in 1390, vol. I, page 302, but in 1391 at page 299. Ducas, 7, and Chalcoeondylas, 33, agree in placing it in the reign of Bayezid ; yet Ameilhon, Lebeau, xx. 460, gives the date 1379; and the work of Ken, which shows that the author paid some attention to the chronology of this period, dates it in *1374.-Imperatores* Orientis compendio exhibiti a Constantine *Magno* ad Constantinum ultimum. Studio F. Borgie Keri e Soc. Jesu. Sac, Tyrnavio, 1744, folio, 530.

[212] George Finlay, *History of the Byzantine and Greek Empires: From MLVII to MCCCCLIII* [1057-1453] (Edinburgh-London: William Blackwood and Sons, 1854), 585-6.

[213] The portal of the Sultan's audience-hall or tent was already the official waiting-place of princes and the acts of the Othoman government were already dated from this porte, or entrance to the Sultan's presence. - Ducas, 27th edit. Par. Quoted in George Finlay, *History of the Byzantine and Greek Empires: From MLVII to MCCCCLIII* [1057-1453] (Edinburgh-London: William Blackwood and Sons, 1854), 587-8.

Lemnos. John had already placed the Greek empire in a state of <u>vassalage</u> to the Tartar conqueror; Manuel ratified the treaty, and paid to Timor the tribute which he had formerly paid to Bayezid."[214]

1422: "At last the pretender Mustapha, whom Manuel had supplied with money to cause a revolt against his brother, began to stir up such trouble in Asia Minor, that the Sultan determined to raise the siege and march against him. He granted Manuel peace, on the condition that he ceded all his dominions save the cities Constantinople, Thessalonica and the Peloponnesian province. Thus the empire once more sank back into a state of <u>vassalage</u> to the Ottomans (1422)....

"Manuel II. died three years after, [1425] at the age of seventy-seven. He was the last sovereign of Constantinople who won even a transient smile from fortune. The tale of the last thirty years of the empire is one of unredeemed gloom.

"To [*sic*] Manuel succeeded his son John VI., whose whole reign was passed in peace, without an attempt to shake off the Turkish yoke; such an attempt indeed would have been hopeless, unless backed by aid from without."[215]

Ducas (1400-1462) was a Byzantine historian who flourished under Constantine XI. He is a very important primary source for the last decades and fall of Constantinople. Ducas informs us of the amount of annual tribute that the Byzantine Emperor Manuel II paid to the Sultan:

"Manuel also engaged to pay the sultan an annual tribute of 300,000 aspers."[216]

1448: "John [VI] even contrived to avoid taking any part of the war carried on against the sultan by his brother Constantine in Greece, and succeeded in preserving uninterrupted peace until his death in 1448. During his inglorious reign of twenty-three years he never forgot that he was a <u>vassal</u> of the Ottoman Empire."[217]

1448: "The incident of securing the Sultan's consent hardly seems to stand out from other and even more formal acknowledgements of vassalage to the Turk. And it occurs in 1448. Besides this, Constantine was really less of a vassal to the Turk than his predecessors: 'A prince whose heroism throws a sunset glory on the close of the long-clouded series of the Byzantine annals.'"[218]

Like the other emperors before him, Emperor Constantine XI sought the consent of the Sultan in 1448 to ascend to the throne, a fact we acknowledged earlier. His coronation took place on January 6, 1449. Since John V, in fact, all emperors were "compelled" to submit or face the repercussions. So here we see there has not been one thread of truth or fact to the claims of Josiah Litch for his

---

[214] George Finlay, *History of the Byzantine and Greek Empires*: From MLVII to MCCCCLIII [1057-1453] (Edinburgh-London, William Blackwood and Sons, 1854), 601.
[215] Charles William Chadwick Oman, *The Byzantine Empire* (New York-London: G.P. Putnam's Sons, 1892), 339.
[216] George Finlay, *History of the Byzantine and Greek Empires: From MLVII to MCCCCLIII* [1057-1453] (Edinburgh-London, William Blackwood and Sons, 1854), 613. [Finlay references Ducas in his footnote and expands his documentation.]
[217] Ibid., 619.
[218] Williams, Henry Smith, *Historians' History of the World* (London and New York: Hooper & Jackson, 1908, c1907), 24:327.

predictions involving the year 1449 that we have surveyed alongside the primary sources. In fact, we just read that "Constantine was really less of a vassal to the Turk than his predecessors."

We furnish one more document for the sake of honesty and closure. Uriah Smith, in writing his *Daniel and the Revelation,* gave the following reference in his 1897 edition that we wish to acknowledge. The 1944 edition and newer ones do not reference this footnote; they have been heavily edited. (To download a copy of this early 1897 edition of *Daniel and the Revelation* by Uriah Smith, see my website at www.thesourcehh.org.) On page 576 Uriah Smith says the following in his footnote, concerning the predicted event of 1449:

> "Some historians have given this date as 1448, but the best authorities sustain the date here given, 1449. See Chamber's Encyclopedia, art. Paleologous."

To be totally fair and ethical, we are going to submit the entire article referenced in Smith's footnote relative to the 1449 date, because truth can withstand investigation and closure is the sole motive of this book:

> "John VII. [John VI] (1425-1449), on being pressed by the Turks, again held out to the pope the old bait of the union of the Greek and Western Churches under his sway, and even presented himself at the council of Florence, where, in July 1439 the union of the churches was agreed to. But on his return to Constantinople, the opposition of the Greek ecclesiastics to the union, supported by the people, rendered the agreement of Florence a dead letter. The pope, however, saw that it was for his interest to fulfill his part of the agreement, and accordingly stirred up Wladislas of Hungary to attack the Turks (see JAGELLONS), but this act only hastened the downfall of the Palaeologi. John's brother, Constantine XIII, [Constantine XI] (1449-1453), a heroic action of a degenerate race, accepted the crown after much hesitation, knowing his total inability to withstand the Turks, and even then took the precaution of obtaining the sultan's consent before he exercised the imperial authority; but some rebellions in Caramania which now occurred, baffling Sultan Mohammed II's efforts to quell them, the emperor was willingly persuaded by his rash advisors that the time had now arrived for rendering himself independent of the Turks. The attempt, however, only brought swifter destruction on the wretched remnant of the Byzantine empire, for Mohammed invested the capital by sea and land, and after a siege, which lasted from 6th April to 29th May 1453, Constantinople was taken by storm, and the last of the Paleaologi fell fighting bravely in the breach. A branch of this family ruled Montferrat in Italy from 1306, but became extinct in 1533. The Palaeologi were connected by marriage with the ruling families of Hungary, Servia, and the last of the family married Ivan, Czar of Russia- a fact which the Czars of Russia have persisted till lately in bringing forward as a claim in favor of their pretensions to the possession of European Turkey. It is said that direct descendants of the Palaeologi exist to the

present day in France. (For further information, see the separate articles on some of the emperors, and Byzantine Empire.)"[219]

As one can clearly see, this article cited by U. Smith is inaccurate and is largely no more than surface reading. It by no means proves to be of the "best authorities," as claimed by Uriah Smith, when compared to the primary sources. An example for "best authorities" among the international academic community would be Hadschi Chalfa's *Historic Chronology*. If one would care to open its pages to the Hegira year 853/1449,[220] one will find it completely blank. Why? Because nothing whatsoever of any historical significance took place in the year 1449. The reader may now insert the three-year, ten-day discrepancy, only to compound the math and the futility of finding a suitable event. One may continue to search for some historical event that could be claimed for a forced fulfillment for July 27, 1449, but it will be in vain, for neither the primary sources nor the annals nor the chronological tables will bring the desired result!

---

[219] *Chambers Encyclopedia*, "Paleologous" (Philadelphia-Edinburgh: J.B. Lippincott, 1869), 7: 901.
[220] Hadschi Chalfa, *Cronologia Historica* [*A Historic Chronology*] (Italy: Andrea Poletti, 1697), 130.

5

Square Pegs and Round Holes

We have just honestly surveyed all the critical written works of Josiah Litch pertaining to the fifth and sixth trumpets of the Millerite movement. When October 22, 1844, came and went with no return of Christ in the clouds of heaven, the disappointment was too much for the majority. The Millerite movement came to an end, while the Advent movement was commanded to "prophecy again" (Rev. 10:11). Among those who forsook the cause shortly thereafter was Josiah Litch, who returned to his evangelical faith. Josiah Litch publicly repudiated his former belief and especially his exposition of the fifth and sixth trumpets of Revelation. In 1873 he wrote another book entitled *A Complete Harmony of Daniel and the Apocalypse*. In chapter nine Litch gives us his exposition of "The Fifth and Sixth Trumpets." No longer does Litch read the Ottoman Empire into the text. In fact, he makes an honest attempt by using the Scriptures, which we find commendable. We supply the reader with this entire exposition of the fifth and sixth trumpets by a man who had the integrity to admit his error:

CHAPTER IX.

LOCUSTS FROM THE WELL PIT

"*Verses* 1-11. 'And the fifth angel sounded, and I saw a star fall from heaven unto the earth: and to him was given the key of the bottomless pit. And he opened the bottomless pit; and there arose a smoke out of the pit, as the smoke of a great furnace; and the sun and the air were darkened by reason of the smoke of the pit. And there came out of the smoke [162] locusts upon the earth: and unto them was given power, as the scorpions of the earth have power. And it was commanded them that they should not hurt the grass of the earth, neither any green thing, neither any tree; but only those men which have not the seal of God in their foreheads. And to them it was given that they should not kill them, but that they should be tormented five months: and their torment *was* as the torment of a scorpion, when he striketh a man. And in those days shall men seek death, and shall not find it; and shall desire to die, and death shall flee from them. And the shapes of the locusts *were* like unto horses prepared unto battle; and on their heads *were* as it were crowns like gold, and their faces *were* as the faces of men. And they had hair as the hair of women, and their teeth were as *the teeth* of lions. And they had breastplates, as it were breastplates of iron; and the sound of their wings *was* as the sound of chariots of many horses running to battle. And they had tails like unto scorpions, and there were stings in their tails: and their power *was* to hurt men five months. And they had a king over them, *which is* the angel of the bottomless pit, whose name in the Hebrew tongue *is* Abaddon, but in the Greek tongue hath *his* name Apollyon.'

"In this instance it is evident, from the action performed, that the '*star*' which is said to have 'fallen from heaven unto the earth,' is a symbol of an angelic messenger, for a star is frequently used as the symbol of an angel or messenger, whether human or superhuman, and the context must decide which, if reference is had to either. The *seven stars* in Christ's right hand are the 'angels of the churches.' The [163] dragon's tail drew a third part of '*the stars of heaven,*' and cast them to the earth. This, no doubt, refers to the angels whom Satan seduces, and who share his fate. (See Matt. xxv. 41) It is not natural for a *star* to receive, hold, or use a key.

" '*Fallen from heaven unto the earth.*' The writer did not see this *star* angel in the act of falling, but saw him as already *fallen*. It may be the dragon after his defeat by Michael, and his expulsion from heaven with his angels into the earth; or it may be a subordinate angel. But whatever he is, his name is *Apollyon,* and his mission is to open the bottomless pit, and let loose its hordes of locusts; marshal and govern them in their work of tormenting men.

" '*To him was given the key of the bottomless pit.*' Φρεατος – well, pit, cistern. Αβυσσον – deep profound, bottomless, abyss, place of the dead, hell. Paul uses it in the sense of *place of the dead.* 'Who shall descend into the Αβυσσον, that is, to bring up Christ again from the dead.' It was the Αβυσσον from which the ejected demons desired Christ to spare them until their time. It is the place into which Satan is to be cast and bound for a thousand years. (Rev. xx.)

" '*Key of.*' Key is the symbol of power. This angel is invested with power to open the '*well of the abyss.*' It was opened when Korah, Dathan, and Abiram, with their company, went down alive into it.

[164] " 'He opened.' 'There arose a great smoke,' so great that the sun and the air were darkened 'by reason of the smoke of the pit.' That such a transaction as this will take place, there is no more reason to doubt, than there is to doubt the history of Korah and his company.

" 'Locusts upon the earth.' Probably they arose in the smoke proceeding from the pit. That they are not natural locusts, whose nature it is to devour all green things, is evident from the fact that these do not eat any green thing; their only mission being to *torment men*, not to devour any vegetation.

" '*Seal of God.*' These infernal locusts are not to torment *men* indiscriminately. God has provided a mark for certain characters, and these are exempted from the plague, just as Israel was in Egypt, while protected by the blood of the Passover lamb from the sword of the destroying angel. Is it not to this protection our Saviour refers when he says, 'Watch ye, therefore, and pray always that ye may be accounted worthy to escape all these things that shall come to pass, and to stand before the son of man'? (Luke xxi.)

" '*Not kill them.*' Their mission was restricted. They were not to kill the subjects of their torments, nor would they be able to die, however much they desired it; '*death shall flee from them.*' A fearful picture is here presented – a torment so great as to [165] induce men to long for the approach of the 'king of terrors;' indeed, to *seek* for death, but yet not able to find it, not escape from the torment which they must bear. 'Their torment is as the torment of a scorpion when he striketh a man.' The scorpion sting produces an inflammation and redness of the parts, accompanied with the most terrible pain, inducing the subject to roll on the ground in his anguish. But it can not be escaped by death, for death itself flies away. The description of these locusts is so unearthly as to strike the stoutest heart with terror – like horses in shape, hair like women, faces like men, crowns like gold, breastplate like iron, teeth like lions, tails like scorpions, and stings in their tails, all marshaled like an army of cavalry rushing to battle, producing a sound with their wings like the chariots of many horses running to battle. 'Their power was to torment men five months,' or just one hundred and fifty days, under the command of *king* Apollyon, the destroyer, whose name is derived from the Greek verb Απολλυυι, to destroy. And be it observed that torment is the only destruction which he has power to inflict. He is the angel of the bottomless pit. If he governs it, has he more power than with his legions of hellish locusts on earth? Who can read the description of the plagues under these trumpets, and not be reminded of our Saviour's description of the time which shall precede [166] his coming in a cloud? 'There shall be signs in the sun, and in the moon, and in the stars; and upon the earth distress of nations, with perplexity; the sea and waves roaring; men's hearts failing them for fear, and for looking after those things which are coming on the earth.' In regard to the numerous theories which have been advanced from time to time as affording the *most reasonable* solution of this *'confessedly difficult passage,'* we have simply to say that they do not meet the requirements of the prediction. Perhaps that which has gained for itself the largest number of adherents among the advocates of an historical interpretation of this book, is that these locusts symbolize the Mohammedan invasion of Europe and other lands, under Mohammed and his successors. It is true that in some things there are points of coincidence which have given a certain coloring of plausibility to the theory; but it can bear no searching analysis. Let us examine one or two points out of the many that exist in contravention of this theory. The prediction is very positive that these locusts, in going forth 'upon the face of the earth,' 'should not hurt the grass nor any green thing.' It is true that one of the invaders gave the command to the Saracen army invading the East, *'Destroy no palm trees nor burn any fields of corn; cut down no fruit trees.'* But this very command shows that this was an exception to the general rule; and besides, it is absurd even to [167] think of armies, such as went forth under Mohammedan leaders, abstaining from the injury of trees, which were necessary for fuel, and grass, necessary for the pasturage of their horses. These locusts were to have power, not to kill, but to torment. And besides all that, even this power was limited to all who had not the *'seal of God in their foreheads.'* Whereas the whole mission of these fanatical hordes which spread themselves abroad in certain parts of Europe and the East, was to kill and destroy the saints of God. When Mohammed wrote his Koran he delivered this command: 'When ye encounter the unbelievers, strike off their heads, until ye have made a great slaughter among them.... As for the infidels, let them perish.' Here, then, we have ample reason for refusing credence to a theory which is in so evident an opposition to facts. For not only were these locusts prohibited from touching those possessing the seal of God, but their power was limited to *torment*. They had no power to inflict death. It is true that the ground has been taken that this command, *'not to kill men,'* has been interpreted as meaning 'not to annihilate them as a political Christian body.' But this reasoning has met its answer in the reply of

Dean Alford to one of the advocates of this theory. He says, 'If, then, the same rule of interpretation is to hold, the sixth verse must mean that the "political Christian body" will be so sorely beset by [168] Mohammedan locusts that it will vehemently desire to be annihilated, and not find any way. For it surely can not be allowed that *the killing of men* should be said of their annihilation as a political body in one verse, and their *desiring to die* in the next should be said of something totally different, and applicable to their individual misery.'

"But it is said that these Mohammedans in their mighty array, in the bustling, confusing sound made by them upon the march, the character of their dress and accouterments of war, their long hair, their horses, their turbans, breastplates, and shields, all rendered the resemblance between them and these *so-called* 'symbolical locusts' so complete that it is impossible to mistake the allusion. 'But how could turbans be like gold?' Or even admitting this general resemblance, when the character of their work differs so essentially from that spoken of in the prophecy, why should a few petty details, in which there may *appear* something of a coincidence, be taken as affording conclusive reasons for the adoption of an interpretation so strained as this?"

THE SECOND WOE

THE SIXTH TRUMPET

"Verses 12-21. 'One woe is past; *and,* behold, there come two woes more hereafter. And the sixth angel sounded, and I heard a voice from the four horns of the golden altar which is before God, saying to the sixth angel which had the trumpet, Loose the [169] four angels which are bound in the great river Euphrates. And the four angels were loosed, which were prepared for an hour, and a day, and a month, and a year, for to slay the third part of men. And the number of the army of the horsemen *were* two hundred thousand thousand: and I heard the number of them. And this I saw the horses in the vision, and them that sat on them, having breastplates of fire, and of jacinth, and brimstone: and the heads of the horses *were* as the heads of lions: and out of their mouths issues fire, and smoke, and brimstone. By these three was the third part of men killed, by the fire, and by the smoke, and by the brimstone, which issued out of their mouths. For their power is in their mouth, and in their tails: for their tails *were* like unto serpents, and had heads, and with them they do hurt. And the rest of the men which were not killed by these plagues yet repented not of the works of their hands, that they should not worship devils, and idols of gold, and silver, and brass, and stone, and of wood: which neither can see, nor hear, nor walk: neither repented they of their murders, nor of their sorceries, nor of their fornication, nor of their thefts.'

"None who read and believe the description of the work of the locusts in tormenting men, will doubt but what it will be a 'woe' on the inhabiters of the earth. But it will be past ere the second woe is introduced; clearly, then, they are consecutive.

" 'Loose the four angels which are bound in,' or *by,* as an instrument, bond, or limit, 'the great river Euphrates.' That four angels or messengers of wrath are restrained *by* the literal *River Euphrates,* [170] the eastern boundary of the Roman empire, awaiting the time appointed for their action within its bounds, there is no reason for doubting. They are those bound by angelic order, as recorded in chapter vii.3. The command to loose them is said to come 'from *one* of the four horns of the golden altar which is before God,' and on which were offered the prayers of all the saints with much incense. This action denotes the nature of those prayers, by the answer that is given in letting loose the judgments of God already prepared, but awaiting the proper moment to be introduced. *'And the four angels were loosed.'* The exact hour for them to be loosed was fixed. They were prepared *unto* an hour, day, month, and year. That is, the exact time for their loosing was fixed, to a year, a month, a day, and an hour; it is not an exact period during which they should act. 'To slay the third part of men.' To what extent is not stated, whether on the whole globe, or the Roman empire – the dominion of the beast, or the land of Israel. But to whatever extent their commission runs, one third part of men are to be killed by this woe. The agents of destruction under these four angels were to be horsemen, and the horses they ride.

"This army is announced to be two hundred millions in number – an army equal to all the men on earth able to bear arms. John heard the number stated; he did not count them himself. Not only did he hear [171] the number, but saw the horses, and those who sat on them, and he proceeds to describe them as he saw them. Their riders had breastplates of fire, and jacinth, and brimstone. Jacinth is the color of the blue flame of brimstone. The heads of the horses were as the heads of lions, and out of their mouths issued fire, and smoke, and brimstone. Their power lay in their mouths and tails. By the fire, smoke, and brimstone suffocating those they approached, the third part of men was killed.

" 'Their tails were like serpents, having heads,' and with those heads attached to the serpent-like tail, they do hurt. It is not said that any are killed by the tails, but they are hurt by them, and killed by what proceeds from their mouths.

"These beings, like the horses and chariots of fire which filled the mountains in the days of Elisha, must be supernatural beings, of which heaven and hell are full. The two witnesses of Rev. ii. are said to do much the same thing; but then they are endowed by God for their work.

"One would suppose that such judgments would lead men to repent of their sins and seek mercy. But as it was in Egypt in the days of Pharaoh, so will it be in this instance; instead of being convinced, and softening their hearts, they are rather rendered hard and more obdurate than before; and so continue to worship demons and idols, to commit murders, fornications, [172] and thefts. Such is human nature when left to itself. Mercies and judgments alike fail to move men without the influence of the Holy Ghost. All the plagues of these six trumpets are unavailing to produce repentance. Nothing remains, then, but for the final or third woe, which is to bring the judgment of the dead, and 'destroy them that destroy the earth.' (See chapter xi. 15-19.)

These agents, it should be remembered, were shown John in his vision in heaven. Whether, in the days of the fulfillment, these agencies will be any more visible or tangible to the natural senses than were the horses and chariots of fire which Gehazi's eyes were opened to see in the days of Elisha, admits of doubt. But that such instrumentalities are in reserve for that dreadful day, admits of no doubt. How the prophet Elisha was defended by the fiery horses, we do not know; how his enemies were smitten with blindness by their agency, we can not comprehend; but yet the fact remains – they were the prophet's defense; and the blindness came, and his enemies were made an easy prey. So we may be left in doubt and uncertainty about many things in regard to the demon cavalry; but the wicked will one day feel their power, while the saints will have protection."[221]

The words of Josiah Litch speak for themselves and require no further commentary.

There are two main schools of thought and hermeneutics employed among Seventh-day Adventists today when expounding upon the seven trumpets of Revelation. These two schools are not presented sarcastically, but in a straight-forward display so as to reinforce the reader the quality of the fruit that can be expected as a result from each:

1. One ideology is based upon the traditions of the fathers, claiming to be historicist in its methods of exposition, while at the same time using Jesuit futuristic hermeneutics, literal-local, for their identity and interpretation.

2. The other ideology is based upon the Scriptures and its motto is "the Bible is its own interpreter." It strictly follows the historicist method of interpretation and does not incorporate Jesuit hermeneutics into its exposition of the text.

"Hermeneutics" is an all-encompassing term used by theologians to mean a mode or method employed for interpreting prophetic scripture. It includes, in part, symbols, time and place, as we will illustrate. We must remember that the books of Daniel and Revelation contain an array of symbols that only the Bible can interpret, because the Bible is its own interpreter. Forgetting this principle causes many to stray into false interpretations. They incorporate private or human reasoning above the Biblical mandate that has been clearly set before us all. That Biblical hermeneutical principle is simply this:

> "The things of God before the cross are always taken in a literal and local sense; after the cross, in a symbolic or spiritual and worldwide sense. An example of this is in the last vision of Daniel, chapters 10-12. When we read in Daniel 10:14 and 11:14, we interpret 'thy people' as meaning the literal Jews, and rightly so. But then we come to Daniel 12:1, which is part of the vision of chapter 11, for there is no break in the original text and, in fact, the vision does not contextually conclude till verse 3 of chapter 12. In Daniel 12:1, we interpret 'thy people' as the saints of God, born-again Christians, spiritual Israel, the Christian Church at the very end of probationary time.
> "So the great question that naturally would be asked is this: How can we move in our interpretation from literal-local to spiritual-worldwide? Wouldn't such interpretations appear inconsistent or contrived? It is well-known that futurists like many evangelicals and others teach that 'thy people' in Daniel 12:1 refers to the

---

[221] Josiah Litch, *A Complete Harmony of Daniel and the Apocalypse* (Philadelphia: Claxton, Remsen & Haffelfinger, 1873), 161-172.

literal Jews. On the surface, this literal interpretation seems to be consistent and logical. So why do Seventh-day Adventists differ from that approach?

"We restate the hermeneutical principle: Before the cross, we interpret the prophetic symbols literally. After the cross and up to the time of the Second Coming, we interpret the prophetic symbols spiritually. In answer to the question above, we have the divine endorsement for doing so in the writings of Paul. In the book of Romans, written after the cross, Paul explains that a Jew is not someone who is such merely by birth, but a Jew is the person who is circumcised or renewed in heart. This is the born-again Christian. He or she has become a spiritual Jew. The term Jew under this dispensation now has a spiritual, worldwide application, as does the city Jerusalem, which is now interpreted and understood to be the Christian Church.

"Also, the prophetic principle is that after the Second Coming, we return to literal time. The thousand-year millennium is literally 1000 years. So it is with Babylon. After the cross, Babylon is no longer understood and confined in a literal, local, geographical location. No, Babylon, like the Jew and Jerusalem, is understood as spiritual, worldwide Babylon. And the same Biblical hermeneutical principle applies to the King of the South as well as to the King of the North. Before the cross: literal, local. After the cross: spiritual, worldwide. After the second coming: literal, local."[222]

In order to counter the Protestant Reformation in its identification of the papacy as the harlot of Revelation and the little horn in the book of Daniel, the Catholic Church had to come up with a way to shift the prophecies of Daniel and Revelation from herself and place them on something or someone else. One of the two Jesuit priests who were foremost in the counter-attack was Louis de Alcazar. In 1614, he introduced the preterist interpretation: all of the prophecies had their fulfillment by the end of the first century. In this way papal Rome could not be implicated, for it had not yet been established. (How convenient!) In 1590 the other Jesuit priest, Francisco Rivera, set in motion the futurist interpretation: all prophecies are to be fulfilled at the very end of time, conveniently after the so-called man-made rapture that the Bible knows nothing about. In this way Rome could not be seen to be the Antichrist. (Again, how convenient.) This Jesuit counter-attack interprets everything in Scripture in its "literal-local" context. In other words Babylon, of course, is no longer spiritual-worldwide Babylon, but is literal Babylon, all the way to the second coming. So it is with the Jew, the city of Jerusalem, the "great river Euphrates," and the list goes on and on. Futurism is the trap that ensnared William Miller, Josiah Litch, Uriah Smith in their day. All those who yet today expound on the trumpets of Revelation in the same train as Josiah Litch are guilty of incorporating these Jesuit futuristic hermeneutics, at least in part. "How?" you may rightly ask. Let us give you an example.

Many are deceived if they think they have a foundation for the trumpets in the *Daniel and the Revelation* by Uriah Smith. I have received numerous inquiries and much feedback in the last year or so from laypersons to academics because of the Islam-centered interpretation that is being promoted by some Seventh-day Adventists. But imagine, if you can, giving an exposition on the first six trumpets and never using the Bible for one text to sustain your interpretations of those trumpets. That is exactly what you have in the *Daniel and the Revelation*. Please show me just one text in that book that is used to identify any of the symbols in the first six trumpets…. That's right. There are no scriptures given at all to interpret any of the first six trumpets, yet it is called a commentary of the Bible on the book of Revelation. Have we missed something here? A perfect illustration of what this

---

[222] Heidi Heiks, *King of the North* (Brushton, New York: Teach Services, 2009), 4-5.

commentary does on the first six trumpets by Uriah Smith, and what those who follow in his method of hermeneutics do, is substitute human reasoning above divine revelation. For example, they claim the fire and smoke and brimstone of Rev. 9:18 represent the gunpowder used by Mohammedans in their cannon barrage against Constantinople. Not only is this intellectually offensive, but it also bears no Scripture support, because there is none. Since when has the Bible stopped being its own interpreter?

Seventh-day Adventists as a whole have been very good about *sola scriptura*:

> "But God will have a people upon the earth to maintain the Bible, and the <u>Bible only</u>, as the standard of <u>all doctrines</u> and the basis of <u>all reforms</u>."[223]

But I have found that when the majority come to a delineation of the trumpets of Revelation, there seems to be this bewitching spell cast upon the minds of the people, orbiting them to a land without reason. If we cannot prove what we believe from Scripture (and history, if and when appropriate), then how can we conscientiously stand before a multitude and pawn off our private interpretations as Biblical doctrine? Yet this is how many, even today (and perhaps unconsciously) employ Jesuit hermeneutics to identify the many symbols of the trumpets with "literal-local" human reasoning. More examples will be forthcoming in their appropriate time.

With this background established, we now want to focus on some of the fruits produced by this school of thought, so the reader can intelligently discern between these two schools when he or she reads, or studies to gain, an interpretation of the contents of chapter 6. Once again, truth can withstand investigation.

What is taking place is that some are unwittingly serving Satan's cause, running ahead, presenting a false, horizontal or earth-focused conflict (pagans fighting pagans, Matt. 24:6-8) before the final, genuine, vertical, Great Controversy conflict is to take place between Christ Jesus in the persons of His believers and Antichrist Satan in the persons of his followers (Matt. 24:9-14). In doing so, true Adventist understanding is preempted, which is Satan's objective. Then when the "so-called" SDA Islam prophecy has proven itself false (as it surely will), that interpretation and its interpreters will be ridiculed by the world, and true Adventist understanding will be discredited and rejected by association. How, then, will the masses receive the true message (the three angels' messages) when they perceive it coming from the same source? Let us seriously think on these things!

Thankfully, I am not the only one that understands the seriousness of this Islam fanaticism that is now also presenting new interpretations of the books of Daniel and Revelation, along with other newly-claimed supportive Scriptures that are wholly untenable. I have heard from about half a dozen of the best academic minds in Adventism, men who hold top theological positions in the church, and who have the responsibility to steer the theology of the church in the right direction. All of them speak with one voice in opposition to Islam fulfilling prophecy in Revelation. The following short evaluation was sent to me from just such an individual, whose name I choose not to disclose. It is not the man but the perspective he shares with other well-respected leaders in Adventism that is our focus.

---

[223] Ellen G. White, *The Great Controversy* (Nampa, ID: Pacific Press, 1911), 395.

"Evaluation of

"Tim Roosenberg's *Islam and Christianity in Prophecy*

"General Remarks:

"This book is the latest in a series of books and articles dealing with Daniel 11. It is published by Review and Herald; therefore, it merits closer inspection. It has fourteen chapters and four appendices, of which the first one is the most significant because it is a comparison of Daniel 11:2-12:4 with historical events. The main thrust of the book, as the title indicates, is to show that Daniel 11 is largely a history of the wars between Christianity and Islam. Putting aside the issue of Islam for the moment, the book contains some excellent material on the Sabbath, the state of the dead, and the Second Coming. It is basically an evangelistic book with appendix C 'A Gospel Appeal' as the altar call at the end of the evangelistic series. The author is to be commended for his adherence to the basic Adventist doctrines and for the evangelistic emphasis in the book.

"This may just be a typo – 'temple' for 'Jerusalem,' but on page 28 Roosenberg says, 'The book of Ezra announces the decree that authorizes the rebuilding of the Temple. Archaeology has pinned that date to 457 B.C.' The temple was finished in 515 BC. In 457 BC a decree was issued to restore Jerusalem (Dan 9:25), not the temple.

"Another mistake is the statement on page 100 that says, 'God sent in [to Israel] the descendants of Ishmael (Midianites, Ammonites, and Moabites –the children of the East) to punish Israel.' Neither the Midianites nor the Ammonites nor Moabites were descendants of Ishmael. The Midianites were descendants of Midian, the son of Abraham and Keturah (Gen 25:2) and the Ammonites and Moabites were the descendants of Lot's sons Ben-Ammi and Moab (Gen 19:37, 38).

"Islam and Daniel 11

"Roosenberg's basic outline of Daniel 11 is found on pages 203-212:

"Verses 2   Medo-Persia

"Verses 3-4   Greece

"Verses 5-19   Wars between the Seleucids and the Ptolemies

"Verses 20-22   Romans

"Verses 23-24   Rise of the papacy

"Verses 25-28   Second conflict between Christianity and Islam during the time of the Reformation

"Verses 40-45   Third and future conflict between Christianity and Islam

"This outline presents some problems:

1.   "On page 12, Roosenberg claims that Daniel 11 predicts three holy wars between Christianity and Islam: The first he sees in the Islamic conquest and the crusades. However, when he comes to the text in Dan 11:25-28 (p. 207) he finds no room for the Islamic conquest and begins with the crusades. Therefore, on page 91 he calls the crusades the 'first conflict between the papacy and Islam.' This is historically problematic! If Daniel 11 describes the wars between Christianity and Islam it does not mention the most important war in the past – the Islamic conquest in the 7th and 8th century AD which wiped out Christianity in the Middle East. If Daniel 11 deals with the conflict between Christianity and Islam, why is the greatest conflict ignored?

2.   "Much of the interpretation of Daniel 11 is based on subjective conjectures rather than on exegesis. For example, within the Seventh-day Adventist Church this chapter has received a variety of interpretations. The differences between the various authors concern primarily the question, 'At what points in the story do the Romans and the papacy enter the picture?' F. D. Nichol and M. Maxwell see the Roman entry in verse 14; R. A. Anderson, G. M. Price and W. H. Shea believe the Romans come on the scene in verse 16. J. B. Doukhan believes that the Romans appear briefly only in verse 4, from verse 5 he has the papacy as the King of the North until the end of the chapter. Maxwell applies verses 21-45 to the papacy; Shea has the papacy enter the story in verse 23; Price in verse 30; and Nichol and Anderson believe that not until verse 31 can we discern the activities of the papacy. Roosenberg differs from all of them. He has Rome appearing in verse 20, the papacy in verse 23, and Islam in verse 25. This variety indicates the subjectivity of the various interpretations. Hence we need to be careful and not be dogmatic when it comes to the interpretation of this chapter.
    "Exegetically we can say that in Daniel 11 five points provide the basic outline for Daniel 11. These points in the chapter are fairly clear and straightforward and they can be supported by using the principle 'scripture interprets scripture, one passage being the key to other passages' (Ev 581).

a.   "At the beginning of Daniel 11 the angel refers to Persian and Greek kings.
b.   "The next clearly identifiable event is the death of the Messiah in AD 31 (v. 22)
c.   "The third event which can be interpreted by comparing Scripture with Scripture is the taking away of the daily and the setting up of the abomination of desolation in verse 31. The 'taking away of the daily' is exactly the same expression that is used in 8:11, where it refers to the taking away of the intercessory ministration of Christ in the heavenly sanctuary through the papal priesthood. And the 'abomination of desolation' refers to the vast system of beliefs and practices of the papacy and it's joining forces with the power of the state in 508 (the beginning of the 1290 years of

Dan 12:11).

d. "The fourth expression which provides a chronological marker in the story is the expression 'time of the end' in 11:40, which began in 1798.

e. "The fifth point that is easily understood is the resurrection in connection with the Second Coming (12:2).
"All the other historical events mentioned in the chapter must fit into this chronological framework.

"Roosenberg claims that the prophecies in Daniel are historically sequential, i.e., nations or events follow each other chronologically. He says, for example, that Daniel 11:2-12:3 'starts in the time of Daniel (seventh century B.C.), moves in a straightforward way through human history, and concludes with the end of the world....' (p. 13). However, his explanations do not move chronologically through history. He has the crusades (1095-1291) in verses 25-28 (pp. 12, 207), and he agrees that verse 31 refers to the same event as 8:11-13 (p. 208). But the events in 11:31 ('taking away of the daily' and 'abomination of desolation') took place 500 years before the crusades in 11:25-28 (see under point c above). His interpretation destroys the chronological sequence of the prophecy at this point.

3. "The difficulty of correctly interpreting Daniel 11:23-30 is shown by the fact that Bible-believing historicists have come to completely different interpretations. Among Adventists we find the following interpretations for 11:23-30:

a. "The Roman history from the 'league of friendship' between the Romans and Jews in 161 BC to Emperor Constantine in the 4th century AD (Smith, McCready Price, Swearingen[224]).

b. "The history of Antiochus Epiphanes (171-165 BC) (D. Ford, F. Laiu[225]).

c. "The Roman History following the crucifixion in AD 31 until Emperor Constantine (Haskell).

d. "The wars of the crusades (Shea, Roosenberg).

e. "The spread of Christianity after the crucifixion (Nelson[226]).

"It is not the exegesis of the text that provides these different interpretations; rather the interpreters try to fit the text into certain historical events. And the fact that the text can somehow be made to fit these different interpretations must caution us against being dogmatic, claiming that a particular interpretation is the only valid one. This does not mean that the text can have a double application, it only has one correct interpretation, but the question is which one is the correct one?

4. "For Roosenberg the 'time of the end' begins in 1844 (p. 209). This phrase is found

---

[224] Marc Alden Swearingen, *Tidings out of the Northeast* (Coldwater MI: Remnant Publications, 2006).

[225] F. Laiu, "Sanctuary Doctrine: a critical-apologetic approach," unpublished paper, 18.

[226] Edward Nelson, "Daniel 11:23-39 – The Connection Between Ancient and Modern Israel: A Hermeneutical Key," unpublished paper.

only in the book of Daniel, once in the vision of Daniel 8 (v. 17) and four times in connection with Daniel's last vision (11:35, 40; 12:4, 9). The visions of Daniel 8 and 11 both reach to 'the time of the end,' at which, according to Daniel 12:2, a resurrection takes place. Daniel 12:4 indicates that just prior to the end of history people will study and search out the Danielic visions just as Daniel himself searched out the 70 year prophecy (9:2). And in the epilogue to the book of Daniel (12:5-13) Daniel is told that 'the words are shut up and sealed until the time of the end.' At that time knowledge of these visions will increase and their meaning will be understood (vs. 4, 10).

"From history we know that in the 19th century, after the end of the 1260 years of Daniel 7:25, knowledge of the Danielic prophecies increased dramatically. 'The prophetic days of Daniel had been understood as calendar years by only seven writers in the 16th century, and by only twelve in the 17th, but they were correctly understood by twenty-one of the twenty-two who wrote in the 18th, and by over one hundred of the one hundred and nine who wrote on Daniel between 1800 and 1850.'[227] It is reasonable, therefore, to conclude that the time of the end began with the fall of the papacy in 1798. This means, the events from Daniel 11:40 onwards must be sought in the time between the deadly wound of the papacy in 1798 and the resurrection at the end of time.

5. "Roosenberg insists that Daniel is literal/geopolitical from beginning to the end (p. 213). But this ignores the fact that with the death of Jesus prophetic elements change. For example, in the New Testament the land of Canaan becomes the heavenly Canaan; Jerusalem becomes the heavenly Jerusalem; the temple becomes a spiritual temple, the church; Israel becomes spiritual Israel, the church. Hence, in Daniel 11 after the death of Jesus in verse 22 the literal/geopolitical elements also change: the king of the North becomes a spiritual power, the papacy; the king of the South also becomes a spiritual or ideological entity; the beautiful land in verse 41 is no longer Israel but the church.

Interesting parallels

6. "Roosenberg considers Daniel 11:40-45 as the third war between Christianity and Islam in the future. Time will tell if his prophecy will come true. Exegetically, this passage reflects the Exodus story. A. Rodriguez has put together an interesting list of parallels:

a. "Daniel refers to Egypt as the 'land of Egypt.' This phrase is used frequently in Exodus to designate Egypt (Exod 6:13, 26, 28; 7:3, 4, 19; 8:5, etc.).

b. "In Exodus the hand of the Lord is against Egypt; in Daniel the king of the North is against Egypt.

c. "Water is an important element in both narratives. In Exodus the Red Sea became an army of the Lord fighting against the Egyptians. In Daniel the army of the king of the North is described as a flood overflowing the lands (Dan 11:40 NIV).

---

[227] Le Roy Edwin Froom, *The Prophetic Faith of Our Fathers*, 4 vols. (Washington, D.C.: Review and Herald, 1950-1954), 2:528, 784; 3:270. *Charts - must study later*

125

d. "The reference to chariots and horsemen (Dan 11:40) recalls the Egyptian army during the Exodus that also consisted of chariots and horsemen (Exod 14:9, 17, 18, 23, etc.).

e. "Edom, Moab, and Ammon (Dan 11:41) are mentioned in the narrative of the wilderness wandering of the Israelites (Num 20:14; 22:3; Deut 2:37). The Israelites did not conquer them and neither did the king of the North.

f. "The Israelites took silver and gold from the Egyptians (Exod 12:35, 36). In Daniel the king of the North takes silver and gold from them (Dan 11:43)

g. "The Israelites left Egypt to meet the Lord at the holy mountain - Mt Sinai (Exod 3:12; 19:20-23). In Daniel the king of the North leaves Egypt to go to the holy mountain (Dan 11:45).

h. "The Israelites were commanded to exterminate (*charam*) the Canaanites (Deut 7:2). The king of the North leaves Egypt to exterminate (*charam*) God's people (Dan 11:44). In both cases reference is to the law of extermination (*cherem*).[228]

"In the Exodus story Egypt stands for human hubris and independence. 'Pharaoh said, "Who *is* the LORD, that I should obey His voice to let Israel go? I do not know the LORD, nor will I let Israel go." (Exod 5:2).' While the king of the North wants to usurp God's place, the king of the South does not care. He 'represents the nations of the earth that do not take into consideration the Lord and live by their own rules. Today we will probably refer to them as non-Christian societies and nations where secularism or atheism prevails. In the final conflict these nations will join the king of the north in his opposition against the Lord.'[229] If this conclusions is correct, some of the elements of Daniel 11:40-45 may already have found a fulfillment (see Swearingen, 254).

"Conclusion

"Roosenberg's book on Daniel 11 is an interesting interpretation of one of the most difficult chapters in the Bible, but it is by no means exegetically as solid as he believes. It seems to be another attempt to interpret Scripture with the newspaper. As indicated in point 2, we can be certain of five points which we can establish exegetically. Beyond these five points we have to tread lightly."

That evaluation was very well-said. If the reader has Tim Roosenberg's book, he will find the above analysis it to be an honest assessment. Our sole objective is the proclamation of the truth, and a bold and public declaration of anything that is not.

There is so much more that could be said here, but that would require another book. To bring some resolution to this topic under discussion, I direct the reader to my book *King of the North*.[230] It will address all the other issues in the book of Daniel. Essentially, though, Roosenberg follows the same path as Amadon that we witnessed in chapter 3. Like her example before him, he likewise

---

[228] A. Rodriguez, "Daniel 11:40-45: A Personal View," unpublished paper, 6.
[229] Ibid., 11.
[230] Heidi Heiks, *King of the North* (Brushton, New York: Teach Services, 2009).

never gives any proof for the existence of Islam from the Scriptures. However, in his book on pages 220-221 he gives the same list as Amadon did of 124 theologians throughout the centuries that supported the identification of Islam as the fulfillment of the fifth and sixth trumpets of Revelation. All through his videos and book, his proof for Islam is that he says so—never Scripture! If I would submit a list of 777 pastors or theologians that say the Sabbath is now Sunday, would that prove or strengthen my case? Of course not. In addition to this, Tim Roosenberg openly admits in his first video of three that were posted on the internet in 2012 that he uses the hermeneutics of Professor George E. Ladd from his book *The Blessed Hope*. Now I understand why Roosenberg is all over the map and anchored nowhere. After watching all three videos, I went online to AbeBooks and purchased a used hardback copy of that book with the dust cover still on it. On the author's dustcover the title of the book reads:

"The Blessed Hope: A Biblical Study of the Second Advent and the Rapture"[231]

George E. Ladd, Ph.D., was associate professor of New Testament at the Fuller [Evangelical] Theological Seminary. That book was reviewed by John F. Walvoord with the following extracted comment:

> "The appearance of this important volume on the return of the Lord just at the time of the completion of the study of 'Premillennialism and the Tribulation' will be of such special interest to readers of *Bibliotheca Sacra* that it justifies an interruption of the series for this review. Dr. George E. Ladd, Professor of New Testament History and Biblical Theology at Fuller Theological Seminary, in this his second book in the field of eschatology, ably presents a spirited defense of post-tribulationism. According to Dr. Ladd himself, 'The central thesis of this book is that *the Blessed Hope is the second coming of Jesus Christ and not a pre-tribulation rapture* (p. 11, italics his).' Dr. Ladd is recognized as a New Testament scholar and on occasion he has contributed articles to *Bibliotheca Sacra*. In offering this review, no personal criticism or discourtesy to the author is intended. The reviewer is convinced that the arguments of the book do not sustain adequately the post-tribulational position, but Dr. Ladd is entitled to be heard. He has marshaled with unusual force the traditional arguments for the post-tribulational theory. It is not too much to say that this is one of the best studies in support of post-tribulationism which has appeared in book form for some time and will probably strengthen the cause of post-tribulationism in contemporary conservative theology."[232]

Jesuit hermeneutics! Need we say more?

Next we need to address a few erroneous suppositions by Dr. Alberto Treiyer. We want the reader to know that Alberto Treiyer is not in the same theological camp with Tim Roosenberg. In fact, Brother Treiyer does inform us that there is no future prophecy that singles out the Muslims in the

---

[231] George E. Ladd, *The Blessed Hope: A Biblical Study of the Second Advent and the Rapture* (Grand Rapids, MI: Wm. B. Eerdmans, 1956).
[232] John F. Walvoord, *A Review of 'The Blessed Hope' by George E. Ladd*, http://bible.org/article/review-blessed-hope-george-e-ladd. Created 2008.

final events, to which we whole-heartedly agree. However, he goes where we cannot when he declares that in the past, Islam had a specified prophetic role to play in the book of Revelation:[233]

> "The only prophecies in the New Testament where the Arabs are intended to have an important role to accomplish are found in Revelation 9. The fifth and sixth trumpets are focused on them"[234]

Dr. Treiyer relates a story in his book *The Seals and the Trumpets*[235] about a scholar that was going to publish his views on the trumpets—views against which Treiyer took issue. But when the brother decided not to publish them, Alberto Treiyer decided not to publish his rebuttal, either. Only if published would the errors need public repudiation. In a Christian rebuttal, one is able to perceive the strengths and weaknesses of reasoning on both sides of an issue, and thereby make intelligent decisions for the truth. A sure foundation of truth will strengthen us if and when we may have to stand alone in the world court. Much could be said here, but the following analysis of Treiyer's book will be confined to certain specifics needful for the reader with regard to standards or principles of interpretation, and with the hope that the author will in due time acknowledge and abide by them.

1. To this very day no one has supplied any Scriptural proof for Islam as the entity of the fifth and sixth trumpets of Revelation chapter 9. However, Brother Treiyer does make an attempt to do so with the following Scripture:

> Isa. 33:4 "And your spoil shall be gathered *like* the gathering of the caterpiller: as the running to and fro of locusts shall he run upon them."[236]

The text itself does not support that application, though, and neither does the *Seventh-day Adventist Bible Commentary*, volume 4, page 227:

> "**4. Your spoil.** This refers to the plundering of the Assyrian camp after the annihilation of the invaders and the precipitate flight of the few survivors. As caterpillars and locusts devour everything green, so the Hebrews would, in due time, strip the haughty Assyrians bare."[237]

2. How does brother Treiyer generally identify the symbols?

> "…The Muslims, who come from the East, appeared from the 'abyss'…. Who could avoid evoking in this context, the symbols of the fifth and sixth trumpets which depict them so well?"[238]

Reference? G. Oncken, *Historia Universal*. Scripture? None. Hermeneutics? Literal, local. Treiyer again:

---

[233] Alberto Treiyer, *The Seals and the Trumpets* (Distinctive Messages, 2005), 324.
[234] Ibid., 286.
[235] Ibid., 291.
[236] Ibid., 295.
[237] F. D. Nichol, *The Seventh-day Adventist Bible Commentary* (Review and Herald, 1978, 2002), 4: 227.
[238] Alberto Treiyer, *The Seals and the Trumpets* (Distinctive Messages, 2005), 290.

"The description of the locust which come out from the smoke, paints a vivid picture of the Muslim hordes which spread out over the earth (Rev 9:3, 7-9)."[239]

3. The hermeneutics of brother Treiyer vary, but the following is rather consistent throughout his book:

"The era of the cannons was beginning, announced by Rev. 9:17."[240]

4. Alberto Treiyer (A. T.) states: "In fact, the beginning of Turkish authority over the Christian and European world began in 1449; the beginning of Christian and European authority over the Turkish Empire began in 1840, putting an end to the Turkish domination in the Mediterranean world."[241]

Heidi Heiks (H. H.) states: "In fact, the beginning of Turkish authority over the Christian or Eastern European world began in 1370. In chapter 4 of this book, we read for ourselves from the primary sources that John V became a vassal to the Ottoman Empire in AD 1370. That act would involve in submission every successive emperor until the overthrow of Constantinople on May 29, 1453. The beginning of Christian and European authority over the Turkish Empire began in 1827, not 1840, thus putting an end to the Turkish domination in the Mediterranean world that we witnessed from the primary sources in chapter 2."

5. A. T. states: "If we carefully read the description of the fifth trumpet, we will see that it predicts two invasions encompassing the same period of time.[242] Whereas the first invasion reflects a paradox of combined mercy and torment, the second places more emphasis on its destructive character (Rev 9:4-5, I0-11). This was what precisely took place with the two Muslim invasions of the Roman Empire, namely, that of the Arabian Saracens during the 7th and 8th centuries, and that of the Ottoman Turks during the 14th and 15th centuries."[243]

H. H. states: "As we have already witnessed in chapter 4, this breaks the prophetic chain of Revelation 9. The Ottoman Empire or Turkey was the sole entity of the fifth and sixth trumpets, according to Josiah Litch. The two were added together and made 541 years and 15 days, and reckoned from July 27, 1299, straight on to August 11, 1840. The Saracens, we noted, had ceased to be an aggressive power nearly five centuries earlier, making this application untenable, along with the fact that this was never part of Josiah Litch's exposition, but is most certainly being pawned off as such today. This fact was well-known then and today, but nevertheless is still being presented by some as legitimate history.

---

[239] Ibid., 293.
[240] Ibid., 325.
[241] Ibid., 336.
[242] [Treiyer's footnote:] "Let us emphasize here that the apocalyptic prophecies do not have a dual fulfillment. Sometimes when we go to the historical fulfillment, we find more than one event related to the same authority under consideration. Those events and their dates can be related under the principle of a 'sliding scale,' which offers a wider scope on the nature and importance of the portrayed historical facts. For more examples, see A. Treiyer, *The Seals and the Trumpets*, Excursus I, 89-118."
[243] Alberto R. Treiyer, *The Mystery of the Apocalyptic Trumpets Unraveled* (Distinctive Messages, 2012), 50.

6. A. T. states: "The hour of judgment for the sixth trumpet expired on August 11, 1840, or, according to the sliding scale principal applied to practically all prophetic dates, March 21, 1844. It is then that we find a parenthesis between the sixth and seventh trumpets. This parenthesis shows an angel with a little scroll who swears by the Creator that 'there should be [prophetic] time no longer!' (Rev 10:1-2, 5-6, KJV). The time had come to open the prophetic scroll that Daniel was told to seal up. Everything pertaining to the 'time of the end' that Daniel could not understand (Dan 8:17, 19, 26; 12:4-9), must now be made clear. From that point on, there were to be no more prophetic dates, and what Daniel esteemed to be an incomprehensible mystery could now be understood."[244]

H. H. states: " 'According to the sliding scale principal applied to practically all prophetic dates.'
I had never heard of such a thing (and neither has the Bible). I therefore emailed Brother Treiyer and asked him what the 'sliding scale principle' is. I received a reference, but no explanation. From the reference I was directed to this footnote:

> "Let us emphasize here that the apocalyptic prophecies do not have a dual fulfillment. Sometimes, when we go to the historical fulfillment, we find more than one event related to the same authority under consideration. Those events and their dates can be related under the principle of a 'sliding scale,' which offers a wider scope on the nature and importance of the portrayed historical facts. For more examples, see A. Treiyer, *The Seals and the Trumpets,* Excursus I, 89-118."[245]

H. H. states: "With Treiyer's 'sliding [shifting] scale principal applied to practically all prophetic dates,' we end up with new dates and events for the fifth and sixth trumpets, with 1453 and 1844, respectively, yet at the same time we are told August 11, 1840, was 'amazingly fulfilled.' Where does one find those Biblical hermeneutics?"

A. T. states: "The date anticipated by Josiah Litch for the conclusion of the sixth trumpet's hour of judgment was amazingly fulfilled, as we have already seen, on August 11, 1840....
"What's interesting is that on that same day, March 21, 1844, the Turkish sultan was signing the 'law of apostasy.' That law essentially ended the policy of killing every convert that apostatized from the Muslim faith (see Rev 9: 15). Consequently, it also ended the sixth trumpet's hour of judgment. However, the Millerites discovered that the correct date should be October 22, 1844, and not March 21."[246]

A. T. states: "All the American and European historicists between the end of the eighteenth century and the first half of the nineteenth century placed the beginning of the sixth trumpet at the fall of Constantinople in 1453, and announced a change of trend in the typical Muslim harassment until 1844."[247]

---

[244] Ibid., 63. Emphasis in the original.
[245] Ibid., 50, footnote 7.
[246] Ibid., 64.
[247] All of them understood that the Muslims had been refrained for centuries by Constantinople, and rightly concluded that they were not "released" until 1453, with the fall of Constantinople. Consequently, they predicted the time of judgment represented by the sixth trumpet as being concluded in 1844. Among the numerous examples we may mention E. W. Whitaker (British: 1795); Ch. Buck (British: 1811); W, C. Davis (American: 1811); E. Smith (American: 1811); J.

A. T. states: "As a summary we may recall the dates of 1453 (fall of Constantinople and of the Eastern Roman Empire) + 391 = 1844 (law forbidding to kill the Muslim apostates)."[248]

H. H. states: "Before going any further, a summary is indeed in order here, as we have just witnessed a resurrection from the dead. When the brethren came together for the 1919 Bible conference, we all witnessed the innumerable errors about the fifth and sixth trumpets placed in bold display. However, there was no resolution submitted because, like some still today, they could not bring themselves to entirely relinquish the predominant view of Islam being the main entity in the fifth and sixth trumpets. Also, they did not properly understand Mrs. White's statement in *The Great Controversy*, page 334-5, that was addressed and interpreted in our introduction—a statement that has now been clarified before all. When the proponents of Islam are pushed, they always run to extremes, as we have seen in their prophetic proclamations. Such was the case with the brethren of the 1919 Bible Conferences in their quest for answers, as history proves they had previously considered the law forbidding to kill Muslim apostates as a possible fulfillment for the prophecy, and even recalculated the date several times till it reached to 1844.

1919 Bible Conference Minutes

[62] John 4:21, 23; 5:25, 28; 5:35; 7:30; 8:20; 12:23; 13:1; 16:2, 4; 17:1; Romans 13:11; 2 Cor. 7:8; Philemon 15; Revelation 3:10; 14:7.

"Now in these texts this same word is translated by these different words, 'time', 'day', 'hour', 'season.' But in all these cases it cannot refer to, and does not refer to, a 1/24 part of a day. It is an <u>indefinite</u> period.

"Now I wish to call attention to two special passages. John 5:35. Christ speaking of John the Baptist says, 'He was a burning and a shining light: and ye were willing for a <u>season</u> to rejoice in his light.' For a <u>season</u>. It is not definite as to the time. That is the same word and the same construction.

"In Second Corinthians 7:8 you have the same thing. 'For though I made you sorry with a letter, I do not repent, though I did repent: for I perceive that the same epistle hath made you sorry, though it were but for a <u>season</u>.' – Referring to a <u>duration</u> of time, an indefinite time and not a fixed period.

"F. W. WILCOX: Then 'a day, a year an hour' would be in apposition with or explanatory to 'season.'

"PRESCOTT: Yes.

"And those who read the Greek text will note that the <u>article</u> used is used with the word denoting 'hour' or 'season' while omitted with the word for day, month, year. That is, 'prepared for the season, namely, a day, a month and a year.' The <u>season</u> is

---

Fry (British: 1822); J. A. Brown (British: 1823); J. R. Park (British: 1825); Th. R. Robertson (American, 1826); "c. E. S." [Chr. Obser.] (British: 1826); Th. White (British, 1828); Ph. Homan (British: 1829); "J. G. 0." [Jew. Exp.] (British: 1832); M. Habershon (British, 1834); Prot. Vindicator (American, 1836); J. Cox (British, ?); J. Scott (British, ?); R. C. Shimeal (American, ?). Cf. L. E. Froom, *The Prophetic Faith of Our Fathers* (RH Publishing Association, Washington, 1946-54), IV, 1124-25.
Dr. Alberto Treiyer, *The Seals and the Trumpets* (Distinctive Messages, 2005), 333.
[248] Ibid., 343.

here limited to a definite time, and the <u>definite article</u> is used. In the other cases, the definite article is not used.

[63] "VOICE: The month and year would be translated the same way as 'hour and day and month'?

"PRESCOTT: No. I would translate, 'They were prepared for the season.' Then define it: 'even a day, a month, and a year.' The indefinite season now becomes definite in these words, a day a month and a year, -- which gives us 391 years.

[64] "PRESCOTT: I would translate it, 'They were prepared for the season' – Then defined – namely, 'The hour, even a month, a day, a year.' The indefinite season now becomes definite in those terms day, month, year. It would be interpreted and give us the 391 years.

"LACEY: A very interesting incident occurred in the University of Nebraska right on this point. We were reading Demosthenes and the head of the Department of Greek pointed out a similar instance exactly in one of the orations of Demosthenes. In that case it is a series of three nouns, and the first noun has the article, then came the other two nouns introduced by the conjunction *kai*, and these latter two were to be considered as explaining the first. When you have the group, and the first articled, that comprises all that follows. We predicate those, put them under it, and they explain it. There is an exactly analogous case with Revelation 9.

"PRESCOTT: Now, then, taking it that way, we have no further necessity of establishing a day for the beginning or a day for the close. <u>Beginning with 1453, the siege of Constantinople, 391 years brings us to 1844, of course a notable date with us in our expositions. That is to say, this killing power is limited to that time when this message rises. Just exactly as this message arose, at the close of those periods assigned in Daniel, 1260 days, 1290 days, 2300 days. At the end of those periods this message arose. At the end of this period, no, this message would rise in the same way and these powers that were to hinder, to stand in the way of the gospel till 1844, would mark the end of that limitation. Then you ask me, what happened in 1844 that would in any way fulfill this [65] prophecy? That remarkable edict of toleration issued by the Mohammedan power under the pressure of the Christian powers. These facts were printed in the *Review* of February, 1918.</u> Don't you remember Brother Spicer had an article 'A wonderful Providence' in which he gives the extracts relating to this matter, that this decree of toleration was demanded under the leadership of the English representative at Constantinople. It was flatly refused. It was said that to grant that would be to destroy Islam. It is contrary to the absolute principle of the Koran. We can't possibly do it. But the ambassador would not be denied. He held to it unto he obtained it, and one extract is from Doctor Barton's work 'Daybreak in Turkey.' He dwells upon it. One extract I have in my file says that this event was greater than any political event of the period, because it marked a concession which struck at the very foundation principles of Islam. Now that, Brother Chairman, is just that bare outline of the statement.

"F M WILCOX: Have we any time prophecy in the Bible in which the day of beginning or ending is indicated? This would be an exception, would it not…?[249]

---

[249] Transcript of the 1919 Bible Conference of the General Conference of Seventh-day Adventists, July 17, 1919 (Silver Spring, MD), 62-65. [Emphasis mine]

H. H. states: "Emphasis mine. After the 1919 Review and Herald board's appointed committee admitted they could go no further, [250] in the GC archives I found this same line of reasoning in the works of Prescott, Benson and Spicer that they had, in all probability, submitted to the General Conference Committee in Council. This is just one example of an old controversy being resurrected. I think Inspiration addresses this issue very well:

> "In history and prophecy the Word of God portrays the long-continued conflict between <u>truth</u> and <u>error</u>. That conflict is yet in progress. Those things which <u>have been</u> will be <u>repeated</u>. <u>Old controversies</u> will be <u>revived</u>, and <u>new theories will be continually arising</u>. But God's people, who in their belief and fulfillment of prophecy have acted a part in the proclamation of the first, second, and third angels' messages, <u>know where they stand</u>."[251]

H. H. states: "Let's get straight to the point; this is confusion compounded and nothing more than private interpretation. And for another, the text can only have one correct interpretation. However, sometimes there will be seen certain texts having a double application or even multiple future applications, as given by Ellen White, but the contexts of the given specifications will determine time and place of fulfillment. This Biblical premise I will show, illustrate and expand in chapter 6.

7. A. T. states: "The sixth trumpet starts with a voice coming from the altar of the Holy Place (Rev 9: 13). The seventh trumpet starts with the heavenly judgment in the Most Holy Place, which, according to the prophecy of Dan 8:14, should also begin in 1844 (Rev 11:15, 18-19)."[252]

H. H. states: "Does the sixth trumpet start with a voice coming from the altar of the Holy Place, Rev 9: 13? No! Does the seventh trumpet start with the heavenly judgment in the Most Holy place? No, absolutely not!"

A. T. states: "The last trumpet has to do with the period corresponding to the time of the end. It is the time when the 'mystery of God' is 'accomplished' (Rev 10:7). It is the time when the nations concentrate their final effort to reunite themselves into a world empire (Rev 16: 13-14). The purpose of the nations in attaining such union is the re-establishment of the 'image of the beast,' that is to say, the recovering of the intolerant united political and clerical system of the Middle Ages (Rev 13: 12-17; 17: 12-14). It is under this renewed, characteristic system of government of the Middle Ages that the nations intend to unite themselves to restore the old and universal Roman Empire, in agreement with the decrees of Rome over the earth (Rev 17:5-18; 18:24).

"That time coincides with the appearance of the Son of Man before His Father in the Most Holy Place of the heavenly sanctuary, to receive the kingdoms of this world and to vindicate the saints (Rev 11: 15-19; cf. 4-5; Dan 7:9-10,13-14). In addition, the death wound of the *beast* caused by the secular powers of the world and its healing takes place during that time (Rev 13:3-10, 12, 14). It is just at the time of the political healing of the papacy when the final confrontation of the wrath of

---

[250] Ibid., 50-1.
[251] Ellen White, *Manuscript Releases* (Washington, DC: Review and Herald, 1981), 1:47.
[252] Ibid., 343.

God with the wrath of the nations is consummated (Rev 11: 18; cf. Dan 11:44-45; Rev 17: 14; 19:11-21)."[253]

H. H. states: "Although this very issue is covered in chapter 6, the above is so grossly misapplied, I must address it here as well:

"We observe that the gospel or salvation is still obtainable under the sixth trumpet:

"Neither **repented** they of their murders, nor of their sorceries, nor of their fornication, nor of their thefts." Rev. 9:21.

"We also take notice that the sixth trumpet extends to the closing of the gospel invitation, when the mystery of God should be finished (Eph. 6:19, Col. 4:3, Eph. 3:3,6), the close of probation:

"But in the days of the voice of the seventh angel, when he shall begin to sound, the mystery of God should be finished, as he hath declared to his servants the prophets." Rev. 10:7.

"This is also confirmed when the seventh trumpet begins to sound:

"And the seventh angel sounded; and there were great voices in heaven, saying, The kingdoms of this world are become [the kingdoms] of our Lord, and of his Christ; and he shall reign for ever and ever." Rev. 11:15

"When do the kingdoms of this world become the kingdoms of our Lord, and of his Christ? It is not until the solemn declaration has gone forth and every case has been forever fixed for eternal life or eternal death. *Then* Jesus receives his kingdom; hence, the close of human probation:"

"I saw Jesus, who had been ministering before the ark containing the ten commandments, throw down the censer. He raised His hands, and with a loud voice said, 'It is done.' And all the angelic host laid off their crowns as Jesus made the solemn declaration, 'He that is unjust, let him be unjust still: and he which is filthy, let him be filthy still: and he that is righteous, let him be righteous still: and he that is holy, let him be holy still.'
"Every case had been decided for life or death. While Jesus had been ministering in the sanctuary, the judgment had been going on for the righteous dead, and then for the righteous living. Christ had received His kingdom, having made the atonement for His people and blotted out their sins. The subjects of the kingdom were made up. The marriage of the Lamb was consummated. And the kingdom, and the greatness of the kingdom under the whole heaven, was given to Jesus and the heirs of salvation, and Jesus was to reign as King of kings and Lord of lords."[254]

"The close of the sixth trumpet brings in the close of human probation. At the commencement of the seventh trumpet, Christ receives His kingdom; that event is followed by the seven last plagues."

---

[253] Ibid., 361.
[254] Ellen White, *Early Writings* (Washington, D.C: Review and Herald, 1945), 279-280.

8. A. T. states: "For some, her statement of the 'prediction' as having been fulfilled 'exactly," has to do with the prediction of Litch, not necessarily with the prediction of the sixth trumpet. Either way, we cannot ignore her former statement at the beginning of the previous paragraph: '*another remarkable fulfillment of prophecy.*' This cannot be confined to the prediction of Litch."[255]

H. H. states: "Let us read the *Great Controversy* statement in its context:"

> "In the year 1840 another remarkable fulfillment of prophecy excited widespread interest. Two years before, Josiah Litch, one of the leading ministers preaching the second advent, published an exposition of Revelation 9, predicting the fall of the Ottoman Empire. According to his calculations, this power was to be overthrown 'in A.D. 1840, sometime in the month of August;' and only a few days previous to its accomplishment he wrote: 'Allowing the first period, 150 years, to have been exactly fulfilled before Deacozes ascended the throne by permission of the Turks, and that the 391 years, fifteen days, commenced at the close of the first period, it will end on the 11th of August, 1840, when the Ottoman power in Constantinople may be expected to be broken. And this, I believe, will be found to be the case.'--Josiah Litch, in *Signs of the Times*, and *Expositor of Prophecy*, Aug. 1, 1840."[256]

H. H. states: "This prediction cannot be credited to anyone else but William Miller and Josiah Litch, for they spoke one and the same. The problem comes because Alberto Treiyer has moved the prophetic dates for the fulfillment of the fifth and sixth trumpets from July 27, 1449, to May 29, 1453, and from August 11, 1840, to March 21, 1844, then to Oct. 22, 1844,[257] thanks to Treiyer's sliding or shifting scale principal 'applied to practically all prophetic dates.' We therefore come to a poignant conclusion!

9. A. T. states: "The prophecy is still under the ministry of the Lord before the altar of incense in the Holy Place of the heavenly sanctuary (Rev 9:13: 'a voice coming from the horns of the golden altar….')."[258]

H.H. states: "No! The prophecy is under the ministry of the Lord in the Most Holy Place of the heavenly sanctuary. This we will show to be conclusive in chapter 6."

10. A. T. states: "…The final preaching of the gospel during *a time without computation* (Rev 10:6: 'there shall be [prophetic] time no longer')…."[259]

H. H. states: "Let's clarify here. Josiah Litch, remember, used the term, 'No more season of mercy.' We must also remember that the 1844 movement believed that the sanctuary was the earth and it was to be cleansed by fire at the Lord's second coming. Therefore the 'daily' had to be something earthly as well. All prophecies had to be fulfilled before that time and this is why the 6th trumpet had to

---

[255] Dr. Alberto Treiyer, *The Seals and the Trumpets* (Distinctive Messages, 2005), 335.
[256] Ellen White, *The Great Controversy* (Nampa, ID: Pacific Press, 1911), 334-5.
[257] Dr. Alberto Treiyer, *The Seals and the Trumpets* (Distinctive Messages, 2005), 340.
[258] Ibid., 340.
[259] Ibid., 329.

have a forced fulfillment before that time as well. Josiah Litch did come out here relatively on the right side of the issue, in that the close of probation does extend all the way to the close of the sixth trumpet of Revelation:"

> "It would appear from this, that upon the fall of the Turkish empire which will take place on the closing up of the 'sixth vial' and 'trumpet,' that the day of probation will close." [260]

"However, as we likewise just witnessed from point 7 of this chapter and from the last 4 chapters of this book, this is the only sentiment of truth that could withstand investigation in Josiah Litch's exposition of the fifth and sixth trumpets of Revelation, except his application was premature. Nevertheless, Josiah Litch confuses the issue with an unwarranted interpretation of another clause of Scripture, 'There shall be time no longer.'[261] (Rev. 10:6) Seeing the need for clarity on a much-misunderstood section of Scripture even to this very day with its far-reaching ramifications, we have decided to briefly mention a few important points:"

> "This message announces the end of the prophetic periods."[262]

> "This time, which the angel declares with the solemn oath, is not the end of this world's history, neither of probationary time, but of prophetic time, which would precede the advent of our Lord, i.e., the people would not have another message upon definite time. After this period of time, reaching ... to 1844, there can be no definite tracing of the prophetic time. The longest reckoning reaches to the autumn of 1844." [263]

"The context is Rev. 10 and the little book open is the book of Daniel. The prophetic periods spoken of by Ellen White are the four prophetic periods found in the book of Daniel. They are called prophetic periods because prophetic periods have specified, calculated beginning and ending dates. They consist of the 1260, 1290, 1335, and 2300 day/year time prophecies. This does not mean that the day/year principle in Bible prophecy ceased in 1844. It means any time periods remaining, such as the 'half-hour' silence in heaven (Rev. 8:1.), the 'one hour' for Rev. 17:12, and the 'one day' for the seven last plagues (Rev. 18:8), etc., must still be applied according to the year-day principle. In other words, we recognize their symbolic time span, but we are given no calculated beginning or ending dates from which to measure. To say otherwise renders the text totally meaningless. The absurd notion that the 'half hour,' 'one hour,' or the 'one day,' etc., may be rendered to mean simply a short period of time is intellectually offensive, at best. Humanity has never been left to flaunt human elevation above divine revelation. God always means what He says and says what He means. But there are those who want us to believe that the pen of inspiration has included that the 'year for a day' principal ceased at 1844, as well. To do so, these people encounter a serious problem. They violate the hermeneutical principles of interpretation laid down for us in the Scriptures, which keep

---

[260] Josiah Litch, *Signs of the Times*, Boston, August 1, 1840.
[261] Josiah Litch, *The Probability of the Second Coming of Christ About A.D. 1843* (Boston: David H. Ela, 1838), 158-159.
[262] Ellen White. *Selected Messages* (Hagerstown, MD: Review & Herald, 1958), 2:108.
[263] Ellen White, Manuscript No. 59, 1900, *SDA Bible Commentary* (Hagerstown, MD: Review & Herald, 1957), 7:971.

us from falling into either the Jesuit preterist or futuristic methods of interpretation. Symbolic prophecy extends until the Second Advent. After the Second Advent, symbols cease. Therefore symbolic time (day for a year) likewise ceases at the Second Advent. As proof, the 1,000 years of Revelation 20 are now literal years. This, then, cancels out all date-setting after 1844 for any event whatsoever, as far as Bible prophecy is concerned. But their dilemma does not stop there. Turning to the *Seventh-day Adventist Bible Commentary,* volume 7, page 787, we read regarding 'half an hour' (Rev.8:1) that Ellen White applies this seven and a half days yet in the future. In fact, she uses the 'year-day' principle, as can be seen in *Early Writings* page 16. It is the very hermeneutical principle they say she supposedly did away with in 1844. However, it is this very principle she applies in Revelation 8:1, that finds its fulfillment <u>after</u> 1844!"

11. A. T. states: "But what specific date in 1449 would he choose as a starting point, in order to obtain the exact day of expiration of the 391 remaining years of the sixth trumpet? Surprisingly, he did not choose January 6, but July 27, without any specific event from history."[264]

H. H. states: "Litch never had a choice once he accepted July 27, 1299, for his commencement of the fifth trumpet! Treiyer fully admits that no historical event was ever specified for July 27, 1449, and we can attest to the fact from my personal study and our study of chapter 4 that no historical event for July 27, 1449, could be produced from either the European or Ottoman sources, whether historian or chronologist. Then in his next breath…:"

12. A. T. states: "This does not mean that the dates held by the Millerites to fulfill the sixth trumpet in 1840 were not important. Though several Adventist authors have recently disagreed with those dates, the more I read the criticisms of these two historic events (1449-1840), the more convinced I have become that the Millerites were well-founded in choosing them. I believe that those who criticize these two dates do not know the history well, or do not see the tremendous meaning they have. In fact, they do not see the great implications of both events for today."[265]

H. H. states: "Treiyer has shifted to 1453 and 1844 using his own private 'sliding scale principal' for the fulfillment of the two claimed historic events for the fifth and sixth trumpets. Then he said the following: *'This does not mean that the dates held by the Millerites to fulfill the sixth trumpet in 1840 were not important.'* Why should these 'dates' of 1449 and 1840 still be important to us, when he has replaced them for himself with 1453 and 1844? Let's get past the semantics of mind-conditioning here and stay focused on the facts, please. And the fact of the matter is simply this: the primary sources have pointed us in another direction. The honest in heart have been encouraged with the following promise:"

> "He who reads every heart and tries every motive will leave <u>none</u> who desire a knowledge of the <u>truth</u>, to be <u>deceived</u> as to the issues of the controversy."[266]

---

[264] Dr. Alberto Treiyer, *The Seals and the Trumpets* (Distinctive Messages, 2005), 333.
[265] Ibid., 335, footnote 17.
[266] Ellen White, *The Great Controversy* (Nampa, ID: Pacific Press, 1911), 605. [Emphasis mine]

"None will be deceived except those who want to be deceived. Such is the fruit that is produced when we still try to force square pegs into round holes. Chapter 6 will prove to the reader a breath of fresh air, because this is the very first exposition on the sixth trumpet of Revelation that uses the Scriptures and allows the Bible to be its own interpreter. Enjoy!"

6

An Exposition of the
6th Trumpet of Revelation 9:13-21

Pastor
Stephen P. Bohr

Acknowledgments

Pastor Stephen P. Bohr has served the Seventh-day Adventist Church faithfully for over thirty years and has contributed greatly to the cause of truth. One of his latest contributions to the church and to the international community is an exposition of the seven trumpets of Revelation. With the sixth trumpet having its application in force until the close of probation (Rev. 10:7), it is little wonder that demand exists for clarity on the topic. In recognition of the need for sound interpretation of the trumpets of Revelation, Pastor Bohr is the first to identify the symbols from the Scriptures, letting the Bible interpret itself.

With this book that you have in your hands, I have fulfilled my own promise to deliver a considerable array of related historical documentation from primary and secondary sources. The reader will see how it fully sustains Pastor Bohr's scriptural interpretation of the sixth trumpet. These two independent works indeed complement one another, each separately supporting the same conclusion: that Islam plays no part in prophetic fulfillment, whether in Revelation or elsewhere in scripture. My editorial comments in Pastor Bohr's article are in bracketed paragraphs; it will be seen that he and I view the issues in the same light. Readers are encouraged to obtain Pastor Bohr's entire exposition on the seven trumpets of Revelation. Pastor Bohr has made his findings available for all to obtain in CD and MP3 format at *Secrets Unsealed*, with optional study notes available.

Heidi Heiks, editor, 2012

PASTOR
STEPHEN P. BOHR

Secrets Unsealed
PO Box 6545
Fresno, CA 93703-6545

559-264-2300
888-REV-1412
(888-738-1412)
www.SecretsUnsealed.org

Hours of Operation:
Monday-Thursday 8:30 a.m.-5:30 p.m.
Friday 8:00 a.m.-12:00 p.m. Pacific Time

Overview of the Period of the Sixth Trumpet

The sixth trumpet (Revelation 9:13-21) is a vivid description of the **gathering or mustering of the wicked** by Satan's three symbolic angels for the final battle against God's remnant (Revelation 16:13-16). This final gathering, which began in 1844, will intensify until the close of probation.

Immediately before the close of probation, when the seventh angel is about to blow his trumpet, Satan will bring about a great counterfeit Pentecostal revival (Revelation 13:13). The purpose of this revival will be to preempt and counterfeit the true revival that will take place at the outpouring of the latter rain. Inspiration tells us that the false prophet (apostate Protestantism) will even make fire come down from heaven in the sight of men, a miracle that parodies the falling of fire from heaven in the days of Elijah, and the manifestation of tongues of fire on the day of Pentecost (see Revelation 13:13; GC p. 464). This gathering of the wicked during the sixth trumpet (in Revelation 9:13-21) is further amplified in Revelation 12:17, 13:11-18, 14:18-20 and 16:13-16.

Immediately after the conclusion of the gathering of the wicked during the sixth trumpet (in Revelation 9:21), chapter 10 presents the flip side of the coin by going back in time to describe the global **gathering of the righteous** by the message that comes forth from the little book. We know that this judgment-hour message, which began with events surrounding the year 1844, is global because the angel places one foot on the land and the other on the sea. This gathering of the righteous by the message that comes from the little book is further amplified in Revelation 14:6-12, which is the "prophesying again" of Revelation 10:11.

In the midst of Satan's counterfeit revival, God will bring about a genuine revival of primitive godliness among His people. This message is known as the message of the fourth angel; it brings the final latter-rain loud-cry (Revelation 18:1-4) revival of the Holy Spirit to God's remnant (GC p. 464). The gathering of both the righteous and the wicked is then further described in the harvest scene of Revelation 14:14-20.

Structure of Revelation 9:13-14:20

Revelation 9:13-21	The gathering of the wicked from 1844 till the close of probation.
Revelation 10:1-11:1	The gathering of the righteous from 1844 until the close of probation.
Revelation 12:17; 13:11-18	The gathering of the wicked before the close of probation.
Revelation 14:6-12	The gathering of the righteous before the close of probation.
Revelation 14:14-20	The wicked and righteous have been gathered inside and outside of the symbolic city, spiritual Jerusalem.

Ellen White and the Two Gatherings

Ellen White describes the final gathering of both the righteous and the wicked under the genuine and the counterfeit Pentecostal revivals:

*"Notwithstanding the widespread declension of faith and piety, there are true followers of Christ in these churches. Before the final visitation of God's judgments upon the earth, there will be among the people of the Lord such a **revival of primitive godliness** as has not been witnessed since apostolic times. The Spirit and power of God will be poured out upon His children. At that time many will separate themselves from those churches in which the love of this world has supplanted love for God and His word. Many, both of ministers and people, will gladly accept those great truths which God has caused to be proclaimed at this time to prepare a people for the Lord's second coming. The enemy of souls desires to hinder this work; and **<u>before the time for such a movement shall come</u>**, he will endeavor to prevent it by introducing a counterfeit. In those churches which he can bring under his deceptive power, he will make it appear that God's special blessing is poured out; there will be manifest what is thought to be **great religious interest**. Multitudes will exult that God is working marvelously for them, when the work is that of another spirit. Under a religious guise, Satan will seek to extend his influence over the Christian world."[267]*

*"Servants of God, with their faces lighted up and shining with holy consecration, will hasten from place to place to proclaim the message from heaven. By thousands of voices, all over the earth, the warning will be given. Miracles will be wrought, the sick will be healed, and signs and wonders will follow the believers. **Satan also works, with lying wonders, even bringing down fire from heaven in the sight of men.** Revelation 13:13. Thus the inhabitants of the earth will be brought to take their stand."[268]*

With that inspired foundation laid before us in bold view, we are prepared to begin our exposition of the sixth trumpet of Revelation 9:

Rev. 9:13: And the sixth angel sounded, and I heard a voice from the **four horns of the golden altar** which is before God....

Does Revelation 9:13 indicate whether Christ is ministering in the first or second apartment when the sixth trumpet sounds?

"As in vision the apostle John was granted a view of the temple of God in heaven, he beheld there 'seven lamps of fire burning before the throne.' He saw an angel 'having a golden censer; and there was given unto him much incense, that he should offer it with the prayers of all saints upon the golden altar which was before the throne.' Revelation 4:5; 8:3. Here the prophet was permitted to behold the first

---

[267] Ellen White, *The Great Controversy* (Nampa, Idaho: Pacific Press, 1911), 464.
[268] Ibid., 612.

apartment of the sanctuary in heaven; and he saw there the 'seven lamps of fire' and the 'golden altar' represented by the golden candlestick and the altar of incense in the sanctuary on earth. Again, 'the temple of God was opened' (Revelation 11:19), and he looked within the inner veil, upon the holy of holies. Here he beheld 'the ark of His testament' (Revelation 11:19), represented by the sacred chest constructed by Moses to contain the law of God."[269]

[Although Ellen White was plainly in agreement with a first-apartment setting for Revelation 4:5 and 8:3, and with a second-apartment setting for Revelation 11:19, nothing in that quotation above allows for any movement of Christ from one apartment to another within any of the visions, for that would be confusion compounded. In addition, she said nothing in that quotation regarding Revelation 9:13. However, we know that in each of John's visions under discussion (Rev. 4:5, 8:3, 9:13, 11:19), Christ's location in the heavenly sanctuary after His ascension is designated. We have no freedom to place Him where He is not, nor does Christ move during any of the visions. He remains solely within either one or the other apartment. All the specifications of a given prophecy must be fulfilled, whether in the time period from Christ's inauguration to 1844, or from 1844 to the close of probation. The prophecies of each vision clearly describe time and place in the chain of events that take place while Jesus performs his priestly functions in the designated apartment of the heavenly sanctuary. Having completed His inauguration and the anointing of the heavenly sanctuary (Rev. 4-5), Christ began only His first apartment functions, terminating them in 1844. The second-apartment priestly services of Christ, which began the investigative judgment as well, commenced on October 22, 1844, and will terminate at the close of human probation.

We observe that the gospel or salvation is still obtainable under the sixth trumpet:]

> "Neither **repented** they of their murders, nor of their sorceries, nor of their fornication, nor of their thefts." Rev. 9:21.

[We also take notice that the sixth trumpet extends to the closing of the gospel invitation, when the mystery of God should be finished (Eph. 6:19, Col. 4:3, Eph. 3:3,6), which is the close of human probation:]

> "But in the days of the voice of the seventh angel, when he shall begin to sound, the mystery of God should be finished, as he hath declared to his servants the prophets." Rev. 10:7.

[The timing and message of the seventh trumpet confirm that point:]

> "And the seventh angel sounded; and there were great voices in heaven, saying, The kingdoms of this world are become *the kingdoms* of our Lord, and of his Christ; and he shall reign for ever and ever." Rev. 11:15

[When do the kingdoms of this world become the kingdoms of our Lord, and of his Christ? It is not until the solemn declaration has gone forth, and every case has been forever fixed for eternal life

---

[269] Ellen White, *Patriarch and Prophets*, (Nampa, ID: Pacific Press, 1958), 356.

or eternal death. *Then* Jesus receives his kingdom; hence, the close of human probation must occur first:]

> "I saw Jesus, who had been ministering before the ark containing the ten commandments, throw down the censer. He raised His hands, and with a loud voice said, 'It is done.' And all the angelic host laid off their crowns as Jesus made the solemn declaration, 'He that is unjust, let him be unjust still: and he which is filthy, let him be filthy still: and he that is righteous, let him be righteous still: and he that is holy, let him be holy still.'
> "Every case had been decided for life or death. While Jesus had been ministering in the sanctuary, the judgment had been going on for the righteous dead, and then for the righteous living. Christ had received His kingdom, having made the atonement for His people and blotted out their sins. The subjects of the kingdom were made up. The marriage of the Lamb was consummated. And the kingdom, and the greatness of the kingdom under the whole heaven, was given to Jesus and the heirs of salvation, and Jesus was to reign as King of kings and Lord of lords."[270]

[The close of the sixth trumpet parallels the close of human probation. At the commencement of the seventh trumpet, Christ receives His kingdom. That event is followed by the seven last plagues.

We now return to our initial question as to in which apartment we should look for Christ to be ministering at the beginning of the sounding of the sixth trumpet. The answer will be made clear when we contrast the Scriptures alongside these two texts:]

> Rev. 8:3 "And another angel came and stood at the **altar**, having a golden censer; and there was given unto him much incense, that he should offer *it* with the prayers of all saints upon the **golden altar** which was before the throne."

> Rev. 9:13 "And the sixth angel sounded, and I heard a voice from the **four horns of the golden altar** which is before God...."

[Attention to detail is important, and heaven is calling our attention to the differences in those two texts. Revelation 8:3 is without question a first apartment description as Scripture, history, (time and place of events) and Ellen White confirm. However, that is not the case with Revelation 9:13, our text under scrutiny. Yes, the golden altar is in the first apartment. However, notice the importance that is being placed upon the "four horns" of that altar. That specific detail must be kept in mind when we compare type and antitype within the established parameters of our "time and place" of Scriptural emphasis:]

> Ex. 30:10 "And Aaron shall make an atonement upon the <u>horns of it once in a year</u> with the blood of the sin offering of atonements: <u>once in the year</u> shall he make atonement upon it throughout your generations: it *is* most holy unto the LORD."

> Lev. 16:16 "And he shall make an atonement for the holy *place*, because of the uncleanness of the children of Israel, and because of their transgressions in all their

---

[270] Ellen White, *Early Writings* (Washington, D.C: Review and Herald, 1945), 279-280.

sins: and so shall he do for the tabernacle of the congregation, that remaineth among them in the midst of their uncleanness.

v.17 "And there shall be no man in the tabernacle of the congregation when he goeth in to make an atonement in the holy *place*, until he come out, and have made an atonement for himself, and for his household, and for all the congregation of Israel.

v.18 "And he shall go out unto the altar that *is* before the LORD, and make an atonement for it; and shall take of the blood of the bullock, and of the blood of the goat, and put *it* upon the horns of the altar round about.

v.19 "And he shall sprinkle of the blood upon it with his finger seven times, and cleanse it, and hallow it from the uncleanness of the children of Israel."

[We have established already from the Scriptures that the sixth trumpet extends to the close of probation. Then, rightly understanding type and antitype with the emphasis on the "four horns" of the golden altar, it is an indisputable fact that Jesus is in the second apartment of the heavenly sanctuary. Moreover, we will shortly demonstrate from Revelation 9:15 that the sixth trumpet had its orientation in the second apartment of the heavenly sanctuary, as well. That being so, there can be no movement of Christ from one apartment to another during the sounding of the sixth trumpet. The point I wish to establish here is that when Christ is presented by Ellen White in Revelation 4:5, for example, in the first apartment, He does not move from that apartment to the second apartment during the entire scope of *that* vision. That holds true also for the visions of 8:3, 9:13, and 11:19. When Christ is presented in the second apartment, as in Revelation 11:19, we cannot say he goes back through the door He has shut, into the first apartment. No, the visions reveal that if he is pictured as in the first apartment, then the initial specifications of that prophecy must find their fulfillment between the first century AD up to 1844, and never beyond. That is because the text can only have one correct interpretation.

However, there can and sometimes will be seen certain texts that will have a double application, or even multiple future applications, as given by Ellen White. Regardless, the contexts of the given specifications will determine time and place of fulfillment. This will likewise hold true with a second apartment description, from 1844 to the close of probation. Revelation 4:5, 8:3, 9:13, and 11:19 constitute the key that establishes in which apartment of the heavenly sanctuary Christ is presiding. The given specifications of Revelation 4:5 and 8:3 will demonstrate that their Scriptural and historical fulfillments will be established between the first century AD and Oct. 22, 1844. This key is given to help the reader place parameters on the specifications, in order to stay within the prophecies' designated time and place. The scriptural and historical specifications of Revelation 9:13 and 11:19 will demonstrate that their fulfillment will take place while Christ is presiding in the second apartment of that heavenly sanctuary-- from Oct. 22, 1844, to the close of probation.

It must be understood that while there are some places in the visions where we are given other *applications* by Ellen White, they are not additional prophecies. In Daniel 11: 31-36 (MR 13:394), for example, in quoting these verses that speak of the Dark Ages, she told us these *Scriptures* will be repeated-- but not the prophecy. The same can be said about the "souls under the altar." This prophecy with its given specifications was fulfilled during the 1260 years. However, it has another application given to it by Ellen White under Revelation 18:1-5; nevertheless, that second application is not the fulfillment of that prophecy. The same may also be said for the praise anthem of Rev. 5:11-14, as the specifications given for the prophecy do not take us past the first century. Nevertheless, Ellen White gives the praise anthem multiple future applications.

At this point, let us clarify the significance of the "four horns of the golden altar." The first-apartment ministry does not stop when the second apartment ministry begins in 1844. Otherwise, nobody could be saved after 1844. Salvation comes through the first apartment ministry and continues through the second; they run together after 1844. Judgment, however, comes from the second apartment alone. Note that in Leviticus 16, the *daily* was performed before and after the special services of the Day of Atonement in the earthly sanctuary, in preparation for the New Year's services. The anointing of the horns takes place on the Day of Atonement, because the priest goes the deepest into the sanctuary, into the Most Holy Place, and atones for it. Then he atones for the Holy Place, including the four horns. Then he atones for the altar in the courtyard. This is the complete cleansing service, and then the accumulated defilement of sin is sent away on the scapegoat. The priest goes the deepest and then <u>backs out</u>, atoning for each as he goes. This yearly activity does not negate the daily use of the altar of incense.

Ellen White wrote what would happen at the end of human history, as Jesus completes His heavenly ministrations on behalf of the fallen race. She said the end will come more quickly than many think, surprising even Seventh-day Adventists. At that time the "three-fold union" will be at its peak:]

"But there is a day that God hath appointed for the close of this world's history. 'This gospel of the kingdom shall be preached in all the world for a witness unto all nations; and then shall the end come.' Prophecy is fast fulfilling. More, much more, should be said about these tremendously important subjects. The day is at hand when the destiny of every soul will be fixed forever. This day of the Lord hastens on apace. The false watchmen are raising the cry, 'All is well;' but the day of God is rapidly approaching. Its footsteps are so muffled that it does not arouse the world from the deathlike slumber into which it has fallen. While the watchmen cry, 'Peace and safety,' 'sudden destruction cometh upon them,' 'and they shall not escape,' 'for as a snare shall it come on all them that dwell on the face of the whole earth.' It overtakes the pleasure-lover and the sinful man as a thief in the night. When all is apparently secure, and men retire to contented rest, then the prowling, stealthy, midnight thief steals upon his prey. When it is too late to prevent the evil, it is discovered that *some door* or window was not secured. ["When we make any reserve, we are leaving open *a door* through which Satan can enter to lead us astray by his temptations." Ellen White, *Mount of Blessings*, 92.] 'Be ye also ready: for in such an hour as ye think not the Son of man cometh.' People are now settling to rest, imagining themselves secure under the popular churches; but let all beware, lest there is a place left open for the enemy to gain an entrance. Great pains should be taken to keep this subject before the people. The solemn fact is to be kept not only before the people of the world, but before our own churches also, that the day of the Lord will come suddenly, unexpectedly. The fearful warning of the prophecy is addressed to every soul. Let no one feel that he is secure from the danger of being surprised. <u>Let no one's interpretation of prophecy rob you of the conviction of the knowledge of events which show that this great event is near at hand.</u>"[271]

---

[271] Ellen White, *Fundamentals of Christian Education*, (Hagerstown, MD: Review and Herald, 1923), 335-6.

[When all are thinking peace and prosperity, then sudden destruction comes. That destruction reveals that human probation has closed. What we witness here are simply the final steps of the cleansing of the sanctuary itself.]

Verse 14: "Saying to the sixth angel which had the trumpet, Loose the **four angels** which are **bound** in the **great river Euphrates**."

"Four" in the Scriptures denotes universality, or global extent:

Eze. 7:2 "Also, thou son of man, thus saith the Lord GOD unto the land of Israel; An end, the end is come upon the <u>four corners of the land</u>."

Matt. 24:31 "And he shall send his angels with a great sound of a trumpet, and they shall gather together his elect from the <u>four winds, from one end of heaven to the other</u>."

Rev. 7:1 "And after these things I saw four angels standing on the <u>four corners of the earth</u>, holding the <u>four winds of the earth</u>, that the wind should not blow on the earth, nor on the sea, nor on any tree.
Rev. 7:2 "And I saw another angel ascending from the east, having the seal of the living God: and he cried with a loud voice to the <u>four angels</u>, to whom it was given to hurt the earth and the sea...."

These are evil angels that are waiting for God to release them so that they can wreak havoc on mankind, as can be seen in the succeeding context.

A related point is this: If these evil angels nee6d to be *released,* it must mean that they have been *restrained.* What is it that has restrained these angels from manifesting their destructive power? Revelation 12:16 explains what has restrained them: the earth. The papacy received a deadly wound in 1798 and the civil governments of the world have kept that wound in place since then. But when the beast from the earth gives civil power back to the papacy, then the restraint will be removed and the final display of Satan's power will be manifested.

The meaning of "bound" is "to restrain:"

Rev. 20:1 "And I saw an angel come down from heaven, having the key of the bottomless pit and a great chain in his hand.
Rev. 20:2 "And he laid hold on the dragon, that old serpent, which is the Devil, and Satan, and <u>bound him</u> a thousand years...."

Though "bound" to some degree yet, Malachi Martin in *The Keys of This Blood* had this to say about papal intentions for earthly dominance:

"In this timely and provocative new book, best-selling author Malachi Martin reveals the untold story behind the Vatican's role in the collapse of the Iron Curtain, as well as Pope John Paul II's far-reaching assessment of the three-way contest now unfolding among the global powers--the Soviet Union under Mikhail Gorbachev, the capitalist nations of the West, and the Pope's own universal Roman Church--a winner-take-all race against time and each other to establish, maintain, and control the first one-world government that has ever existed on the face of the earth.

"**From the first moment of his pontificate, it was John Paul's purpose to free the papacy from the straitjacket of inactivity in world affairs imposed upon it by the major secular powers for 200 years.** It was his purpose to end the morally toxic and humanly untenable balance-of-power arrangements that had led in our century to the slaughter of two world wars and countless smaller conflicts worldwide. And it was his purpose to end the division of nations into two warring camps that for nearly half a *century* had condoned the enslavement and starvation of millions and had condemned the world to the terror of nuclear brinksmanship."[272]

"Let the **restraints** now imposed by <u>secular governments</u> be <u>removed</u> and Rome be reinstated in her former power, and there would speedily be a revival of her tyranny and persecution."[273]

[The event involving the "great river Euphrates" of Revelation 9:14 and the event of Revelation 16:12-14[274] are one and the same, with further specifications of Babylon's persecuting objectives. In 1798 Rome's tyrannical power ceased to flow, symbolized by the "great river Euphrates" being dried up. Her church-state monopoly over the Western world was abruptly taken away. However, Rome's oppressive power is going to have a resurrection, and the "great river Euphrates" is going to flow again. Separation of church and state will become politically inconvenient history, and history's narrative of papal persecution will resume. Some have sought to find an application of the sixth trumpet to the phenomenal growth of radical Islam, because the river Euphrates is mentioned. The question that begs to be asked is this: What hermeneutical principle allows them to say that the Euphrates in Revelation 9 is referring to a literal geographical location in the Middle East, while the Euphrates of Revelation 16 refers to the multitudes of the whole world under the control of spiritual Babylon? In other wording, why is the Euphrates in Revelation 16:12 to be understood as symbolic, while the Euphrates in Revelation 9 is to be understood as literal, when both of them apply to the same period of the end time (sixth trumpet and sixth plague)? Are not geographical restrictions removed after the cross? Our analysis of verse 15 will cement the fact that this marshaling of Satan's forces has gradually been building momentum since October 22, 1844. (For a more delineated work on "**the great river Euphrates,** see Study Notes at the end of the chapter):]

"**Already** the inhabitants of the earth **are** marshalling under the leading of the prince of darkness."[275]

Notice how Ellen White understands Revelation 16:13, 14:

---

[272] Malachi Martin, *The Keys of this Blood* (New York: Simon and Schuster, 1990), dust jacket.
[273] Ellen White, *The Great Controversy* (Nampa, Idaho: Pacific Press, 1911), 564.
[274] To correctly understand who are the "three unclean spirits" of Rev. 16:13-14, obtain Pastor Bohr's 6th Trumpet CD's or see my book, *King of the North* (Brushton, New York: Teach Services, 2009), 45-50. <u>www.thesourcehh.org</u>.
[275] Ellen White, *Testimonies for the Church* (Boise, ID: Pacific Press, 1948), 8:49.

"The Spirit of God **is** gradually withdrawing from the world. Satan **is** also **mustering** his forces of evil, going forth 'unto the kings of the earth and of the whole world,' to gather them under his banner, to be trained for 'the battle of that great day of God Almighty.'"[276] [Revelation 16:14]

"Satan **is** marshalling his **forces** for the **last great struggle** [the Battle of Armageddon], 'to make war with the **remnant of her seed**, which keep the commandments of God, and have the testimony of Jesus Christ.' If we would be true to God, we cannot escape the conflict. But we are not left in doubt as to the issue. Beyond the **smoke and heat** [smoke, fire and brimstone] of the **battle**, we behold 'them that had gotten the victory' **standing on Mount Zion** with the Lamb."[277]

Verse 15: "And the **four angels were loosed**, which were prepared for an ["**the**" (the article *teen*)] **hour, and day, and month, and year**, for to **slay the third part of men**." Rev. 9:15.

"**Four angels were loosed.**" As we substantiated earlier from the Scriptures for verse 14, the number "four" in the Bible signifies universality, or global extension. As we also noted earlier, Revelation 16:14 tells us that the entire world will be gathered together in rebellion against God by the spirits of devils.

"**[The]** (the article *teen*) **hour, and day, and month, and year.**" What is meant by the expression "the hour, the day, the month and the year"? A careful study of Revelation indicates that the "hour" is "the hour of God's judgment"--that is, when His judgment begins:

Rev. 14:6 "And I saw another angel fly in the midst of heaven, having the everlasting gospel to preach unto them that dwell on the earth, and to every nation, and kindred, and tongue, and people,

Rev. 14:7 "Saying with a loud voice, Fear God, and give glory to him; for the hour of his judgment is come: and worship him that made heaven, and earth, and the sea, and the fountains of waters."

While the sixth trumpet is presented in the context of the sanctuary, other parts of Scripture indicate that the "day" refers to the tenth day of the month of Tishri (the seventh month):

Lev. 23:27 "Also on the tenth *day* of this seventh month *there shall be* a day of atonement: it shall be an holy convocation unto you; and ye shall afflict your souls, and offer an offering made by fire unto the LORD."

And the "year" is 1844:

---

[276] Ellen White, *Last Day Events* (Boise, ID: Pacific Press, 1992), 249.
[277] Ellen White, *Review and Herald,* July 18, 1882.

Dan. 8:14 "And he said unto me, Unto two thousand and three hundred days; then shall the sanctuary be cleansed."

Rev. 3:7 "And to the angel of the church in Philadelphia write; These things saith he that is holy, he that is true, he that hath the key of David, he that openeth, and no man shutteth; and shutteth, and no man openeth;

Rev. 3:8 "I know thy works: behold, I have set before thee an open door, and no man can shut it: for thou hast a little strength, and hast kept my word, and hast not denied my name.

Rev. 3:9 "Behold, I will make them of the synagogue of Satan, which say they are Jews, and are not, but do lie; behold, I will make them to come and worship before thy feet, and to know that I have loved thee."

"The article [*teen*], once only before all the [time] periods, implies that the hour in the day, and the day in the month, and the month in the year, and the year itself, had been definitely fixed by God."[278]

Heaven has hereby foretold the moral fall of apostate Protestantism: October 22, 1844.

"Slay the third part of men." "Third" represents a partial judgment:

Eze. 5:1 "And thou, son of man, take thee a sharp knife, take thee a barber's razor, and cause *it* to pass upon thine head and upon thy beard: then take thee balances to weigh, and divide the *hair*.

5:2 "Thou shalt burn with fire a third part in the midst of the city, when the days of the siege are fulfilled: and thou shalt take a third part, *and* smite about it with a knife: and a third part thou shalt scatter in the wind; and I will draw out a sword after them.

5:3 "Thou shalt also take thereof a few in number, and bind them in thy skirts.

5:4 "Then take of them again, and cast them into the midst of the fire, and burn them in the fire; *for* thereof shall a fire come forth into all the house of Israel."

5:12 "A third part of thee shall die with the pestilence, and with famine shall they be consumed in the midst of thee: and a third part shall fall by the sword round about thee; and I will scatter a third part into all the winds, and I will draw out a sword after them."

Zechariah 13:8 "And it shall come to pass, *that* in all the land, saith the LORD, two parts therein shall be cut off *and* die; but the third shall be left therein.

13:9 "And I will bring the third part through the fire, and will refine them as silver is refined, and will try them as gold is tried: they shall call on my name, and I will hear them: I will say, It *is* my people: and they shall say, The LORD *is* my God."

---

[278] Jamieson, Fausset, and Brown Commentary, Electronic Database. Copyright 1997, 2003, 2005, 2006 by Biblesoft, Incorporated

[The fact that this is not the final and total destruction of the wicked after the close of probation is indicated by the fact that only a third of humanity is killed by this devastating army of demons. The supposition that it refers to a third of the Roman Empire is of human origin, and has no foundation in the Scriptures.]

Verse 16: "And the number of the army of the horsemen *were* two hundred thousand thousand: and I **heard the number of them**."

200 million! The number of the enemy is huge in comparison to the 144,000 of Revelation 7:4:

> "**And I heard the number of them** which were sealed: *and there were* sealed an hundred *and* forty *and* four thousand of all the tribes of the children of Israel."

These are the only two verses in Revelation where John uses the expression "*I heard the number of them*," so they must be related in some way. Revelation 7:4 transpires during the sixth seal and Revelation 9:16 occurs during the period of the sixth trumpet. Notice how Ellen White contrasts the number of God's followers with those of Satan:

> "The remnant church will be brought into great trial and distress. Those who keep the commandments of God and the faith of Jesus will feel the ire of the dragon and his hosts. Satan numbers the world as his subjects, he has gained control of the apostate churches; but here is a little company that are resisting his supremacy. If he could blot them from the earth, his triumph would be complete."[279]

Verse 17: "And thus I saw the horses in the vision, and them that **sat on them**, having breastplates of **fire** [red], and of **jacinth** [blue], and **brimstone** [yellow]: and the heads of the horses *were* as the heads of **lions**; and out of their **mouths** issued **fire and smoke and brimstone**."

This is clearly an army that rises from hell. These are the same spirits of demons in Revelation 16:14 that are released to gather the "kings of the earth and of the whole world" against God's people. They are also the demons that are mentioned in connection with the fourth angel's message in Revelation 18:2-3.

An Army from Hell:

> Ps. 11:6 "Upon the wicked he shall rain snares, fire and brimstone, and an horrible tempest: *this shall be* the portion of their cup."

> Eze. 38:22 "And I will plead against him with pestilence and with blood; and I will rain upon him, and upon his bands, and upon the many people that *are* with him, an overflowing rain, and great hailstones, fire, and brimstone."

---

[279] Ellen White, *Testimonies for the Church* (Boise, ID: Pacific Press, 1948), 9:231.

Rev. 14:10 "The same shall drink of the wine of the wrath of God, which is poured out without mixture into the cup of his indignation; and he shall be tormented with <u>fire and brimstone</u> in the presence of the holy angels, and in the presence of the Lamb:"

Rev. 19:20 "And the beast was taken, and with him the false prophet that wrought miracles before him, with which he deceived them that had received the mark of the beast, and them that worshipped his image. These both were cast alive into a lake of <u>fire burning with brimstone</u>."

Rev. 20:10 "And the devil that deceived them was cast into the lake of <u>fire and brimstone</u>, where the beast and the false prophet *are*, and shall be tormented day and night for ever and ever."

Rev. 21:8 "But the fearful, and unbelieving, and the abominable, and murderers, and whoremongers, and sorcerers, and idolaters, and all liars, shall have their part in the lake which burneth with <u>fire and brimstone</u>: which is the second death."

Lions, a symbol of Satan and Babylon:

2Tim. 4:17 "Notwithstanding the Lord stood with me, and strengthened me; that by me the preaching might be fully known, and *that* all the Gentiles might hear: and I was <u>delivered out of the mouth of the lion</u>."

1Pet. 5:8 "Be sober, be vigilant; because your adversary <u>the devil</u>, as a <u>roaring lion</u>, walketh about, seeking whom he may devour:"

Rev. 13:2 "And the beast which I saw was like unto a leopard, and his feet were as *the feet* of a bear, and <u>his mouth as the mouth of a lion</u>: and the dragon gave him his power, and his seat, and great authority."

Eze. 38:13 "Sheba, and Dedan, and the merchants of Tarshish, with all the <u>young lions</u> thereof, shall say unto thee, Art thou come to take a spoil? hast thou gathered thy company to take a prey? to carry away silver and gold, to take away cattle and goods, to take a great spoil?"

Leviathan:

Job 41:1 "Canst thou draw out leviathan with an hook? or his tongue with a cord *which* thou lettest down?"

Job 41:19 "Out of his mouth go burning lamps, *and* sparks of fire leap out.
Job 41:20 "Out of his nostrils goeth smoke, as *out* of a seething pot or caldron.
Job 41:21 "His breath kindleth coals, and a flame goeth out of his mouth."

Job 41:31 "He maketh the deep to boil like a pot: he maketh the sea like a pot of ointment."

Job 41:34 "He beholdeth all high *things*: he *is* a <u>king over all the children of pride</u>."

Job 1-2 = Satan

Isa. 27:1 "In that day the LORD with his sore and great and strong sword shall punish leviathan the piercing <u>serpent</u>, even <u>leviathan that crooked serpent</u>; and he shall slay the <u>dragon</u> that *is* in the <u>sea</u>."

Rev. 12:7 "And there was war in heaven: Michael and his angels fought against the <u>dragon</u>; and the <u>dragon</u> fought and his angels,
Rev. 12:8 "And prevailed not; neither was their place found any more in heaven.
Rev. 12:9 "And the <u>great dragon</u> was cast out, that old <u>serpent</u>, called the <u>Devil</u>, and <u>Satan</u>, which deceiveth the whole world: he was cast out into the earth, and his angels were cast out with him."

Verse 18: "By these **three** was the third part of men killed, by the **fire**, and by the **smoke**, and by the **brimstone**, which issued out of their **mouths**."

What comes out of the mouths is what kills the wicked. In the book of Revelation, fire, brimstone and smoke are identified with those who worship the beast and his image and who receive the mark:

Rev. 14:9 "And the third angel followed them, saying with a loud voice, If any man worship the beast and his image, and receive *his* mark in his forehead, or in his hand,
Rev. 14:10 "The same shall drink of the wine of the wrath of God, which is poured out without mixture into the cup of his indignation; and he shall be tormented with <u>fire</u> and <u>brimstone</u> in the presence of the holy angels, and in the presence of the Lamb:
Rev. 14:11 "And the <u>smoke</u> of their torment ascendeth up for ever and ever: and they have no rest day nor night, who worship the beast and his image, and whosoever receiveth the mark of his name."

Notably Revelation 16:13 explains that the evil spirits come out of the mouths of the threefold union.

Verse 19: "For their power is in their **mouth**, and in their **tails**: for their tails *were* like unto **serpents**, and had heads, and with them they do hurt."

The horses have mouths like **lions**. Elsewhere in the Bible, Babylon is portrayed as a devouring lion (Daniel 7:2, 4), as is its king, Nebuchadnezzar (Jeremiah 4:7). Satan is described as a devouring lion who seeks whom he may devour (1Pet 5:8).

Dan. 7:2 "Daniel spake and said, I saw in my vision by night, and, behold, the four winds of the heaven strove upon the great sea."

Dan 7:4 "The first *was* like a lion, and had eagle's wings: I beheld till the wings thereof were plucked, and it was lifted up from the earth, and made stand upon the feet as a man, and a man's heart was given to it."

Jer. 4:7 "The lion is come up from his thicket, and the destroyer of the Gentiles is on his way; he is gone forth from his place to make thy land desolate; *and* thy cities shall be laid waste, without an inhabitant."

1Pet. 5:8 "Be sober, be vigilant; because your adversary the devil, as a roaring lion, walketh about, seeking whom he may devour:"

Revelation 16:13-14 clarifies that the false doctrines come out of the mouths of the three counterfeit angels in order to gather the wicked for the final battle against God. The tail is a symbol of lies (Revelation 12:3-4; John 8:44; Isaiah 9:15). Notice that the mouth is in the tail.

Rev. 12:3 "And there appeared another wonder in heaven; and behold a great red dragon, having seven heads and ten horns, and seven crowns upon his heads.
Rev. 12:4 "And his tail drew the third part of the stars of heaven, and did cast them to the earth: and the dragon stood before the woman which was ready to be delivered, for to devour her child as soon as it was born."

John 8:44 "Ye are of *your* father the devil, and the lusts of your father ye will do. He was a murderer from the beginning, and abode not in the truth, because there is no truth in him. When he speaketh a lie, he speaketh of his own: for he is a liar, and the father of it."

Isa. 9:15 "The ancient and honourable, he *is* the head; and the prophet that teacheth lies, he *is* the tail."

Verse 20: "And the rest of the men which were not killed by these plagues yet repented not of the works of their hands, that they should not **worship devils**, and **idols of gold, and silver, and brass, and stone, and of wood: which neither can see, nor hear, nor walk**:"

Rev. 18:2 "And he cried mightily with a strong voice, saying, Babylon the great is fallen, is fallen, and is become the <u>habitation of devils, and the hold of every foul spirit, and a cage of every unclean and hateful bird</u>.
Rev 18:3 "For all nations have drunk of the wine of the wrath of her fornication, and the kings of the earth have committed fornication with her, and the merchants of the earth are waxed rich through the abundance of her delicacies."

The expression "idols of gold, silver, brass, stone, and wood, which can neither see nor hear nor walk" comes almost verbatim from Daniel 5:23. Daniel 5 is discussing the fall of Babylon when the Euphrates was dried up. Thus three passages are linked: The fall of Babylon in Daniel 5, the drying up of the Euphrates in Revelation 16:12 and the sixth trumpet of Revelation 9:20.

Dan. 5:23 "But hast lifted up thyself against the Lord of heaven; and they have brought the vessels of his house before thee, and thou, and thy lords, thy wives, and thy concubines, have drunk wine in them; and thou hast praised the gods of silver, and gold, of brass, iron, wood, and stone, which see not, nor hear, nor know: and the God in whose hand thy breath *is*, and whose *are* all thy ways, hast thou not glorified:"

Verse 21: "Neither repented they of their **murders**, nor of their **sorceries**, nor of their **fornication**, nor of their **thefts**."

Revelation 17:6; 18:20, 24 describes Babylon as a **murderer** of God's people.
Revelation 18:23 refers to the **sorceries** of Babylon as one of the reasons for her fall.
Revelation 17:2 portrays the adultery or **fornication** of the harlot with the kings of the earth.
Revelation 18:10-13 describes this system as **greedy** and enslaving, stealing from the poor and favoring the rich. This greediness is described in James 5:1-8.

Since 1844 the armies of both the wicked and the righteous have been in the process of being gathered. God's three angels have been gathering the righteous (Rev. 14:6-12) while Satan's three angels have been gathering the wicked (Rev. 16:13-14). The sixth trumpet in Revelation 9:13-21 describes the gathering of the wicked for battle, while Revelation 10 describes the gathering of the righteous on God's side. Rev.18:1-5 describes the final gathering of the righteous under God's fourth angel. However, before that time, Satan's "fourth angel" will try to prevent it by introducing a counterfeit.[280]

There are only three places in Revelation where the word "demons" or "devils" appears: in Revelation 9:20, 16:14, and 18:1-5. Furthermore, the "great river Euphrates" appears only in Revelation 9 and Revelation 16. By these parallels we know that there is a link between these two passages.

Murderer:

Rev. 17:6 "And I saw the woman drunken with the blood of the saints, and with the blood of the martyrs of Jesus: and when I saw her, I wondered with great admiration."

Rev. 18:20 "Rejoice over her, *thou* heaven, and *ye* holy apostles and prophets; for God hath avenged you on her."

Rev. 18:24 "And in her was found the blood of prophets, and of saints, and of all that were slain upon the earth."

Sorceries:

Rev. 18:23 "And the light of a candle shall shine no more at all in thee; and the voice of the bridegroom and of the bride shall be heard no more at all in thee: for thy merchants were the great men of the earth; for by thy sorceries were all nations deceived."

---

[280] Ellen White, *The Great Controversy* (Nampa, Idaho: Pacific Press, 1911), 464.

Fornication:

Rev. 17:2 "With whom the kings of the earth have committed fornication, and the inhabitants of the earth have been made drunk with the wine of her fornication."

Rev. 19:1 "And after these things I heard a great voice of much people in heaven, saying, Alleluia; Salvation, and glory, and honour, and power, unto the Lord our God:
Rev. 19:2 "For true and righteous *are* his judgments: for he hath judged the great whore, which did corrupt the earth with her fornication, and hath avenged the blood of his servants at her hand."

Thefts:

Rev. 18:10 "Standing afar off for the fear of her torment, saying, Alas, alas, that great city Babylon, that mighty city! for in one hour is thy judgment come.
Rev. 18:11 "And the merchants of the earth shall weep and mourn over her; for no man buyeth their merchandise any more:
Rev. 18:12 "The merchandise of gold, and silver, and precious stones, and of pearls, and fine linen, and purple, and silk, and scarlet, and all thine wood, and all manner vessels of ivory, and all manner vessels of most precious wood, and of brass, and iron, and marble,
Rev. 18:13 "And cinnamon, and odours, and ointments, and frankincense, and wine, and oil, and fine flour, and wheat, and beasts, and sheep, and horses, and chariots, and slaves, and souls of men."

Jas. 5:1 "Go to now, *ye* rich men, weep and howl for your miseries that shall come upon *you.*
Jas. 5:2 "Your riches are corrupted, and your garments are motheaten.
Jas. 5:3 "Your gold and silver is cankered; and the rust of them shall be a witness against you, and shall eat your flesh as it were fire. Ye have heaped treasure together for the last days.
Jas. 5:4 "Behold, the hire of the labourers who have reaped down your fields, which is of you kept back by fraud, crieth: and the cries of them which have reaped are entered into the ears of the Lord of sabaoth.
Jas. 5:5 "Ye have lived in pleasure on the earth, and been wanton; ye have nourished your hearts, as in a day of slaughter.
Jas. 5:6 "Ye have condemned *and* killed the just; *and* he doth not resist you.
Jas. 5:7 "Be patient therefore, brethren, unto the coming of the Lord. Behold, the husbandman waiteth for the precious fruit of the earth, and hath long patience for it, until he receive the early and latter rain.
Jas. 5:8 "Be ye also patient; stablish your hearts: for the coming of the Lord draweth nigh."

"Thefts" will also include a repeat of the confiscation of people's assets, as was done during the Dark Ages, and as was confirmed by Ellen White.

[There can be no doubt as to the identity of the aggressive "plague" (Rev. 9:20) of the sixth trumpet that will be permitted to destroy a significant number of people during the period of the sixth trumpet. In Revelation 9 God has exposed modern Babylon so that none need be charmed by her sorceries or beguiled by her lies, to eternal destruction. Nevertheless, we are told in verse 20 that "the rest of the men which were not killed by these plagues yet repented not." Sadly, some will be unwilling to perceive the character of Babylon and will remain under her spell. May this work in your hand serve to remove the scales from human eyes. May the Lord find us all prepared for the final crisis.]

STUDY NOTES

BY

Pastor Stephen P. Bohr

-THE GREAT EUPHRATES RIVER-

The Relevance of Revelation 16:12-16

Revelation 16:12-16 is to be understood as an enlargement and amplification of Revelation 9:13-21. The key that links these two passages together is the reference to the **River Euphrates**. These are the **only two places** in the book of Revelation where this river is explicitly named although we shall notice that it is strongly **alluded to** in the parallel passage of Revelation 12:13-15.

In order to understand the relationship between these two passages (Revelation 9:13-21 and 16:12-16) we must go back to Revelation 12 to get a little historical context. In Revelation 12:13-15 we are told that the dragon spewed water out of his mouth like a river with the intention of drowning God's faithful remnant during the 1260 years of Papal persecution.

> *"Now when the dragon saw that he had been cast to the earth, he persecuted the woman who gave birth to the male Child. But the woman was given two wings of a great eagle, that she might fly into the wilderness to her place, where she is nourished for a time and times and half a time, from the presence of the serpent. So the serpent spewed **water** out of his mouth like a **flood** after the woman that he might cause her to be carried away by **the flood**."* (Revelation 12:13-16)

In **Joshua 24:2, 3, 14, 15** the Euphrates River is described under the euphemism of "the Flood." **Genesis 15:18** depicts the Euphrates as "the great River" (see also Isaiah 8:7, 8; 17:12, 13; 59:19). Thus in Revelation 12 we are to understand **the** River (with the definite article in the Greek) or Flood that the dragon spews out his mouth as the river Euphrates.

Even though the Greek word translated "flood" and "river" in the New Testament are the same, many contemporary Bible versions have seen the relationship between "the flood" and "the river" and thus use them interchangeably. Notice only one example of many, the English Standard Version (ESV):

> *"The serpent poured water like a **river** out of his mouth after the woman, to sweep her away with a **flood**. 16 But the earth came to the help of the woman, and the earth opened its mouth and swallowed **the river** that the dragon had poured from his mouth."*

It will be noticed that the flow of the persecuting waters of the River Euphrates were dried up when the earth (the territory of the United States from which France later acquired many of the principles that led to the French Revolution) dried up the waters and provided refuge for the persecuted woman:

> *"But the earth helped the woman, and the earth opened its mouth and **swallowed up the flood** which the dragon had spewed out of his mouth."* (Revelation 12:16)

Revelation 12:17 explains that after persecution ceased for a while, the dragon will once again persecute the remnant of the Seed of the woman, in other words, the remnant of Jesus. This is another way of saying that the dragon will once again spew the waters of the symbolic River Euphrates out of his mouth.

Revelation 9:13-21 and 16:13-16 describe the time when the waters of the Euphrates which were dried up by the democratic principles of the United States and the French Revolution, will begin flowing once again when the deadly wound is healed. This will lead to oppressive enactments against God's people.

Revelation 17 further describes how the waters of the Euphrates will flow once again under the dominion of the harlot who sits on many waters. As long as the waters of the river flow all goes well for the harlot who is full of the blood of the saints (Revelation 17:6). But immediately after describing the meaning of the waters upon which the woman sits (Revelation 17:15), we are told that the kings will turn on her (Revelation 17:16). In other words, they will dry up on her (Revelation 16:12). This will be the final drying up of the Euphrates River.

Ellen White graphically describes the events that lead up to this climactic moment:

> "With shouts of triumph, jeering, and imprecation, throngs of evil men are about to rush upon their prey, when, lo, a dense blackness, deeper than the darkness of the night, falls upon the earth. Then a rainbow, shining with the glory from the throne of God, spans the heavens and seems to encircle each praying company. **The angry multitudes are suddenly arrested**. Their mocking cries die away. The objects of their murderous rage are forgotten. With fearful forebodings they gaze upon the symbol of God's covenant and long to be shielded from its overpowering brightness." <u>GC</u> pp. 635, 636.

A little further on in The Great Controversy, Ellen White amplifies what she means by the expression "the angry multitudes are suddenly arrested":

> "The people see that they have been deluded. They accuse one another of having led them to destruction; but all unite in heaping their bitterest condemnation upon the ministers. Unfaithful pastors have prophesied smooth things; they have led their hearers to make void the law of God and to persecute those who would keep it holy. Now, in their despair, these teachers confess before the world their work of deception. The multitudes are filled with fury. "We are lost!" they cry, "and you are the cause of our ruin;" and they turn upon the false shepherds. The very ones that once admired

them most will pronounce the most dreadful curses upon them. The very hands that once crowned them with laurels will be raised for their destruction. The swords which were to slay God's people are now employed to destroy their enemies. Everywhere there is strife and bloodshed." GC pp. 655, 656.

Thus Revelation 9:13-21 describes how the wicked angels united with wicked men are released at the Great River Euphrates to wreak global havoc on humanity and Revelation 16:12 describes the moment when they will eventually lose the support of the waters.

In summary

- Revelation 8:12; 12:13-15; 13:1-9: The persecuting waters of the symbolic River Euphrates flowed against God's people for 1260 years.

- Revelation 9:1-11; 12:16; 13:3, 10: The persecuting waters were dried up by the earth and by the French Revolution which acquired many of its principles from the "American Experiment".

- Revelation 9: 13-21; 12:17; 16:13-15; 17:1, 2, 15: The persecuting waters flow once again when the lamb-horned beast from the earth gives the sword back to the beast.

- Revelation 11:15-17; 16:12; 17:16: The persecuting waters dry up against Babylon for the final time when Jesus overcomes them and takes over the kingdoms of the world.

Comments on Verse 12

*"Then the sixth angel poured out his bowl on the **great river Euphrates**, and its **water was dried up**, so that the way of the **kings from the east** might be prepared."*

Note: We know for certain that the drying up of the Euphrates at the time of the sixth plague occurs after the close of probationary time because the seven bowls of God's unmingled wrath will be poured out after the close of probation (see Revelation 15:5-8 and 16:1)

Comments on Verse 13

*"And I saw three **unclean spirits** like frogs coming out of the **mouth** of the dragon, out of the mouth of the beast, and out of the mouth of the false prophet."*

Note: It is vitally important to underline that the events of verses 13-16 occur chronologically before those of verse 12. In other words, verse 12 describes the sixth plague after the close of probationary time while verses 13-16 describe the events that led up to that climax during probationary time.

The frog in ancient Egypt was considered the **God of immortality**. These unclean spirits are to be understood as **three symbolic fallen angels** (see Luke 4:33 where the evil spirits or angels that Jesus cast out are called demons). Notice that the three unclean spirits come out of the **mouth** of the dragon, the beast and the false prophet. It has been common among Adventists to interpret the dragon in this verse as spiritualism. But we notice that all three are controlled by spiritualism because the evil spirits come out of the mouths of all three. These three fallen angels (actually these three angels represent Satan's people who spread his lies) will **speak** on behalf of the counterfeit trinity. The dragon (or civil powers of the world according to Testimonies to Ministers, p. 39) is a parody of God the Father. The beast counterfeits the ministry of the Jesus Christ the Son. And the false prophet counterfeits the work of the Holy Spirit.

Notice how Ellen White connects the false prophet of Revelation 13:13 with the message of Revelation 16:13, 14:

> "*John, upon the Isle of Patmos, saw the things which should come upon the earth in the last days. **Revelation 13:13; 16:14**: "And he doeth great wonders, so that he maketh fire come down from heaven on the earth in the sight of men." "For they are the spirits of devils, working miracles, which go forth unto the kings of the earth and of the whole world, to gather them to the battle of that great day of God Almighty."* Con p. 89.

Comments on Verse 14

> "*For they are **spirits of demons**, performing signs which go out to the kings of the earth and of the whole world to gather them to the battle of that great day of God Almighty.*"

Note: The purpose of the message of these three symbolic angels and the signs they perform is to gather the kings of the earth and the whole world against God and His people. One can't help but see that under the sixth trumpet the angels at the four corners at the River Euphrates are released while here we are told that the spirits of demons go to the kings of the earth and the whole world.

Notice how Ellen White understands Revelation 16:13, 14:

> "*The Spirit of God **is** gradually withdrawing from the world. Satan **is** also mustering his forces of evil, going forth "unto the kings of the earth and of the whole world," to gather them under his banner, to be trained for "the battle of that great day of God Almighty*" [Revelation 16:14] LDE p. 249.
> "*The line of distinction between professed Christians and the ungodly is now hardly distinguishable. Church members love what the world loves and are ready to join with them, and Satan determines to **unite them in one body** and thus strengthen his cause by **sweeping all into the ranks of spiritualism**. Papists, who boast of miracles as a certain sign of the true church, will be readily deceived by this **wonder-**

*working power; and Protestants, having cast away the shield of truth, will also be deluded. **Papists**, **Protestants**, and **worldlings** will alike accept the form of godliness without the power, and they will see in this union a grand movement for the conversion of the world and the ushering in of the long-expected millennium."* <u>GC</u> p. 588, 589.

*"**Already** the inhabitants of the earth **are** marshalling under the leading of the prince of darkness."* <u>8T</u> p. 49.

*"Let us earnestly prepare for the conflict that is before us, for Satan's armies **are** marshalling for the **last great struggle**."* <u>19MR</u> p. 376.

*"In these perilous times, when the forces of evil **are** marshalling their **hosts** to thwart, if possible, the efforts of God's servants in the earth, it is vitally necessary for every laborer to walk humbly with God. Daily he is to maintain a close connection with heavenly agencies."* <u>North Pacific Union Gleaner, January</u> 27, 1910.

*"Satan **is** marshalling his **forces** for the **last great struggle** [the Battle of Armageddon], "to make war with the **remnant of her seed**, which keep the commandments of God, and have the testimony of Jesus Christ." If we would be true to God, we cannot escape the conflict. But we are not left in doubt as to the issue. Beyond the **smoke and heat** [smoke, fire and brimstone] of the **battle**, we behold "them that had gotten the victory" **standing on Mount Zion** with the Lamb."* <u>RH</u> July 18, 1882.

*"I was shown that a terrible condition of things **is** seen to exist in our world. The angel of mercy **is folding** her wings, **ready to depart**. **Already** the Lord's restraining power **is being withdrawn** from the earth, and the power of Satan **is working** in the world to **stir up the religious elements**, under the training of the great deceiver, to work with all deceivableness of unrighteousness in the children of disobedience. **Already** the inhabitants of the earth **are** marshalling under the leadings of the prince of darkness, and this is **only the beginning of the end**. The law of God **is** made void. We **see** and hear of confusion, perplexities, want and famine, earthquakes and floods; terrible outrages will be committed by men; passion not reason bears sway. The wrath of God is upon the inhabitants of a world that is fast becoming as corrupt as were the inhabitants of Sodom and Gomorrah. **Already** fires and floods are destroying thousands of human beings and the property that has been selfishly boarded by the oppression of the poor."* <u>8T</u> p. 49.

*"So it will be in the great final conflict of the controversy between righteousness and sin. While new life and light and power are descending from on high upon the disciples of Christ, a new life is springing up from beneath, and energizing the agencies of Satan. Intensity is taking possession of every earthly element. With a subtlety gained through centuries of conflict, the prince of evil works under a disguise. He appears clothed as an angel of light, and multitudes are "giving heed to **seducing spirits, and doctrines of devils**." 1 Timothy 4:1."* <u>DA</u> p. 257.

*"The light given me has been very forcible that **many would go out from us**, giving heed to seducing **spirits and doctrines of devils**. The Lord desires that every soul who claims to believe the truth shall have an intelligent knowledge of what is truth. False prophets will arise and will deceive many. Everything is to be shaken that can be shaken. Then does it not become everyone to understand the reasons for our faith? In place of having so many sermons, there should be a more close searching of the Word of God, opening the Scriptures text by text, and searching for the strong evidences that sustain the fundamental doctrines that have brought us where we now are, upon the platform of eternal truth."* Ev pp. 363, 364.

*"He has power to bring before men the appearance of their departed friends. The counterfeit is perfect; the familiar look, the words, the tone, are reproduced with marvelous distinctness. Many are comforted with the assurance that their loved ones are enjoying the bliss of heaven, and without suspicion of danger, they give ear "to **seducing spirits, and doctrines of devils**."* GC p. 552.

*"Many will be confronted by the **spirits of devils** personating beloved relatives or friends and declaring the most dangerous heresies. These visitants will appeal to our tenderest sympathies and will work miracles to sustain their pretensions. We must be prepared to withstand them with the Bible truth that the dead know not anything and that they who thus appear are the **spirits of devils**."* GC p. 560

*"Satan has long been preparing for his **final effort** to deceive **the world**. The foundation of his work was laid by the assurance given to Eve in Eden: "Ye shall not surely die." "In the day ye eat thereof, then your eyes shall be opened, and ye shall be as gods, knowing good and evil." Genesis 3:4, 5. Little by little he has prepared the way for his **masterpiece of deception in the development of spiritualism**. He has not yet reached the full accomplishment of his designs; but it will be reached in the **last remnant of time**. Says the prophet: "I saw three unclean spirits like frogs; . . . they are the **spirits of devils**, working miracles, which go forth unto the kings of the earth and of the whole world, to gather them to the battle of that great day of God Almighty." Revelation 16:13, 14. Except those who are kept by the power of God, through faith in His word, **the whole world will be swept into the ranks of this delusion**. The people are fast being lulled to a fatal security, to be awakened only by the outpouring of the wrath of God."* GC p. 561, 562.

In Early Writings, p. 87 Ellen White describes the importance of understanding the state of the dead:

*"I saw that the saints must get a thorough understanding of present truth, which they will be obliged to maintain from the Scriptures. They must understand the state of the dead; for the **spirits of devils** will yet appear to them, professing to be beloved friends and relatives, who will declare to them that the Sabbath has been changed, also other unscriptural doctrines.'* EW p. 87.

Under the description of a train she then goes on to explain the global nature of the work of these spirits of devils in the last days before the close of probation:

> "*I saw the rapidity with which this delusion was spreading. A train of cars was shown me, going with the speed of lightning. The angel bade me look carefully. I fixed my eyes upon the train. It seemed that **the whole world** was on board, that there could not be one left. Said the angel: 'They are binding in bundles ready to burn.' Then he showed me the conductor, who appeared like a stately, fair person, whom all the passengers looked up to and reverenced. I was perplexed and asked my attending angel who it was. He said, "It is Satan. He is the conductor in the form of an angel of light. He has taken **the world** captive. They are given over to **strong delusions**, to believe a lie, that they may be damned. This agent, the next highest in order to him, is the engineer, and other of his agents are employed in different offices as he may need them, and they are all going with lightning speed to perdition." EW pp. 88, 89.*

Ellen White then described another group that resisted this overwhelming delusion:

> "*I asked the angel if there were none left. He bade me look in an opposite direction, and I saw a little company traveling a narrow pathway. All seemed to be firmly united, bound together by the truth, in bundles, or companies. Said the angel: 'The third angel is binding, or sealing, them in bundles for the heavenly garner.' This little company looked careworn, as if they had passed through severe trials and conflicts. And it appeared as if the sun had just risen from behind a cloud and shone upon their countenances, causing them to look triumphant, as if their victories were nearly won.*"

J. A. Seiss in his Exposition of the Book of Revelation makes the following incisive remark about Revelation 16:13 that agrees fully with the concept of Ellen G. White:

> "*Modern spiritism, or so-called spiritualism, is only a revival of the same thing-a branch of the same iniquity. There doubtless is some reality in it; and it is confessedly a system of contact with the dead, whose spirits are invoked in various forms and methods, to teach wisdom; to dictate faith, religion, and life; to comfort and help in trouble and necessity; and to serve as saviors and as gods. It is demon-worship brought to life again. It claims to have vast multitudes of adherents, even among the baptized and nominally Christian. It is influencing whole communities of men and women, who are prepared to commit themselves body and soul, for time and eternity, into the care of these lying demon guides. It has made inroads upon people of all classes, and is received by many as a distinct and the only true religion. Its oracles are loud and hopeful in the prediction, that it will soon enlist to itself the **governments and reigning classes of the whole world**.*" J. A. Seiss, The Apocalypse: Exposition of the Book of Revelation, Electronic Database. Copyright © 1998, 2003, 2006 by Biblesoft, Incorporated

Comments on Verse 15

*"Behold, I am coming as a **thief**. Blessed is he who **watches**, and keeps his garments, lest he **walk naked** and they **see his shame**."*

Note: Revelation 3:18 uses the same language in the context of the Laodicean Message. But the original sources of this verse are to be found in the parables of Jesus in Matthew 24 and 25 and ultimately in Genesis 3:7, 15, 21.

It bears noting that it would do no good to give this warning to God's people during the period of the sixth plague after probation has closed because at this time probation will have closed and no one can change sides. In fact, verse 15 is God's warning to His people during probationary time to be faithful in resisting the spirits of devils by not gathering with the kings of the earth and the whole world.

Comments on Verse 16

*"And they **gathered** them together to the place called in Hebrew, Armageddon."*

Comments on Revelation 9:13-21

Verse 13:

*"Then the sixth angel sounded: And I heard a voice from the **four horns** of the **altar** which is **before God**. . ."*

Note: The fact that the voice comes from the four horns of the altar of incense is significant. The noted commentator, Albert Barnes, in agreement with virtually all others, stated:

"When it is said that this was 'before God,' the meaning is, that it was directly before or in front of the symbol of the divine presence in the most holy place." Albert Barnes, Electronic Database on Revelation 9:13.

It is obvious that God the Father is not the one who is speaking here from the four horns because the altar is "before God". The one who stands ministering at the altar of incense before God, presenting the prayers of the saints is none other than Jesus Christ Himself, the Mediator (I Timothy 2:5; Hebrews 7:25).

The horns of the altar of sacrifice in the court represented God's mercy and protective power in times of crisis when life was in danger (see I Kings 1:50, 51; 2:28) But if Israel had not repented from her sin, the horns were broken off (Amos 3:14, 15) and no mercy was extended. In the daily service blood was rubbed on the horns of the altar of sacrifice (Leviticus 4:24, 25; Jeremiah 17:1) to indicate that the confessed sins of Israel had been forgiven.

But the altar in view in Revelation 9:13 is not the altar of sacrifice but rather the altar of incense. As we have noted, the sixth trumpet relates to events that transpire between 1844 and the close of probation. Significantly, blood was rubbed on the horns of the altar of incense once a year for an atonement to cleanse the sanctuary from the sins of Israel that had entered there throughout the course of the year (Exodus 30:10; Leviticus 16:16-18).

Verse 14:

> ". . . saying to the sixth angel who had the trumpet: "**Release the four angels** who are **bound** at the **great river Euphrates**."

Note: Some have confused the four angels who hold the winds in Revelation 7:1-4 with these four angels that are released to wreak havoc on mankind. But these four angels are not the good angels that hold back the winds of strife in Revelation 7:1-4. These are evil angels that are waiting for God to release them so that they can wreak havoc on mankind as can be seen in the succeeding context. We are not to understand that only four angels cause the devastation. The number 4 represents universality or global extent (see Ezekiel 7:2; Matthew 24:31; Revelation 7:1, 2). In other words, Satan and his angels go to the whole world to wreak havoc beginning in 1844 but especially intensifying as the close of probation approaches.

The releasing of the winds in Revelation 7

Notably, God has three angels that gather the remnant on God's side and Satan has three angels who gather the wicked on his side. And both God and Satan have a fourth angel that brings a final great "revival" before the end.

As we have mentioned before, the only other time that the name "the great river Euphrates" appears in the book of Revelation is in chapter 16 and verse 12 so there must be a relationship between the sixth trumpet and the sixth plague.

Some have sought to find an application of the sixth trumpet to the phenomenal growth of radical Islam because the river Euphrates is mentioned. The question that begs to be asked is this: What hermeneutical principle allows them to say that the Euphrates in Revelation 9 is referring to a **literal geographical location** in the Middle East while the Euphrates of Revelation 16 refers to the multitudes of the **whole world** under the control of spiritual Babylon. In short, why is the Euphrates in Revelation 16:12 to be understood as symbolic while the one in Revelation 9 is to be understood as literal when both of them apply to the same period of the end time (sixth trumpet and sixth plague)? Are not geographical restrictions removed after the cross?

Going on to another point: If these evil angels need to be **released** it must mean that they were **restrained**. What is it that restrained these angels from manifesting their destructive power? Revelation 12:16 explains what restrained them—the earth. The papacy received a deadly wound in 1798 and the civil governments of the world have kept that wound in place. But when the beast from the earth gives civil power back to the papacy then the restraint will be removed and the final display of Satan's power will be manifested.

In this context we need to understand the meaning of II Thessalonians 2. While the civil power of the Roman Empire ruled, the papacy was restrained. But when the civil power of Rome was removed by the barbarian invasions, the papacy was allowed to wreak havoc during the Middle Ages under the leadership of Satan, the dragon (Revelation 12:13-15).

Notice the interesting terminology that is used by Cardinal Henry Edward Manning:

"[When the barbarians invaded the Roman Empire], The pontiffs found themselves alone, the sole fountains of order, peace, law, and safety. And from the hour of this providential **liberation**, when, by a divine intervention, the **chains fell off** from the hands of the successor of St. Peter, as once before from his own, no sovereign has ever reigned in Rome except the Vicar of Jesus Christ." (Henry Edward Manning, The Temporal Power of The Vicar of Jesus Christ, Preface, pp. xxviii, xxix. London: Burns and Lambert, 1862). Bold is mine.

Manning further explains:

"*It [the papacy] waited until such a time as God should break its **bonds** asunder, and **should liberate it from subjection to civil powers**, and **enthrone it** in the possession of a temporal sovereignty of its own.*" Henry Edward Manning, The Temporal Power of the Vicar of Jesus Christ (London: Burns & Lambert, second edition, 1862), pp. 11-13. Bold is mine

But in the French Revolution the restraint of the civil powers of the world was once again placed on the papacy. Democratic governments, led by the founding principles of the United States, flourished in the western world. The papacy has been restrained for the past 200 years because the civil powers of the world have not allowed the papacy to recover its lost power. Notice the following telling words from Malachi Martin, the Roman Catholic Jesuit priest:

"*[For] **fifteen hundred years** and more, Rome had kept as strong a hand as possible in each local community around the wide world. . . . By and large, and admitting some exceptions, that had been the Roman view until **two hundred years of inactivity** had been **imposed** upon the papacy **by the major secular powers** of the **world**.*" Quoted in Christianity Today (November 21, 1986), p. 26.

But when the lamb-horned beast restores the sword to this beast by making an image to and of it and commanding everyone to worship it and receive its mark, the restraint placed on the papacy will be removed and she will wreak havoc once again. Ellen White described what will lead to the unbinding of the papacy in the future:

"*Let the **restraints** now imposed by **secular governments** be removed and Rome be reinstated in her former power, and there would speedily be a **revival** of her tyranny and persecution.*" GC p. 564.

The sixth trumpet is primarily pointing to this period when the papacy, apostate Protestantism and the civil rulers of the world will unite to oppress God's people. But the process of gathering these powers against God's people began in 1844.

Verse 15:

"*So the **four** angels, who had been prepared for the **hour and day and month and year**, were released to kill a third of mankind.*"

166

Note: The number four in the Bible denotes universality or global extension. As we have noted, Revelation 16:14 tells us that the entire world will be gathered together in rebellion against God by the spirits of devils.

What is meant by the expression 'the hour, the day, the month and the year? A careful study of Revelation indicates that the hour is 'the hour of God's judgment' (14:6, 7). Other parts of Scripture indicate that the day refers to the 10th day, the month is Tishri (the seventh month), and the year is 1844 (see Leviticus 23:27; Daniel 8:14).

> *"The article [teen], once only before all the periods, implies that the hour in the day, and the day in the month, and the month in the year, and the year itself, had been definitely fixed by God."* <u>Jamieson, Fausset, and Brown Commentary</u>, Electronic Database. Copyright © 1997, 2003, 2005, 2006 by Biblesoft, Incorporated

The fact that this is not the final and total destruction of the wicked after the close of probation is indicated by the fact that only a third of humanity is killed by this devastating army of demons.

Verse 16:

> *"Now the number of the **army** of the horsemen was **two hundred million** [literally: 'twice ten thousand times ten thousand']; I **heard the number of them**. . ."*

Note: The number of the enemy is huge in comparison to the 144,000 of Revelation 7:4. These are the **only two verses** in Revelation where John uses the expression *"I heard the number"* so they must be related in some way. Revelation 7:4 is transpiring during the sixth seal and Revelation 9:16 is occurring during the period of the sixth trumpet. Notice how Ellen White contrasts the number of God's followers with those of Satan:

> *"The remnant church will be brought into great trial and distress. Those who keep the commandments of God and the faith of Jesus, will feel the ire of the dragon and his hosts. Satan **numbers the world as his subjects**; he has gained control of the apostate churches; but here is a **little company** that are resisting his supremacy. If he could blot them from the earth, his **triumph would be complete**."* <u>9T p. 231</u>.

Revelation 18:1-4: the whole point is to call the 144,000 out of Babylon so that they can join the remnant.

Verse 17:

> *"And thus <u>I saw</u> the horses in the vision: those who **sat on them** had breastplates of **fiery red**, hyacinth **blue**, and sulfur **yellow** and the heads of the horses were like the heads of **lions**; and out of their **mouths** came fire, smoke, and brimstone."*

Note: This is clearly an army that rises from hell. These are the same spirits of demons in **Revelation 16:14** who are released to gather the kings of the earth and the whole world against God's people. They are also the demons that are mentioned in connection with the fourth angel's message in **Revelation 18:2, 3**.

Clearly we have here a picture of Satan and the wicked which are always portrayed in the context of the lake of fire (Psalm 11:6; Ezekiel 38:22; Revelation 14:10; 19:20; 20:10; 21:8).The fire and smoke coming out of the mouths of the horses reminds us of the story of Leviathan in the book of Job where he has smoke and fire come from His mouth (Job 41:19-21, 31-34). Elsewhere in the Bible Leviathan is identified with the dragon, the ancient serpent, the devil and Satan (Isaiah 27:1; Revelation 12:7-9)

Verse 18:

*"By these **three plagues a third** of mankind was killed — by the fire and the smoke and the brimstone which came out of their **<u>mouths</u>.**"*

Notice that what comes out of the **mouth** is what kills the wicked. In the book of Revelation, fire, brimstone and smoke are identified with those who worship the beast and his image and receive the mark. Notably Revelation 16:13 explains that the evil spirits come out of the mouth of the threefold union.

Verse 19:

*"For their power is in their **<u>mouth</u>** and in their **<u>tails</u>** for their tails are like **<u>serpents</u>**, having heads; and with them they **<u>do harm</u>**."*

Note: The horses have mouths like **lions**. Elsewhere in the Bible Babylon is portrayed as a devouring lion (Daniel 7:2) as is its king, Nebuchadnezzar (Jeremiah 4:7) and Satan is described as a devouring lion who seeks whom he may devour (James 5:8).

Revelation 16:13, 14 clarifies that the false doctrines of the three counterfeit angels come out of the mouth and they gather the wicked for the final battle against God. The tail is a symbol of lies (Revelation 12:34; John 8:44; Isaiah 9:14). Notice that the mouth is in the tail.

Verse 20:
*"But the **<u>rest</u>** of mankind, who were not killed by these plagues, **<u>did not repent</u>** of the works of their hands, that they should not worship **<u>demons</u>** [Revelation 18:2, 3], and **<u>idols</u>** of gold, silver, brass, stone, and wood, which can neither see nor hear nor walk."*

Note: The expression "idols of gold, silver, brass, stone, and wood, which can neither see nor hear nor walk" comes almost verbatim from Daniel 5:23. Daniel 5 is discussing the fall of Babylon when the Euphrates was dried up. Thus three passages are linked: The fall of Babylon in Daniel 5, the drying up of the Euphrates in Revelation 16:12 and the sixth trumpet of Revelation 9:20.

Verse 21:

*"And they did not repent of their **murders** or their **sorceries** or their **sexual immorality** or their **thefts**."*

Note: Revelation 17:6; 18:20, 24 describes Babylon as a **murderer** of God's people
Revelation 18:23 refers to the **sorceries** of Babylon as one of the reasons for her fall
Revelation 17:2 portrays the adultery or **fornication** of the harlot with the kings of the earth
Revelation 18:10-13 describes this system as **greedy** and enslaving, stealing from the poor and favoring the rich. This greediness is described in James 5:1-8.

Summary of the Sixth Trumpet

Since 1844 both armies have been in the process of being gathered. God's three angels have gathered the righteous while Satan's three angels have gathered the wicked. The sixth trumpet in Revelation 9:13-21 describes the gathering of the wicked for battle while Revelation 10 describes the gathering of the righteous on God's side.

The only three places in Revelation where the word "demons" appears is in Revelation 16:14; 9:20 and 18:1-5. Furthermore, the only place where the great river Euphrates appears is Revelation 9 and Revelation 16. Therefore we know that there is a link between these two passages.

Some choice Ellen G. White comments:

"Satan has long been preparing for his final effort to deceive the world. The foundation of his work was laid by the assurance given to Eve in Eden: "Ye shall not surely die." "In the day ye eat thereof, then your eyes shall be opened, and ye shall be as gods, knowing good and evil." Genesis 3:4, 5. Little by little he has prepared the way for his masterpiece of deception in the development of spiritualism. He has not yet reached the full accomplishment of his designs; but it will be reached in the last remnant of time. Says the prophet: "I saw three unclean spirits like frogs; . . . they are the spirits of devils, working miracles, which go forth unto the kings of the earth and of the whole world, to gather them to the battle of that great day of God Almighty." Revelation 16:13, 14. Except those who are kept by the power of God, through faith in His word, **the whole world will be swept into the ranks of this delusion**." DD p. 24.

"Fearful sights of a supernatural character will soon be revealed in the heavens, in token of the power of miracle-working demons. The **spirits of devils will go forth to the kings of the earth and to the whole world**, to fasten them in deception, and **urge them on to unite with Satan in his last struggle against the government of heaven**. By these agencies, rulers and subjects will be alike deceived. Persons will arise pretending to be Christ Himself, and claiming the title and worship which belong to the world's Redeemer. They will perform wonderful miracles of healing and will profess to have revelations from heaven contradicting the testimony of the Scriptures." DD p. 41.

"This scripture points forward to a time when the announcement of the fall of Babylon, as made by the second angel of Revelation 14 (verse 8), is to be repeated, with the additional mention of the corruptions which have been entering the various organizations that constitute Babylon, **since that message was first given, in the summer of 1844. A terrible condition of the religious world** is here described.

With every rejection of truth the minds of the people will become darker, their hearts more stubborn, until they are entrenched in an **infidel hardihood**. In defiance of the warnings which God has given, they will continue to trample upon one of the precepts of the Decalogue, until they are led to persecute those who hold it sacred. Christ is set at nought in the contempt placed upon His word and His people. As the teachings of spiritualism are accepted by the churches, **the restraint imposed upon the carnal heart is removed** [the evil angels are released], and the profession of religion will become a cloak to conceal the basest iniquity. A belief in **spiritual manifestations** opens the door to seducing spirits and doctrines of devils, and thus **the influence of evil angels will be felt in the churches.**" <u>GC</u> pp. 603, 604.

"Spiritualism is about to take the **world captive**. There are many who think that Spiritualism is upheld through trickery and imposture; but this is far from the truth. Superhuman power is working in a variety of ways, and few have any idea as to what will be the manifestations of Spiritualism in the future. The foundation for the success of Spiritualism has been laid in the assertions that have been made from the pulpits of our land. **The ministers have proclaimed, as Bible doctrines, falsehoods that have originated from the arch-deceiver.** The doctrine of consciousness after death, of the spirits of the dead being in communion with the living, has no foundation in the Scriptures, and yet this theory is affirmed as truth. Through this false doctrine the way has been opened for **the spirits of devils to deceive the people** in representing themselves as the dead. **Satanic agencies** personate the dead, and thus bring souls into captivity. **Satan has a religion**; he has a synagogue and devout worshipers. To swell the ranks of his devotees he uses all manner of deception." <u>ST</u> May 28, 1894.

"**Four mighty angels hold back** the powers of this earth till the servants of God are sealed in their conflict, but they are **held in check** by the angels. When this **restraining power is removed** there will come a time of trouble and anguish. Deadly instruments of warfare will be invented. Vessels with their living cargo will be entombed in the great deep. All who have not the spirit of truth will unite under the leadership of satanic agencies, but they are to be **kept under control** till the time shall come for the great battle of Armageddon." <u>LDE</u> p. 238.

"We need to study the pouring out of the **seventh vial** [Revelation 16:17-21: Post-probationary]. The **powers of evil** will not yield up the conflict without a struggle. But Providence has a part to act in the battle of Armageddon. When the earth is **lighted with the glory of the angel of Revelation eighteen [probationary]**, the **religious elements, good and evil, will awake from slumber**, and the armies of the living God will take the field." <u>LDE</u> p. 251.

"The battle of Armageddon is soon to be fought. He on whose vesture is written the name, King of kings and Lord of lords, **leads forth the armies of heaven on white horses**, clothed in fine linen, clean and white [Revelation 19:11-16]." <u>LDE</u> p. 251.

APPENDIX I

Evidence from Scripture and History of the Second Coming of Christ, about the year 1843

Lecture VIII.

William Miller

REV. 8:13

"And I beheld and heard an angel flying through the midst of heaven, saying, with a loud voice, Woe, woe, woe, to the inhabitants of the earth, by reason of the other voices of the trumpet of the three angels which are yet to sound."

In prophetical scripture, the sounding of trumpets is always used to denote the downfall of some empire, nation, or place, or some dreadful battle, which may decide the fate of empires, nations, or places. At the fall of Jericho, the trumpet was the instrument, in the hands of the priest of the mighty God of Jacob, which cast down her walls, destroyed the city, and a curse pronounced against the man that should ever build up her walls again. Again, the trumpet was the instrument by which Gideon put to flight the armies of the aliens. And the prophet Amos says, "Shall a trumpet be blown in the city, and the people not be afraid?" Therefore we may reasonably conclude that a trumpet is the harbinger of destructive wars, and the dissolution of empires, states, or the earth, as the case may be. The seven trumpets mentioned in Revelation, the three last of which are mentioned in our text, indicate the final overthrow of the powers spoken of in the prophecy. The four first had their accomplishment in the destruction of the Jews and their dispersion, in the fall of imperial Rome, in the overthrow of the Asiatic kingdom, and in the taking away of Pagan rites and ceremonies.

The last three trumpets will claim our attention in [116] this discourse; the first four having their accomplishment under Rome Pagan; to the last three under Rome Papal. These three trumpets and three woes are a description of the judgments that God has sent and will send on this Papal beast, the abomination of the whole earth. Therefore we see the propriety of the language of our text, "Woe, woe, woe, to the inhabitants of the earth," meaning the worshippers of this Papal beast, the followers of this abomination. The fifth trumpet alludes to the rise of the Turkish empire under Ottoman, at the downfall of the Saracens. Ottoman uniting under his government the four contending nations of Mahometans, which had long contended for the power during the reign of the Saracen empire, viz., the Saracens, Tartars, Arabs, and Turks. These, all being by profession Mahometans, were ready to follow any daring leader to conquer and drive out from Asia (and even make excursion into Europe) all who professed the Christian faith. They, having embraced the errors of that fallen star, Mahomet, whose principles were promulgated by conquest and the sword, became one and perhaps the only barrier to the spread of the Papal doctrine and power in the eastern world. Here the Roman Church had long held a powerful sway over the minds and consciences of the Christian or Greek church in the east, by the aid of the eastern emperor at Constantinople. But the Turks or Ottomans, whom the Lord suffered to rise up in Bithynia, on or near the head waters of the Euphrates, as a scourge against this Papal abomination, now became a check to the Roman power; and from this time we may reasonably date the declension of Papal authority. Therefore on the sounding of the fifth trumpet, Rome Papal began to show a weakness which in every succeeding age has been more and more manifested, until her civil power has crumbled to ruin, and her ecclesiastical assumption must sink, at the sounding of the seventh trump, to rise no more forever.

In the description of these trumpets we shall be able to apply the prophecy, as the writer believes, to those events designed by the vision which John saw.

Rev. 9:1. "And the fifth angel sounded, and I saw [117] a star fall from heaven unto the earth; and to him was given the key of the bottomless pit." After the downfall of Pagan Rome, and the rise of the anti-Christians abomination, Mahomet promulgated a religion which evidently came from the bottomless pit; for it fostered all the wicked passions of the human heart, such as war, murder, slavery, and lust.

2d verse, "And he opened the bottomless pit, and there arose a smoke out of the pit as the smoke of a great furnace; and the sun and the air was darkened by reason of the smoke of the pit." The figures used in the text are, the bottomless pit, which denote the theories of men or devils, that have no foundation in the word of God. Smoke denotes the errors from such doctrine, which serve to blind the eyes of men, that they cannot see the truth. As the smoke of a great furnace shows the great extent or effect of this error over the world. The sun denotes the gospel, which is the great luminary of the moral world. The air denotes the moral influence on the mind, which is commonly called piety. As air supports or gives to the lungs animation in the physical world, so does the piety of the heart to the moral. This, then, is the true sentiment of this passage. And by reason of the Mahometan errors which would be believed or followed by a great multitude, the gospel and the pious influence of the same would be in a great measure hid or lost to the world.

3d verse, "And there came out of the smoke locusts upon the earth; and unto them was given power, as the scorpions of the earth have power." By these locusts I understand armies. See Joel, 1st and 2nd chapters. Therefore I should read this text thus: And there came out from these Mahometan followers large armies, which should have great power to execute the judgments of God on this anti-Christian beast, which had filled the earth with her abominations.

4th verse, "And it was commanded them that they should not hurt the grass of the earth, neither any green thing, neither any tree, but only those men which have not the seal of God in their foreheads." By grass, green [118] things, and trees, Ps. 72:16, Hosea 14:8, I understand the true church, or people of God. By those men having not the seal of God, &c., I understand the anti- Christian church, or Papal Rome. Then this would be the sense: And it was commanded them that they should not hurt the true church, or people of God, but only the anti-Christian best, or powers subject to her.

5th verse, "And to them it was given that they should not kill them, but that they should be tormented five months; and their torment was as the torment of a scorpion, when he striketh a man." To kill is to destroy. Five months is in prophecy 150 years. To torment as a scorpion, &c., is to make sudden incursions and irruption into the country, &c. Then this is the sentiment to me conveyed in the text: And the Turkish armies would not have power to destroy the Papal powers for 150 years, but would make sudden and quick incursions into their territories, and harass and perplex the nations under the Papal control.

6th verse, "And in those days shall men seek death, and shall not find it; and shall desire to die, and death shall flee from them." About this time the Greek church, in Constantinople, was so harassed by the Papal authority, that it gave rise to a saying among them, that they "had rather see the Turkish turban on the throne of the Eastern Empire, than the Pope's tiara." And anyone who has read the history of the 14th century, will see that this text was literally accomplished.

7th verse, "And the shapes of the locusts were like unto horses prepared unto battle; and on their heads were, as it were, crowns like gold, and their faces were as the faces of men." In this verse we have a description of the Turkish armies. In the first place they are represented as being all horsemen. This was true with the Turks, and no other kingdom since Christ's time, that we have any knowledge of, whose armies were all horsemen. They wore on their heads yellow turbans, which can only apply to the Turks, looking like crowns of gold.

8th verse, "And they had hair as the hair of women, and their teeth were as the teeth of lions." They wore [119] long hair attached to their turbans, and they fought with javelins like the teeth of lions.

9th verse, "And they had breastplates, as it were breastplates of iron; and the sound of their wings was as the sound of chariots of many horses running to battle." By their breastplates I understand shields, which the Turks carried in their battles; and history tells us that when they charged an enemy, they made a noise upon them like the noise of chariot wheels.

10th verse, "And they had tails like unto scorpions, and there were stings in their tails; and their power was to hurt men five months." The Turkish horsemen had each a cimeter which hung in a scabbard at their waist, that they used in close combat after they had discharged their javelins, with which they were very expert, severing a man's or even a horse's head at a blow. And from the time that the Ottoman power or Turkish empire was first established in Bithynia, until the downfall of the Greek or Eastern Empire, when the Turks took Constantinople, was five prophetic months, or one hundred and fifty years.

11th verse, "And they had a king over them, which is the angel of the bottomless pit, whose name in the Hebrew tongue is Abaddon, but in the Greek tongue hath his name Apollyon." The Turkish government had a king when they began, as before mentioned, and he was a follower of the Mahometan faith, and truly a servant or messenger of this doctrine of the bottomless pit. The name of their first king, who is styled in history the founder of the Turkish empire, was Othoman or Ottoman, from whom the empire took its name, and has been called to this day the Ottoman empire. And great has been the destruction which this government has executed upon the world; and well may this empire be styled Destroyer, in prophecy the signification of Abaddon or Apollyon.

12 verse, "One woe is past; and behold, there come two woes more hereafter." This closes the fifth trumpet and the first woe, commencing at the foundation of the Turkish empire in Bithynia, in the year A. D. 1298, and lasting five prophetic months, or 150 years, which carries us down to the year A.D. 1448. When we take into [120] view the object and design of God in sending this judgment or scourge upon the men who have not the seal of God on their foreheads; the anti-Christian beast, who profess to be Christians, but are not; when we compare the history of those times with the prophecy–we have been examining, and the events which have transpired concerning the Ottoman empire, with the descriptive character given of them in this prophecy,–we cannot, I think, hesitate for a moment to apply the fulfillment of this trumpet and woe, to these events, time, and place; and must be led to admire the agreement between the prophecy and fulfillment, and to believe this book of Revelation to be indicted by the unerring wisdom of the Divine Spirit; for no human forethought could have so exactly described these events, dress, manners, customs, and mode of warfare 1200 years beforehand, except the wisdom of God had assisted him. And if these things are revealed by God himself unto us, surely no one will dare to say that it is non-essential whether we believe this part of the revealed will of God or not. Shall God speak and man disregard it? Forbid it, O Father; and let us have "ears to hear what the Spirit saith to the churches."

We shall now follow the revelation of God into the sixth trumpet and second woe; and may we have the Spirit of God to assist us and lead our minds into the truth of these things.

13th verse, "And the sixth angel sounded, and I heard a voice from the four horns of the golden altar which is before God," 14th verse, "Saying to the sixth angel which had the trumpet, loose the four angels which are bound in the great river Euphrates." By the sounding of the trumpet, I understand the commencing of those judgments which were poured out upon the earth under this trumpet; and by the "voice from the four horns of the golden alter," the agreement of all the powers of heaven and earth to execute the design of God in this thing. By losing the four angels which are bound in the great river Euphrates, I understand that God was now about to suffer the four principal nations of which the Ottoman empire was composed, which had in vain [121] attempted to subdue the Eastern Empire at Constantinople, and made but little progress in conquering Europe, now to take Constantinople, and to overrun and subdue one third part of Europe, which was the fact about the middle of the fifteenth century.

15th verse, "And the four angels were loosed, which were prepared for an hour, and a day, and a month, and a year, to slay the third part of men." The four angels, we may reasonably conclude, are a representation of the four nations that had embraced the Mahometan religion, and were now under the control of the Ottoman, viz., Turks, Tartars, Arabs, and Saracens. The time expressed in the last-mentioned verse is 391 years and 15 days. "To slay the third part of men," is to destroy and conquer one third part of the governments or kingdoms of which the Papal beast had the control, which was true in the end.

16th verse, "And the number of the army of the horsemen was two hundred thousand thousand; and I heard the number of them." In this verse the precise number of the army of horsemen is given, for John tells us "he heard the number of them." And if we should understand the prophet to mean, as some suppose he does, 200,000, multiplied by a 1000, then the sum total

would be 200,000,000, which would be more men than were ever on our earth at one time capable of bearing arms; therefore I believe this is not the meaning of the prophet, neither do I think that it was a succession of armies during the whole period of 391 years, making the sum total of 200,000,000, for this, too, would be incredible; for allowing a standing army of 15,385,000 to be recruited every 30 years, it would only make the two hundred millions; and this sum would be more than five times the number of all the standing armies in the known world. And from these consideration I have for myself given this construction, that the prophet John heard the number of 200,000 repeated, or twice told, which would make an army of 400,000 horsemen; and this would not be incredible. And what is to me strong proof of the fact is, that the history informs us that Mahomet II, came against Constantinople about the year A. D. 1450, with [122] an army of 400,000* horsemen, and after a long siege took the city in the year 1453, and destroyed the Eastern Empire, which had stood more than ten centuries from its foundation by Constantine.

17th verse: "And thus I saw the horses in the vision, and them that sat on them, having breastplates of fire, and of jacinth and brimstone; and the heads of the horses were as the heads of lions, and out of their mouths issued fire, and smoke, and brimstone." 18th verse, "By these three was the third part of men killed, by the fire, and by the smoke, and by the brimstone, which issued out of their mouths." 19th verse, "For their power is in their mouth, and in their tails; for their tails were like unto serpents, and had heads, and with them they do hurt." In these verses which we have now read, we are plainly informed that it was an army of horses, and men on them, which John saw in the vision. And the implements and manner of fighting, such as the trapping of their horses, and the instruments offensive and defensive, gun powder and guns, are as exactly described as any person could describe it without knowing the name by which we describe it at the present day. Fire, smoke, and brimstone, would be the most visible component parts of gunpowder. Fire and smoke we should see, and brimstone we should smell. And who ever saw an army of horsemen engaged in an action but would think of John's description, "out of their mouths issued fire, and smoke, and brimstone," and in the breech of the guns were bullets, "like heads, and with these they do hurt"? Every part of this description is exactly applicable to an army of horsemen with fire-arms; and what is equally strong in the evidence is, that guns and fire-arms were invented but a short time previous to this trump-sounding, and the Turks claimed the honor (if honor it can be called) of inventing gun powder and guns: and it is equally evident by the history that guns were first used by the Turks at the taking of Constantinople, they having one single cannon that took 70 yoke of oxen to draw it at the siege, as says Dr. Gill on this passage.

[123] 20th verse, "And the rest of the men which were not killed by these plagues yet repented not of the works of their hands, that they should not worship devils, and idols of gold, and silver, and brass, and stone, and of wood, which neither can see, nor

hear, nor walk." 21st verse, "Neither repented they of their murders, nor of their sorceries, nor of their fornication, nor of their thefts." In these verses, we have the character of the persons or government on whose account these plagues were sent. In the first place, they are represented as idolaters, as worshipping devils, idols of gold, &c., full of murder, sorceries, fornication, and theft. This exactly agrees with the description John has given of the "woman sitting on the scarlet-colored best, full of names of blasphemy, having seven heads and ten horns. And the woman was arrayed in purple and scarlet color, and decked with gold, and precious stones, and pearls, having a golden cup in her hand full of abominations and filthiness of her fornication. And upon her forehead was a name written, Mystery, Babylon the Great, the Mother of Harlots, and the abominations of the earth." So we see that the fifth and sixth trumpets, and the two first woes, were sent as the judgments of God upon this anti-Christian best, and clearly shows the decline of the power which she had exercised over the kings of the earth and the people of God for more than eight centuries, to the commencing of the sixth trumpet, when the Turks were let loose upon those kingdoms under the control of Papacy, conquered all Asia and about one third part of Europe, and were in the end the means of opening the eyes of many of the inhabitants of the world to see that the Pope's pretension of being the vicegerent of God was not well founded; for, if he could not foresee and resist the inroads of the Turks,–that infidel nation,–surely he could not perform those great miracle which he pretended to perform in order to support his ecclesiastical and civil power: and individuals, and afterward nations, began to disregard his authority, excommunications, and bulls, until his power is now but a little more than a bishop of Rome.

Here we see the wonder-working ways of our God, [124] who, in wisdom and providence, suffers the corrupt and infidel nations of the earth to pull down each other, and to bring about his purposes and designs, and will eventually destroy all the kingdoms of the earth, by such means, and in such ways, as the prophets have foretold; and whoever lives until the year 1839 will see the final dissolution of the Turkish empire, for then the sixth trumpet will have finished its sounding, which, if I am correct, will be the final overthrow of the Ottoman power. And then will the seventh trump and last woe begin, under which the kingdoms of the earth and the anti-Christian beast will be destroyed, the power of darkness chained, the world cleansed, and the church purified.

See the 10th chapter of Revelation, 5th, 6th, and 7th verses, "And the angel which I saw stand upon the sea and upon the earth lifted up his hand to heaven." This is the angel of the covenant, the great Mediator. See the first verse, "And I saw another mighty angel come down from heaven, clothed with a cloud." So is Christ to come in the clouds with power and great glory. "And a rainbow was upon his head." This shows plainly that it is Christ; for the rainbow is a token of the covenant. "And his face was as it were the sun." The same as when he was transfigured, Matt 17:2, "And his feet as pillars of fire." See Rev. 1:15, "His feet like unto fine brass, as if they burned in a furnace." Surely this must be Christ. "And he had in his hand a little book open." None could open the book but the lion of the tribe of Judah–another strong proof that the angel in Rev. 10:5 is Christ. And who but Christ could stand upon the sea and upon the earth, and lift "up his hand to heaven, and swear by Him that liveth forever and ever, who created heaven and the things that therein are, and the sea and the things which are therein, that there should be time no longer"? that is, gospel or mediatorial time should cease. No more time for mercy; no more Spirit to strive with you, sinner; no more means of grace; no more repentance unto life; no more hopes of heaven; for Jesus has sworn by himself, because he could swear by no greater, that your day of [125] probation "should be no longer." For "he that is filthy shall be filthy still." The Bridegroom has come, and shut the door. I know, sinner, you will then cry, Lord, Lord, open unto us; but he will say unto you, Depart from me, ye workers of iniquity, for I know you not: when I called to you to open the door of your hearts, that I might come in and sup with you, ye refused; when I stretched out my arm all the long day of the gospel, ye regarded it not; I will now laugh at your calamity, and mock when your fear cometh. Then will the angel, flying through the midst of heaven, cry, with a loud voice, Woe, woe, woe to the inhabitants of the earth; for, when the last woe is pronounced, and "in the days of the voice of the seventh angel, when he shall begin to sound, the mystery of God should be finished, as he hath declared to his servants the prophets." "The second woe is past, and behold the third woe cometh quickly. And the seventh angel sounded; and there were great voices in heaven, saying, The kingdoms of this world are become the kingdoms of our Lord and of his Christ, and he shall reign forever and ever," Rev. 11:14,15. By these passages we learn that, when the sixth trumpet has done sounding, when the second woe is past, then the third woe comes quickly. The seventh trump begins to sound; the mystery of God is finished–all that has been spoken by the prophets, that is, all that concerns the kingdom of Christ; for then will be brought to pass the saying, Death is swallowed up in victory; for, when the last trumpet shall sound, the dead in Christ shall be raised: "For as in Adam all died, even so in Christ shall all be made alive." "But every man in his own order. Christ the first fruits, afterward they that are Christ's at his coming." "The first man is of the earth, earthy; the second Man is the Lord from heaven." "As is the earthy, such are they also that are earthy; and as is the heavenly, such are they also that are heavenly." "And as we have borne the image of the earthy, we shall also bear the image of the heavenly. Now, this I say, brethren, that flesh and blood cannot inherit the kingdom of God; neither doth corruption inherit incorruption." "Behold, I show you a mystery: [126] we shall not all sleep, but we shall all be changed, in a moment, in the twinkling of an eye, at the last trump, for the trumpet shall sound, and the dead shall be raised incorruptible, and we shall be changed; for this corruptible must put on incorruption, and this mortal must put on immortality." "Then will be brought to pass the saying that is written, Death is swallowed up in victory," 1 Cor. 15:22-54."[281]

---

[281] William Miller, *Evidence from Scripture and History of the Second Coming of Christ, about the year 1843; exhibited in a course of lectures.* (Boston, MA: 1842), 115-126.

APPENDIX II

The Probability of the Second Coming of Christ About A.D. 1843

Josiah Litch

PREFACE

The writer would here acknowledge himself indebted to Mr. William Miller's valuable Lectures, for the leading ideas of the following pages. Although the views of Mr. M. may not be correct on every point, yet, so far as his calculation of time is concerned, the writer can but consider his plan irrefutable. The above-named lectures are worthy the attentive perusal of all lovers of the sacred Scriptures. The writings of Bishop Newton, and of Faber on the Prophecies, have furnished some most valuable information. Also, Smith's Key to Revelations has been read with deep interest, and has afforded many new ideas of the meaning of that deeply interesting book. The [iv] historical authorities who have been principally consulted, are Rollin's Ancient History, Gibbon's Decline and Fall, Sabine's Ecclesiastical History, Mosheim's Ecclesiastical History, and Milner's do., Life of Napoleon, by an American Citizen, Mignet's French Revolution, Hawkins' Ottoman Empire, &c. Several valuable Commentaries have also been consulted on the subjects here discussed. In the interpretation of figurative language, the most approved authors have been consulted, and generally followed. But in some instances the writer has found reasons for dissenting from the views of all authors with whom he has met.

The motive which has called forth this work may be asked. The reply is, the principal reason of its publication is, the scarceness of Mr. Miller's book, together with the importance of the subject. This work, however, is not designed to supercede any existing work on the Prophecies. The writer flatters himself, that he has presented some new views on the subject, and arranged and illustrated former views and facts, so as to render them more clear and striking; however, on that point a candid public must judge.

[v] All pretensions to a spirit of prophecy, or to infallibility in the interpretation of prophecy, are utterly disclaimed. It has often been asked, - If the event does not come out as you believe, what will you then think? Will it not destroy your confidence in the Bible? To this it is replied, Not at all; the writer has, in the course of his research on this subject, seen so much which has been literally fulfilled as predicted, that although all he has written on this subject should prove to have been founded in ignorance, he cannot doubt but the prophecies have a meaning, and that they were written by the unerring Spirit of the Holy One, and will, in due time, be fulfilled. But, at the same time, he must be permitted to express his firm conviction, that these calculations are founded in truth, and will stand the ordeal they must very soon pass – the unerring test of time. In conclusion, a candid examination of the subject is requested of the reader, before judgment is rendered; he is then at perfect liberty to

receive or reject, as the strength of the evidence will dictate. For the purity of his motive in presenting to the public the following, the writer must appeal to that day, of [vi] which he writes. He believes that those, even, who do not accord with the peculiar views herein maintained, will find themselves amply compensated for their pains, in giving the book an attentive perusal.

To God, and the word of his grace, the author would now commend himself, his work, and all who may read; praying that the spirit of wisdom and of a sound mind may be granted us, to lead us into all truth. The exhortation of the king of Judah (2 Chron. xx. 20) may perhaps be appropriate on this occasion. "Hear me, O Judah, and ye inhabitants of Jerusalem; believe in the Lord your God, so shall ye be established; believe his prophets, so shall ye prosper." J.L. *May 30, 1838.*

CHAPTER VI.
SECTION I.

We have now again been brought down to the Great Day, and find the redeemed family before the throne of God, and He that sitteth on the throne dwelling among them. Now a new series of events are about to take place.

Rev. viii. 2. "The seven angels, having seven trumpets, stood before God. And the angels prepared themselves to sound."

This trumpet sounded about A.D. 64, when Nero commenced his persecutions against Christians. This persecution was of short duration, for Nero died A.D. 68, which put an end to the calamities [147] of that persecution, by which, for four years, Christians suffered every indignity and torment, throughout the Roman empire, which ingenious cruelty could invent. The torments are represented as hail and fire mingled with blood. Some of the sufferers are said, by historians, to have been wrapped in combustible clothes, and in the darkness of night they were set on fire. Others were fastened to crosses, and torn to pieces by wild beasts. Thus, like a dreadful tempest of hail, fire, and blood, this persecution burst upon the church. The third part of trees was burnt up, and all green grass was burnt up. By trees, and green grass, living soul, living thing, &c., I understand Christians of various degrees of eminence to be meant. By a third part of any thing, as the expression is so frequently used in this book, I understand a large number, but not all, or even the majority.

It is believed, that in this persecution St. Paul and St. Peter both suffered martyrdom, and with them many other eminent ministers – I know not but one third, - also, an incredible number of Christians, so that it might almost literally be said, that every green thing was burnt up.

"The second angel sounded; and as it were a great mountain burning with fire was cast into the sea; and the third part of the sea became blood." Sea denotes any country in a state of agitation or commotion. The sea here spoken of was the Roman empire. This trumpet sounded when the [148] persecution of the Christians commenced under Domitian, A.D. 94, which continued to rage for most of the time with greater or less rigor, until the days of Constantine, A.D. 312. During that period, it is probable that one third of the Christians who lived, were put to death as martyrs. Ships would mean, if the figure is carried out, churches; one third of these were destroyed. We have no data to get the exact proportion of Christians and churches which suffered;

but propably, if the truth could be known, it would not fall much short of one third of the whole number who lived during that period.

"The third angel sounded, and there fell a great star from heaven, burning as it were a lamp." A fallen star, in figurative language, denotes an apostate minister of the Gospel. This angel sounded as the Arian heresy made its appearance, in the reign of Constantine. Arius fell into grievous and fatal errors, yet he maintained his moral character unimpeachable, burning as it were a lamp. Although he had fallen on an important point of doctrine, yet he shone, or shed some light – if not the brilliancy of a star, yet as the more dim light of a lamp. Says Dr. Miller, "Had he not possessed some apparent virtues, he would not have been able to form so great a design, nor to have proved so formidable an adversary. He who does much mischief in deceiving souls, must at least have a fair appearance of morals." This star fell on a third part of the rivers and fountains of waters. By rivers and fountains of waters, [149] we may understand those streams and fountains of water which feed or are tributary to the sea. The Arian heresy spread itself all over the Christian world, and probably one third of the provinces which were tributary to the Roman empire embraced Arianism. The bitter waters of party strife were engendered in the bosom of the church, and the result of the contention was the death of many of both parties. Also, many of the churches were divided and destroyed. This trumpet ceased sounding about A.D. 538.

"The fourth angel sounded, and a third part of the sun, moon and stars, were darkened; so that the day and night shone not for a third part of them." The sun represents the Gospel, or New Testament; the moon, the Old Testament; the stars, ministers of the Gospel. This trumpet sounded about 538, when the bishop of Rome obtained the supremacy in the church, and began to prohibit the laity from reading the word of God for themselves, or more than some detached passages, prepared or selected for the purpose, with notes. There was a state of darkness came on the church. The word of God was obscured, and the clergy were ignorant and bigoted. This event is the same as the clothing the two witnesses with sackcloth. See the explanation of that event. An angel was then seen flying through the midst of heaven, saying with a loud voice, Woe, woe, woe to the inhabitants of the earth, by reason of the other trumpets which are yet to sound.

[150] "The fifth angel sounded, and a star fell from heaven unto the earth." A star is a fallen minister. The sounding of this trumpet took place about A.D. 606, when the Mahommedan imposture took its rise. This imposture was more the work of a Jew, whom he met in his Syrian journeys, and a Nestorian monk who had been expelled from his cloister, than the work of Mahommed himself. His system is a confused medley of Judaism, Christianity, and heathenism. The exiled monk was probably the principal agent in the work of forming this imposture, and might with propriety or without violence to the figure, be denominated a fallen star. The key of the bottomless pit was given him, and he opened the pit, and there arose a great smoke out of the pit, and the sun (the Gospel,) and the air (the moral influence of the Gospel,) were darkened by reason of the smoke of the pit. And there came locusts out of the smoke upon the earth. Smoke denotes errors, and locusts destructive armies. Mahommed, after he and his accomplices had framed their system, began at first to propagate his religion by peaceable means. But not succeeding to his mind, he soon began to meditate more violent measures, and to do by the sword what he could not do by

argument. They, (the armies of Mahommed) had power, as the scorpions of the earth have power. They tormented men by their sudden attacks, and the wounds and tortures which they inflicted. It was commanded that they should not hurt the grass [151] of the earth, neither any green thing, neither any tree; but only those men who had not the seal of God in their foreheads. Tree, grass and green thing are here used in opposition to those men who have not the seal of God in their foreheads. Says Smith's Key to Revelation, "Among the torments inflicted by these Mahommedan powers upon the conquered, were the following: Infidels, who rejected the Christian religion, and also all idolaters, they forced to receive the Mahommedan religion, upon pain of death. But Jews and Christians, having their Bibles and their religion, they left to the enjoyment of them, upon their paying large sums, which they exacted. But where the payment of such sums was refused, they must either embrace the new religion, or die. But the only alternative for the heathen was, to embrace Mahommedanism, or die. It was commanded them, that they should not hurt the grass or trees or any green thing, meaning the people of God, or Christians, but should let them alone for tribute.

This scene changes in the fifth verse, and power is given them to torment, but not to kill the men who had not the seal of God in their foreheads, for five months. To kill, is to conquer, in figurative language; and to torment, is to harass by sudden excursions and assaults. Five prophetic months are one hundred and fifty years, there being thirty [152] days in a Jewish month. This change in the power of the locusts, when it was given them to torment men for five months, is noticed in the tenth and eleventh verses. It was at the time when they had a king over them whose name is, in Hebrew, Abaddon, but in Greek, Apollyon, which signifies destroyer. For near seven hundred years the Mahommedans were divided into several factions. About the close of the thirteenth century, a powerful leader arose by the name of Ottoman, and united the contending parties under one government, which is still known by the name of the Ottoman empire. This was the first government, since the death of Mahommed, under which his followers were united and as the name Apollyon signifies, great has been the destruction of human life under this government. But to return to the description of these warriors. Their torment was as the torment of a scorpion when he striketh a man. And in those days shall men seek death, and shall not find it, and shall desire to die, and death shall flee from them. Says a noted author, "Their military laws adjudged such a portion of their captives to bondage; and the condition of these, particularly of the women, was so deplorable (being in the power of the most licentious men,) that many would prefer death to their condition." Their treatment of their enemies was the most stinging that could well be imagined. The appearance of the locusts we will note. "The shape of the locusts were like unto horses prepared [153] unto battle." The Turkish armies were principally horsemen. Probably more generally so than any other army which ever existed. "And on their heads *were* as it were crowns like gold, and their faces as the face of a man." The horses were each mounted by a man who wore on his head a yellow turban. "They had hair like the hair of women." They wore their hair long like women, and gave it different twists and dresses, to distinguish different bands of soldiery. They fought with javelins like the teeth of lions. "They had breastplates, as it were breastplates of iron; and the sound of their wings were as the sound of chariots of many horses running to battle." Their breastplates were shields which the Turks carried with them in battle. It is said, that when they charged an enemy, they made a noise on them like the noise of chariot wheels. "They had tails like the tails of scorpions." Each Turkish horsemen had a scimeter hung at his wrist, with which they were so expert, as that, when engaged in close combat, they would sever a man's or even a horse's head at a blow.

It was given them after the rise of the Ottoman empire, to torment or harass and weaken men (the Roman empire in the east) five months. If these are prophetic months as is probable, it would be one hundred and fifty years. But when did that empire rise? Mr. Miller has fixed on A.D. 1298. Others, among whom is Gibbon, in his Decline and Fall of the Roman Empire, 1299. He says – Othman first [154] invaded the territory of Nicomedia on the 27th of July, 1299. He also remarks on the singular accuracy of the date, a circumstance not often found in the history of those times. He says – "The singular accuracy with which this event, is given, seems to indicate some foresight of the rapid growth of the monster."

If we date the origin of this empire in 1299, the hundred and fifty years would end 1449. During that length of time, the eastern empire of Rome was harassed beyond measure by the Ottoman power, but was not subjected entirely to it. The year 1448, Amurath the Turkish sultan, besieged Coria, one of the strongest cities in the Roman empire. The end of the five months would come the next year. We should naturally look for some great defeat of the Christian emperor's army. But was it so? So far from it, that after a long summer's siege and a great loss of men, the fall coming on and rains setting in, the Turks raised the siege and retired. The empire was now left in peace. One would be almost inclined to think the word of prophecy must now fail.

But the time came, and the word of God was confirmed by the event. "John Paleologus emperor of Constantinople, was dead, and his brother, Constantine Deacozes, would not venture to ascend the throne without the permission of Amurath, the Turkish sultan. He sent ambassadors to ask his consent before he presumed to call himself [155] sovereign. This happened A.D. 1449. This shameful proceeding seemed to presage the approaching downfall of the empire. Ducas, the historian, counts John Paleologus for the last Greek emperor, without doubt, because he did not consider as such, a prince who had not dared to reign without the permission of his enemy." *Hawkins' Otto. Emp.* P. 113. Gibbon, an infidel, is so struck with the singular accuracy of the record of the origin of this empire, that he attributes it to some foresight in the historian, of the rapid growth of the monster. But would it not become Christians better, to attribute it to the superintending providence of that Being who had set a bound for that and other empires, which they may not pass? who had *given* them power to harass and torment the empire of Constantinople five months; and to kill or subject it to their own sway, an hour, a day, a month, and a year; the whole being five hundred and forty-one years and fifteen days.

The sixth trumpet sounded; and a voice from the four horns of the golden altar which is before God, said to the sixth angel which had the trumpet - "Loose the four angels which are bound in the great river Euphrates." And the four angels were loosed which were prepared for an hour, a day, and a month, and a year, for to slay the third part of men. The four angels denote ministers of judgment. They refer to the four nations of the Seljukan Turks of which the Ottoman empire was composed, [156] located near the river Euphrates, at Aleppo, Iconium, Damascus and Bagdat. Up to the period of 1449, they had indeed tormented the Christian empire, but could not subject it. When the sixth trumpet sounded, God seems to have overawed the Greek emperor, and all power of independence seems, as in a moment, to have fled. He, in the most strange and unaccountable manner, voluntarily acknowledged that he reigned by the permission of the Turkish sultan. The Turks very soon after this addressed themselves to the work of reducing Constantinople. This they effected, A.D. 1453, four years after the emperor obtained permission to ascend the throne. The last third of the ancient Roman empire was now reduced by Turkish arms. The number of horsemen *were* two hundred thousand thousand; what this number means, expositors have been at a loss to determine. But I am inclined to believe with Mr. Miller, that it means two hundred thousand twice told, making four hundred thousand in all. What makes this probable, is the fact, that the Turks usually had from three to four hundred thousand horsemen in their army. They had, when Constantinople was taken, three hundred thousand, and some say four hundred thousand horsemen, beside many foot, and a fleet.

Since the fifth trumpet sounded, there has been an astonishing change in the arms of the Turks. They then had breastplates of iron, and were armed with dirks and scimeters. Now the scene is [157] changed, and they are prepared with breastplates of fire, and of jacinth and brimstone. And out of the mouths of the horses, proceeded fire, and smoke, and brimstone. Their power was in their mouth and tail; their tails were like serpents; long, cylindrical instruments like serpents with heads in them, (bullets) with which they did hurt. This description has long been considered by expositors as a description of fire arms and gunpowder. And, indeed, I do not know how any one who knew nothing of such instruments, could describe them more clearly. The design of these plagues is stated in the twentieth verse. It was to lead the people on whom these plagues were inflicted, to repent of their sins and break them of devil worship, &c. But they did not repent, neither of their murders, nor their sorceries, nor fornications, nor of their thefts. They, like most on whom the judgments of God fall, remain impenitent to this day; and the Turks continue to oppress them.

But when will this power be overthrown? According to the calculations already made, that the five months ended 1449, the hour, fifteen days, the day, one year, the month, thirty years, and the year, three hundred and sixty years; in all, three hundred and ninety-one years and fifteen days, will end in A.D. 1840, some time in the month of August. The prophecy is the most remarkable and definite, (even descending to the days) of any in the Bible, relating to these great events. It is as singular as the record [158] of the time when the empire rose. The facts are now before the reader, and he must make what disposition of them he thinks best. The sixth woe yet continues, and will till the great river Euphrates is dried up, and the seventh trumpet sounds.

Chapter x. We are here presented with new scenes. A mighty angel from heaven, clothed with a cloud; and a rainbow on his head, and his face shining as the sun, and his feet as pillars of fire. In his hand was a little book open; he set his right foot on the sea and his left on the land, and cried as when a lion roareth. Seven thunders then uttered their voices, and John was about to write. But a voice from heaven said – "Seal up those things which the seven thunders uttered, and write them not." "And the angel which I saw stand on the sea and upon the earth lifted up his hand to heaven, and sware by him that liveth for ever and ever, who created heaven and the things that there are therein, and the earth and the things that therein are, and the sea and the things which are therein, that there should be time no longer. But in the days of the voice of the seventh angel, when he shall begin to sound, the mystery of God should be finished, as he hath declared to his servants the prophets."

There shall be time no longer. This scene is to take place immediately after the end of the three hundred and ninety-one years and fifteen days, or the drying up the great river Euphrates. There [159] shall be no more season of mercy; for in the days of the seventh angel, when he shall begin to sound, the mystery of God shall be finished. The great mystery of salvation by faith shall be ended, and the year of his redeemed will come.

Reader, are you prepared for that event? Have you on a wedding garment? Have you your lamp ttrimmed and oil in your vessel? O be wise NOW, *for* THEN *the* MASTER *will have shut to the* DOOR.

The divine apostle now almost began to imagine his work done. But he heard the voice from heaven the second time, saying, "Go and take the little book, which is open in the hand of the angel which standeth upon the sea and upon the earth. And I went unto the angel and said, Give me the little book. And he said unto me, Take it, and eat it up; and it shall make thy belly bitter, but it shall be in thy mouth sweet as honey. And I took the little book out of the angel's hand, and ate it up; and it was in my mouth sweet as honey, and as soon as I had eaten it, my belly was bitter. And he said unto me, Thou must prophecy again before many peoples and nations and tongues and kings." These events were distant, and John's prophecy of them must go through all the earth.[282]

---

[282] Josiah Litch, *The Probability of the Second Coming of Christ About A.D. 1843.*, (Boston: Published by David H. Ela, No. 19 Washington Street, 1838.), Preface & pgs.146-159.

APPENDIX III

SIGNS OF THE TIMES
AUGUST 1, 1840

[69] "THE CLOSING UP OF THE DAY OF GRACE.

As there has been much enquiry of late on the subject of the closing up of the day of grace, or probation, we here give the scriptures on which this opinion is founded, with some remarks and leave our readers to judge for themselves. Rev.xvi. 12-21. The attentive reader of the foregoing passages, will see that on the pouring out of the "Seventh Vial," a voice "from the throne," proclaimed, - "IT IS DONE." This was after the battle of "Armagedon."   If it is after that, then, the day of grace will continue to the end of the world, or till Christ comes. 1 Cor. Xv. 23,24. "Afterwards they that are Christ's at his coming. Then cometh the End when he shall have delivered up the kingdom to God even the Father." On this passage, Prof. Stewart, of Andover, makes the following remark. "The apostle here represents the End as coming when Christ will deliver up his mediatorial kingdom, after he has put all enemies under his feet, this accomplished his mediatorial work is done; his embassy is completed; his mission therefore comes to an end." Again, Rev. x. 7. "But in the days of the voice of the seventh angel, when he shall begin to sound, the Mystery of God should be finished, as he hath declared to his servants the prophets." When the sixth Trumpet hath ceased to sounds, the seventh begins, and "in the days of the voice of the seventh angel, when he shall BEGIN to sound, the mystery of God, or dispensation of grace shall be finished. It would appear from this, that upon the fall of the Turkish empire which will take place on the closing up of the "sixth vial" and "trumpet," that the day of probation will close. Again, Rev. xi. 15. "And the seventh angel sounded; and there were great voices in heaven, saying, the kingdom of this world are become the kingdoms of our Lord and of his Christ; and he shall reign forever and ever." This most certainly closes up the gospel dispensation, and brings us to the glorified state; for we are to "reign forever and ever." This will take place when the seventh angel shall sound. Here we have this most solemn and momentous subject, as brought to view in the book of Revelation. There is one other passage that we quote, which has an important bearing upon this subject. Mat. Xxv. 10-12. "And while they went to buy, the bridegroom come; and they that were ready went in with him to the marriage, and the DOOR WAS SHUT," We learn that the preparation was made by the wise, when the midnight cry was given: but the foolish deferred the matter until it was too late; for while they went to buy, the bridegroom came, "and the door was shut." Afterwards, the foolish virgins came, saying, Lord, Lord, open unto us. But he answered and said, Verily I say unto you, I know you not. This is the time referred to in Rev. xxii. 11, "He that is unjust, let him be unjust still, and he which is filthy, let him be filthy still; and he that is righteous, let him be righteous still; and he that is holy, let him be holy still."

In conclusion, we solemnly warn our fellow Christians, of all sects and denominations, to trim their lamps, and be in readiness for the coming of the bridegroom. Do not delay. Get ready. It can do no harm to be prepared, even if the master should not come so soon as anticipated by many of his servants.

And the unwise we solemnly warn, to awake from their slumbers, and to arise, and call upon God, repent of your sins, and prepare to meet your Judge: "for in such an hour as YOU THINK NOT, the Son of Man will come."

Our readers will find a more full illustration of this subject as to time, &c. in the two following [70] articles: Mr. Miller will give his views of this matter in a future number.

FALL OF THE OTTOMAN POWER IN CONSTANTINOPLE THE END OF THE SECOND WOE. – Rev. ix.

A very general impression prevails at the present time among all classes and in all countries, so far as we have information, that we are on the point of some great revolution, both in the political and moral world. And it is most strikingly illustrative of the declaration of the Savior, Luke xxi. 25, 26, that there should be "on earth distress of nations, with perplexity. And men's hearts failing them with fear, and for looking after those things which are coming on the earth."

Even the most skeptical, respecting the speedy appearing of the Lord Jesus Christ, are constrained to believe that something is to take place. But what that "something" is to be, can only be known from the Holy Scriptures. What then do they teach us of the events of futurity? should be the serious inquiry of every sincere inquirer after truth The public mind seems at the present time to be directed especially towards the affairs of the east – Constantinople, and the surrounding nations. This state of things has probably been brought about in a great measure by Brother Miller's lectures; and other works on the same subject.

This being the case it is important at the present time, that something definite should be spread before the public in relation to the event we may anticipate. It will not come within the compass of my design to go into a full explanation of the prophecy on which the following calculations are founded; but simply to give a synopsis of the calculations themselves, and some general reasons for them.

The prophecy in question is, 9th chapter of Revelation. That chapter is by general consent applied to the Mahometan Religion, and the Ottoman government, as arising out of the Mahomedan system.

The sounding of the fifth apocalyptic trumpet Rev. 9,1, and the accompanying event, is believed to represent the rise of Mahomedanism, and a host of warlike armies, by which that religion was propagated. These armies were for several centuries led on by the chieftains of the several clans into which they were divided: but in the one of the 13th century the different factions of Mahomedans were gathered under one leader or king, and formed one general government which has continued to the present time; I mean the Ottoman or Turkish empire. From the time of this organization under one leader, and he both a temporal and ecclesiastical ruler, [for he was both king and angel, or minister, of the bottomless pit] they were commissioned to torment men for five prophetic months, or 150 years. They were to be restrained from killing, politically, those who were the subjects of their oppressions; but they had power to torment them five months. The five months were to close up the period of the fifth trumpet. I think it is very generally agreed that the Greek empire was the people whom they were to torment, and ultimately politically to put to death.

When then did the five month of Turkish torment on the Greeks commence? Not until they had a king over them, or were gathered under one government. The Ottoman government was established about A.D. 1298 or 9. And. according to Gibbon, Ottoman first entered the territory of Nicomedia, and commenced his attack on the Greeks on July 27th, 1299. The time, 150 years would bring us to 1449, when the fifth trumpet, would end, and the sixth begin to sound.

"And the sixth angel sounded, and I heard a voice from the four horns, of the golden alter, which is before God, saying to the sixth angel which had the trumpet, loose the four angels which are bound in the great River Euphrates. And the four angels were loosed, which were prepared for an hour, and a day and a month, and a year, to slay the third part of men." Chap iii. verses 13, 15.

According to the prediction, at the termination of the five months, the first woe or fifth trumpet was past; and when the second woe or sixth angel began, the restraining power by which the nation composing the Ottoman empire were held in check and only permitted to torment men, was taken off, and power given them to slay, politically, a third part of men, or the third part of the old Roman empire; that part included in the Greek empire.

Accordingly, from 1299 to 1449, the Turks were continually tormenting the Greeks by petty incursions and wars, yet without conqeoring them. But in 1449 a circumstance took place which strikingly fulfilled the prophecy of the sounding of the sixth angel.

The Greek emperor died in that year and left his throne to his brother. But although it was a time of peace in the empire, before that brother dared ascend the throne of Constantinople and reign, he sent his embassadors to Anereth, the Turkish sultan, and requested and obtained his permission to reign; and was then proclaimed emperor of Greece. Thus voluntarily did he acknowledge that his independence was gone and that the Greek empire only existed by permission of its deadly foe. The Turkish nations were therefore loosed by divine command.

The time during which they were to continue their conquests, was an hour, 15 days, a day, one year, a month, 30 years, and a year 360 years, the whole amounting to 391 years 15 days.

Allowing the first period, 150 years to have been exactly fulfilled before Deacozes ascended the throne by permission of the Turks, and that the 391 years 15 days commenced at the close of the first period, it will end in the 11th of August, 1840, when the Ottoman power in Constantinople may be expected to be broken. And this, I believe, will be found to be the case.

But still there is no positive evidence that the first period was exactly to a day, fulfilled; nor yet that the second period began, to a day, where the first closed. If they began and ended so, the above calculation will be correct. If they did not then there will be a variation in the conclusion; but the evidence is clear that there cannot be a years variation from the calculation; we must wait patiently for the issue.

But what, it is asked, will be the effect on your own mind, if it does not come out according to the above calculation? Will not your confidence in your theory be shaken? I reply, not all. The prophecy in hand is an issolated one; and a failure in the calculation does not necessarily affect any other calculation. But yet, whenever it is fulfilled, whether in 1840, or at a future period, it will open the way for the scenes of the last day. Let no man, therefore, triumph, even if there should be an error of a few months in our calculation on this prophesy.   L.

EVENTS TO SUCCEED THE SECOND WOE.

The question is often asked, Do you believe with Mr. Miller that the day of grace will close in the month of August? To this, I reply, It is impossible for me to tell what will come in the month of August. If the foregoing calculations are correct, however, and the Ottoman power falls we shall be brought to a point where there is no certainty that the day of grace will be continued for one hour. For when the second woe is past the third woe cometh quickly. And when the seventh trumpet sounds, the day of grace will be past. Hence, when any one can prove to me satisfactorily how long a period, "Quickly" is, as used Rev. xi. 14, I will tell them how long the day of grace will last after the fall of the Ottoman empire, and not before. Every one must be his own judge on this point. But this I affirm, it will be a fearful experiment for any one to try, to put off the work of salvation until the 11th of August, or any other time. There is no safety except in Christ.

Reader, are you out of the ark of safety? Then you have no time to lose in seeking that refuge. Behold the Judge standeth before the door! Time is short! The last plagues, the seven vials in which is filled up the wrath of God will soon be poured out, when all who have not the seal of God upon them will feel the fierceness of that wrath.

Professor, have you your lamp trimmed and burning? Have you oil in your vessel with your lamp? Have you on the wedding garment? And are you like the good and faithful servant who is watching for the Bridegroom? Look well to yourselves, lest when he cometh your lamps should be gone out and while you are gone to buy oil he enter in and the door be shut.   L.[283]

---

[283] Signs of the Times, Boston, August 1, 1840.

APPENDIX IV

SIGNS OF THE TIMES
FEBRUARY 1, 1841

[161]THE NATIONS.

And the sixth angel poured out his vial upon the great river Euphrates, and the water thereof was dried up.

We have had numerous questions propounded relative to the fall of the Ottoman power within the three last months, both by the friends and opponents of our cause. As we wish to give a full and distinct answer to them all, we present the following article for the satisfaction of that class of our readers. They will not only find all their questions answered, but we hope their faith in the word of God will be confirmed.

THE ELEVENTH OF AUGUST, 1840. FALL OF THE OTTOMAN EMPIRE.

The time and event above named have excited deep interest in the public mind for more than a year past. It is therefore proper that the whole subject should be carefully reviewed, and the exact state of the care presented.

Has, then, or has not, THE ORIGINAL CALCULATION IN REFERENCE TO THE 11TH OF AUGUST AND THE OTTOMAN EMPIRE BEEN ACCOMPLISHED!

The calculations are founded on the 9th chapter of Revelation. Therefore, without entering into a very minute exposition of the chapter, it will be sufficient to give the outline of the views entertained in reference to it.

1. The fifth trumpet is believed to have introduced the Mohamedan delusion, and the time of its sounding to be divided into two periods. The first devoted to the general spread and establishment of the Mohamedan religion; the second to the wearing out and tormenting of the Greek kingdom, under Othman and his successors, but without conquering it. The period of torment was to be five (prophetic) months, or 150 years; beginning when the Mohamedan powers, of which the Ottoman empire was composed, had a king over them and began under him their assault on the Greeks. But from the time of Mahomet to the days of Othman, they were divided into various factions, under different leaders. Othman gathered those factions and consolidated them into an empire, himself the chief.

2. The sixth trumpet changed the nature of the war carried on between the Turks and Greeks from torment to death, political death, which was to take place at the end of the five months, or 150 years.

With these general remarks I will present the original calculation made on these prophetic periods, that the reader may have distinctly before him what we were to anticipate, and compare it with what has actually taken place. Let it be borne in mind, this was not written in 1840 and after the 11th of August, and so adapted to meet the events of that day; but it was written in May, 1838. It may be found in a book entitled "CHRIST'S SECOND COMING," by J. Litch, published by D.H. Ela, Boston. p. 153-158.

"It was given after the rise of the Ottoman empire, to torment or harass and weaken men (the Roman empire in the east) five months. If these are prophetic months, as is probable, it would be one hundred and fifty years. But when did that empire rise? Mr. Miller has fixed on A.D. 1298. Others, among whom is Gibbon, in his Decline and Fall of the Roman Empire, 1299. He says – Othman first invaded the territory of Nicomedia, on the 27th of July, 1299. He also remarks on the singular accuracy of the date, a circumstance not often found in the history of those times. He says – "The singular accuracy with which this event, is given, seems to indicate some foresight of the rapid growth of the monster."

If we date the origin of this empire in 1299, the hundred and fifty years would end 1449. During that length of time, the eastern empire of Rome was harassed beyond measure by the Ottoman power, but was not subjected entirely to it. The year 1448, Amurath, the Turkish Sultan, besieged Coria, one of the strongest cities in the Roman empire. The end of the five months would come the next year. We should naturally look for some great defeat of the Christian emperor's army. But was it so? So far from it, that after a long summer's siege and a great loss of men, the fall coming on and the ruins setting in, the Turks raised the siege and retired. The empire was now left in peace. One would be almost inclined to think the word of prophecy must now fail.

But the time came, and the word of God was confirmed by the event. "John Paleologus, emperor of Constantinople, was dead, and his brother, Constantine Deacozes, would not venture to ascend the throne without the permission of Amurath, the Turkish Sultan. He sent ambassadors to ask his consent before he presumed to call himself sovereign. This happened A.D. 1449. This shameful proceeding seemed to presage the approaching downfall of the empire. Ducas, the historian, counts John Peleologus for the last Greek emperor, without doubt, because he did not consider as such, a prince who had not dared to reign without the permission of his enemy." Hawkins' Otto. Emp. P. 113. Gibbon, an infidel, is so struck with the singular accuracy of the record of the origin of this empire, that he attributes it to some foresight in the historian, of the rapid growth of the monster. But would it not become Christians better, to attribute it to the superintending providence of that Being who had set a bound for that and other empires, which they may not pass? who had given them power to harass and torment the empire of Constantinople five months; and to kill or subject it to their own sway, an hour, a day, a month, and a year; the whole being five hundred and forty-one years and fifteen days.

The sixth trumpet sounded; and a voice from the four horns of the golden altar which is before God, said to the sixth angel when had the trumpet – "Loose the four angels which are bound in the great river Euphrates." And the four angels were loosed which were prepared for an hour, a day, and a month, and a year, for to slay the third part of men. The four angels denote ministers of judgment. They refer to the four nations of the Seljukan Turks of which the Ottoman empire was composed, located near the river Euphrates, at Aleppo, Iconium, Damascns, and Bagdat. Up to the period of 1449, they had indeed tormented the Christian empire, but could not subject it. When the sixth trumpet sounded, God seems to have overawed the Greek emperor, and all power of independence seems, as in a moment, to have fled. He, in a most strange and unaccountable manner, voluntarily acknowledged that he reigned by the permission of the Turkish Sultan. The Turks very soon after addressed themselves to the work of reducing Constantinople. This they effected, A.D. 1453, four years after the emperor obtained permission to ascend the throne. The last third of the ancient Roman empire was now reduced by Turkish arms. The number of horsemen were two hundred thousand thousand; what this number means, expositors have been as a loss to determine. But I am inclined to believe with Mr. Miller, that it means two hundred thousand twice told, making 400,000, in all. What makes this probable, is the fact, that the Turks usually had from three to four hundred thousand horsemen in their army. They had, when Constantinople was taken, three hundred thousand, and some say, four hundred thousand horsemen, beside many foot, and a fleet.

Since the fifth trumpet sounded, there has been an astonishing change in the arms of the Turks. They then had breastplates of iron, and were armed with dirks and scimetars. Now the scene is changed, and they are prepared with breastplates of fire, and of jacinth and brimstone. And out of the mouths of the horses, proceeded fire, smoke, and brimstone. Their power was in their mouth and tail; their tails were like serpents; long, cylindrical instruments like serpents with heads in them (bullets) with which they did hurt. This description has long been considered by expositors as a description of fire arms and gunpowder. And, indeed, I do not know how any one knew nothing of such instruments could describe them more clearly. The design of these plagues is stated in the twentieth verse. It was to lead the people on whom these plagues were inflicted, to repent of their sins, and break them of devil worship, &c. But they did not repent, neither of their murders, nor their sorceries, nor fornications, nor of their thefts. They, like most on whom the judgments of God fall, remain impenitent to this day; and the Turks continue to oppress them.

But when will this power be overthrown? According to the calculations already made, that [162] the five months ended 1449, the hour, fifteen days, the day, one year, the month, thirty years, and the year, three hundred and sixty years; in all, three hundred and ninety-one years and fifteen days, will end in A.D. 1840, some time in the month of August. The prophecy is the most remarkable and definite, (even descending to the days) of any in the Bible, relating to these great events. It is as singular as the record of the time when the empire rose. The facts are now before the reader, and he must make what disposition of them he thinks best.

From the foregoing extract it will be perceived,

1. That the 150 years began by a simple invasion of a Greek province, by Othman, July 27, 1299.

2. That at the termination of 150 years from that date, the Greeks voluntarily parted with their supremacy and independence, by virtually acknowledging they could not maintain their throne without the permission of the Mahomedans. Thus, from that time the Christian Government of Greece was under Turkish domination; and about three years after, fell a victim to Turkish arms.

3. But what termination of Ottoman power were we to expect, in view of the manner of the origin of the Ottoman power in Constantinople? Most certainly, if we reason from analogy, a voluntary surrender of Turkish supremacy in Constantinople, to Christian Influence.

4. What is the history of the Ottoman power for the last year? The Sultan has been engaged in a quarrel with Mehemet Ali, Pacha of Egypt. The Pacha had rebelled

against his master, the Sultan, declared his independence, and conquered a considerable portion of the Sultan's dominions, together with his fleet. These he refused to surrender.

"Subsequent to the occurrence of the disputes alluded to, and after the reverses experienced, as known to all the world, the embassadors of the great powers at Constantinople, in a collective official note, declared, that their governments were unanimously agreed upon taking measures to arrange the said differences, and the Sublime Port, with a view of putting a stop to the effusion of Musslemen blood and to the various evils which would arise from a renewal of hostilities, accepted the intervention of the great powers. His excellency SHEKIU EFFENDI, the Bey likgiz, was therefore, despatched as plenipotentiary to represent the Sublime Port at the conference which took place in London, (July 15, 1840.) for the purpose in question." (Extract from a translation of an official article from the Moniteur Ottoman, Aug. 22d.)

This conference was composed of England, Russia, Austria, and Prussia. The following extract from the same official document above quoted, shows the decision of the conference.

"It having been felt that all the zealous labors of the conferences of London in the settlement of the Pacha's pretentions were useless, and that the only public way was to have recourse to coercive measures to reduce him to obedience in case he persisted in not listening to pacific overtures, the powers have, together with the OTTOMAN PLENOPOTENTIARY, drawn up and signed a treaty, whereby the Sultan offers the Pacha the hereditary Government of Egypt, and of all that part of Syria extending from the Gulf of Suez to the Lake of Tiberius, together with the province of Acre, for life; the Pacha on his part evacuating all the other parts of the Sultan's dominions, now occupied by him, and returning the Ottoman fleet. A certain space of time has been granted him to accede to these terms, and as the proposals of the Sultan and his Allies, the Four Powers, do not admit of any change or qualification, if the Pacha refuse to accede to them, it is evident that the evil consequences to fall upon him will be attributable solely to his own fault. His Excellency, Rifant Bey, Musteshar for Foreign Affairs, has been despatched to Alexandria in a government steamer, to communicate their ultimatum to the Pacha."

From the foregoing extracts it appears the Sultan felt his weakness and most gladly accepted the intervention of the great christian powers of Europe, to assist him in maintaining his empire. In case war was the result of the decisions of the London conference, it, to all intents and purposes threw his dominions into the hands of those powers. As long as the decision of that conference was in his hands, he maintained his independence: but the ultimatum once suffered to pass from him into Mehemet's hands, and the question of war or peace between Mehemet and his Allies mas beyond his control; and if it did result in war, it must throw him entirely into the hands of the great powers. If Mehemet acceded to the ultimatum and the difficulties were peacefully adjusted, he would still remain independent, and support his own throne. When then was the question put officially within the power of Mehemet Ali?

The following extract of a letter from a correspondent of the London Morning Chronicle of September 18, 1840, dated Constantinople, Aug. 27th, will answer the question. Let it be understood Rifaat Bey left Constantinople for Egypt, August 5th, with the ultimatum.

"By the French Steamer of the 24th, we have advices from Egypt to the 16th; they show no alteration in the resolution of the Pacha. Confiding in the valor of his Arab army, and in the strength of the fortifications which defend his capital, he seems determined to abide by the last alternative; and as recourse to this is, therefore, now inevitable, all hope may be considered at an end of a termination of the affair without bloodshed. Immediately on the arrival of the Cyclops steamer with the news of the convention with the Four Powers, Mehemet Ali, it is stated, had quitted Alexandria to make a short tour through Lower Egypt: the object of his absenting himself at such a moment being partly to avoid conferences with the European Consuls, but principally to endeavor by his own presence to rouse the fanaticism of the Bedium tribes, and facilitate the raising of his new levies. During the interval of this absence, the Turkish government steamer, which had reached Alexandria on the 11th, with the envoy, Rifaat Bey, on board, had been by his orders placed in quarantine , and she was not released from it till the 16th. Previous, however, to the Port's leaving, viz. on the very day on which he had been admitted to pratique, the above named functionary had had an audience of the Pacha, and had communicated to him the command of the Sultan with respect to the evacuation of the Syrian Provinces, appointing another audience for the following day, when in the presence of the consuls of the European powers, he would receive from him his definite answer, and inform him of the alternative of his refusing to obey, giving him the ten days which have been allotted him by the convention to decide on the course he should think fit to adopt. But though this period must still elapse before his reply can be officially received, it may be said, in fact, to be already known, for, nothing daunted by the presence of the Bellerophon, which, with four other vessels, whose names are not given, is stated to have anchored off the port on the 14th, he had at once expressed to Rifaat Bey his resolution of confiding in the success of his army; and the preparations he is making for a determined resistance are a sufficient earnest of his intention to keep to it?"

From this letter, it appears, Rifaat Bey arrived at Alexandria on the 11th of August, and threw the decision of the affair into the hands of Mehemet Ali. And from that time it was out of the Sultan's power to control the affair. It lay with Mehemet Ali to say whether there should be war or peace. True, the Turkish envoy did not have an audience with the Pacha until the 14th, and did not receive his answer until the 15th, yet it was entirely under Mehemet's control, and not the Sultan's, after the 11th.

But was the Sultan's throne in danger from Mehemet, that he needed the support of the great powers, and thus threw himself into their hands for support? Let the following extract from a manifesto he had put forth about the 20th of August and caused to be read in the Mosques, day after day, answer. It is taken from the same letter with the above extracts.

"The Port, in order to counteract this (the pretensions of Mehemet) has deemed it necessary to publish a manifesto, laying before its subjects a statement of affairs from the commencement of the quarrel up to the present period, and proving to them by the clearest arguments, that the Pacha himself is the enemy of their religion, and that the object he is aiming at is to DETHRONE THE SULTAN, and warning them, under the severest penalties, against receiving and circulating the doctrines he (Mehemet) is preaching to them." If we can give any credit to the sincerity of the Sultan in putting forth this manifesto, he did consider his throne in danger from Mehemet. The truth is, the Ottoman power in Constantinople was impotent, and could do nothing toward sustaining itself; and it has been since the 11th of August, entirely under the dictation of the great Christian powers of Europe. Nor can it longer stand at all, than they hold it up. Finally, the London Morning Herald is right when it says. (See, *Signs of the Times*, Jan. 1, 1841.) "The Ottoman government is reduced to the rank of a puppet, and that the sources of its strength are entirely dried up."

In conclusion: I am entirely satisfied that on the 11th of August, 1840, The Ottoman power according to previous calculation, DEPARTED TO RETURN NO MORE. I can now say with the utmost confidence, "The second woe is past and behold the third woe cometh quickly." "Blessed is he that watcheth and keepeth his garments, lest he walk naked and they see his shame." L.[284]

[45]

---

[284] Signs of the Times, Boston, February, 1, 1841.

APPENDIX V

Prophetic Exposition; Or A Connected View Of The Testimony Of The Prophets Concerning The Kingdom Of God And The Time Of Its Establishment

JOSIAH LITCH

[iii] PREFACE.

The writer would here acknowledge himself indebted to Mr. William Miller's valuable Lectures, for the leading ideas of the following pages. Although the views of Mr. M. may not be correct on every point, yet, so far as his calculation of time concerned, the writer can but consider his plan irrefutable. The above-named lectures are worthy the attentive perusal of all lovers of the sacred Scriptures. The writings of Bishop Newton, and of Faber on the Prophecies, have furnished some most valuable information. Also, Smith's Key to Revelations has been read with deep interest, and has afforded many new ideas of the meaning of that deeply interesting book. The [iv] historical authorities who have been principally consulted, are Rollin's Ancient History, Gibbon's Decline and Fall, Sabine's Ecclesiastical History, Mosheim's Ecclesiastical History, and Miller's do., Life of Napoleon, by an American Citizen, Mignet's French Revolution, Hawkins' Ottoman Empire, &c. Several valuable Commentaries have also been consulted on the subjects here discussed. In the interpretations of figurative language, the most approved authors have been consulted, and generally followed. But in some instances the writer has found reasons for dissenting from the views of all authors with whom he has met.

The motive which has called forth this work may be asked. The reply is, the principal reason of its publication is, the scarceness of Mr. Miller's book, together with the importance of the subject. This work, however, is not designed to supercede any existing work on the Prophecies. The writer flatters himself, that he has presented some new views on the subject, and arranged and illustrated former views and facts, so as to render them more clear and striking; however, on that point a candid public must judge.

[v] All pretensions to a spirit of prophecy, or to infallibility in the interpretation of prophecy, are utterly disclaimed. It has often been asked, - If the event does not come out as you believe, what will you then think? Will it not destroy your confidence in the Bible? To this it is replied, Not at all; the writer has, in the course of his research on this subject, seen so much which has been literally fulfilled as predicted, that although all he has written on this subject should prove to have been founded in ignorance, he cannot doubt but the prophecies have a meaning, and that they were written by the unerring Spirit of the Holy One, and will, in due time, be fulfilled. But, at the same time, he must be permitted to express his firm conviction, that these calculations are founded in truth, and will stand the ordeal they must very soon pass – the unerring test of time. In conclusion, a candid examination of the subject is

requested of the reader, before judgment is rendered; he is then at perfect liberty to receive or reject, as the strength of the evidence will dictate. For the purity of his motive in presenting to the public the following, the writer must appeal to that day, of [vi] which he writes. He believes that those, even, who do not accord with the peculiar views herein maintained, will find themselves amply compensated for their pains, in giving the books an attentive perusal.

To God, and the word of his grace, the author would now commend himself, his work, and all who may read; praying that the spirit of wisdom and of a sound mind may be granted us, to lead us into all truth. The exhortation of the king of Judah (2 Chron. xx. 20) may perhaps be appropriate on this occasion. "Hear me, O Judah, and ye inhabitants of Jerusalem; believe in the Lord your God, so shall ye be established; believe his prophets, so shall ye prosper." J.L. May 30, 1838.

[146] CHAPTER VI.

SECTION I.

We have now again been brought down to the Great Day, and find the redeemed family before the throne of God, and He that sitteth on the throne dwelling among them. Now a new series of events are about to take place.

Rev. viii. 2. "The seven angels, having seven trumpets, stood before God. And the angels prepared themselves to sound."

This trumpet sounded about A.D. 64, when Nero commenced his persecutions against Christians. This persecution was of short duration, for Nero died A.D. 68, which put an end to the calamities [147] of that persecution, by which, for four years, Christians suffered every indignity and torment, throughout the Roman empire, which ingenious cruelty could invent. The torments are represented as hail and fire mingled with blood. Some of the sufferers are said, by historians, to have been wrapped in combustible clothes, and in the darkness of night they were set on fire. Others were fastened to crosses, and torn to pieces by wild beasts. Thus, like a dreadful tempest of hail, fire, and blood, this persecution burst upon the church. The third part of trees was burnt up, and all green grass was burnt up. By trees, and green grass, living soul, living thing, &c., I understand Christians of various degrees of eminence to be meant. By a third part of any thing, as the expression is so frequently used in this book, I understand a large number, but not all, or even the majority.

It is believed, that in this persecution St. Paul and St. Peter both suffered martyrdom, and with them many other eminent ministers – I know not but one third, - also, an incredible number of Christians, so that it might almost literally be said, that every green thing was burnt up.

"The second angel sounded; and as it were a great mountain burning with fire was cast into the sea; and the third part of the sea became blood." Sea denotes any country in a state of agitation or commotion. The sea here spoken of was the Roman empire. This trumpet sounded when the [148] persecution of the Christians commenced under Domitian, A.D. 94, which continued to rage for most of the time with greater or less rigor, until the days of Constantine, A.D. 312. During that period, it is probable that one third of the Christians who lived, were put to death as martyrs. Ships would mean, if the figure is carried out, churches; one third of these were destroyed. We have no data to get the exact proportion of Christians and churches which suffered;

but probably, if the truth could be known, it would not fall much short of one third of the whole number who lived during that period.

"The third angel sounded, and there fell a great star from heaven, burning as it were a lamp." A fallen star, in figurative language, denotes an apostate minister of the Gospel. This angel sounded as the Arian heresy made its appearance, in the reign of Constantine. Arius fell into grievous and fatal errors, yet he maintained his moral character unimpeachable, burning as it were a lamp. Although he had fallen on an important point of doctrine, yet he shone, or shed some light – if not the brilliancy of a star, yet as the more dim light of a lamp. Says Dr. Miller, "Had he not possessed some apparent virtues, he would not have been able to form so great a design, nor to have proved so formidable an adversary. He who does much mischief in deceiving souls, must at least have a fair appearance of morals." This star fell on a third part of the rivers and fountains of waters. By rivers and fountains of waters, [149] we may understand those streams and fountains of water which feed or are tributary to the sea. The Arian heresy spread itself all over the Christian world, and probably one third of the provinces which were tributary to the Roman empire embraced Arianism. The bitter waters of party strife were engendered in the bosom of the church, and the result of the contention was the death of many of both parties. Also, many of the churches were divided and destroyed. This trumpet ceased sounding about A.D. 538.

"The fourth angel sounded, and a third part of the sun, moon and stars, were darkened; so that the day and night shone not for a third part of them." The sun represents the Gospel, or New Testament; the moon, the Old Testament; the stars, ministers of the Gospel. This trumpet sounded about 538, when the bishop of Rome obtained the supremacy in the church, and began to prohibit the laity from reading the word of God for themselves, or more than some detached passages, prepared or selected for the purpose, with notes. There was a state of darkness came on the church. The word of God was obscured, and the clergy were ignorant and bigoted. This event is the same as the clothing the two witnesses with sackcloth. See the explanation of that event. An angel was then seen flying through the midst of heaven, saying with a loud voice, Woe, woe, woe to the inhabitants of the earth, by reason of the other trumpets which are yet to sound.

[150] "The fifth angel sounded, and a star fell from heaven unto the earth." A star is a fallen minister. The sounding of this trumpet took place about A.D. 606, when the Mahommedan imposture took its rise. This imposture was more the work of a Jew, whom he met in his Syrian journeys, and a Nestorian monk who had been expelled from his cloister, than the work of Mahommed himself. His system is a confused medley of Judaism, Christianity, and heathenism. The exiled monk was probably the principal agent in the work of forming this imposture, and might with propriety or without violence to the figure, be denominated a fallen star. The key of the bottomless pit was given him, and he opened the pit, and there arose a great smoke out of the pit, and the sun (the Gospel,) and the air (the moral influence of the Gospel,) were darkened by reason of the smoke of the pit. And there came locusts out of the smoke upon the earth. Smoke denotes errors, and locusts destructive armies. Mahommed, after he and his accomplices had framed their system, began at first to propagate his religion by peaceable means. But not succeeding to his mind, he soon began to meditate more violent measures, and to do by the sword what he could not do by

argument. They, (the armies of Mahommed) had power, as the scorpions of the earth have power. They tormented men by their sudden attacks, and the wounds and tortures which they inflicted. It was commanded that they should not hurt the grass [151] of the earth, neither any green thing neither any tree; but only those men who had not the seal of God in their foreheads. Tree, grass and green thing are here used in opposition to those men who have not the seal of God in their foreheads. These expressions must therefore mean those who have the seal of God in their foreheads. Says Smith's Key to Revelation, "Among the torments inflicted by these Mahommedan powers upon the conquered, were the following: Infidels, who rejected the Christian religion, and also all idolaters, they forced to receive the Mahommedan religion, upon pain of death. But Jews and Christians, having their Bibles and their religion, they left to the enjoyment of them, upon their paying large sums, which they exacted. But where the payment of such sums was refused, they must either embrace the new religion, or die. But the only alternative for the heathen was, to embrace Mahommedanism, or die. It was commanded them, that they should not hurt the grass or trees or any green thing, meaning the people of God, or Christians, but should let them alone for tribute.

This scene changes in the fifth verse, and power is given them to torment, but not to kill the men who had not the seal of God in their foreheads, for five months. To kill, is to conquer, in figurative language; and to torment, is to harass by sudden excursions and assaults. Five prophetic months are one hundred and fifty years there being thirty [152] days in a Jewish month. This change in the power of the locusts, when it was given them to torment men for five months, is noticed in the tenth and eleventh verses. It was at the time when they has a king over them whose name is, in Hebrew, Abaddon, but in Greek, Apollyon, which signifies destroyer. For near seven hundred years the Mahommedans were divided into several factions. About the close of the thirteenth century, a powerful leader arose by the name of Ottoman, and united the contending parties under one government, which is still known by the name of the Ottoman empire. This was the first government, since the death of Mahommed, under which his followers were united. and as the name Apollyin signifies, great has been the destruction of human life under this government. But to return to the description of these warriors. Their torment was as the torment of a scorpion when he striketh a man. And in those days shall men seek death, and shall not find it, and shall desire to die, and death shall flee from them. Says a noted author, "Their military laws adjudged such a portion of their captives to bondage; and the condition of these, particularly of the women, was so deplorable (being in the power of the most licentious men,) that many would prefer death to their condition." Their treatment of their enemies was the most stinging that could well be imagined. The appearance of the locusts we will note. "The shape of the locusts were like unto horses prepared [153] unto battle." The Turkish armies were principally horsemen. Probably more generally so than any other army which ever existed. "And on their heads *were* as it were crowns like gold, and their faces as the face of a man." The horses were each mounted by a man who wore on his head a yellow turban. "They had hair like the hair of women." They wore their hair long like women, and gave it different twists and dresses, to distinguish different bands of soldiery. They fought with javelins like the teeth of lions. "They had breastplates, as it were breastplates of iron; and the sound of their wings were as the sound of chariots of many horses running to battle." Their breastplates were shields which the Turks carried with them in battle. It is said, that when they charged an enemy, they made a noise on them like the noise of chariot wheels. "They had tails like the tails of scorpions." Each Turkish horseman had a scimeter hung at his wrist, with which they were so expert, as that, when engaged in close combat, they would sever a man's or even a horse's head at a blow.

It was given them after the rise of the Ottoman empire, to torment or harass and weaken men (the Roman empire in the east) five months. If these are prophetic months as is probable, it would be one hundred and fifty years. But when did that empire rise? Mr. Miller has fixed on A.D. 1298. Others, among whom is Gibbon, in his Decline and Fall of the Roman Empire, 1299. He says – Othman first [154] invaded the territory of Nicomedia on the 27th of July, 1299. He also remarks on the singular accuracy of the date, a circumstance not often found in the history of those times. He says – "The singular accuracy with which this even, is given, seems to indicate some foresight of the rapid growth of the monster."

If we date the origin of this empire in 1299, the hundred and fifty years would end 1449. During that length of time, the eastern empire of Rome was harassed beyond measure by the Ottoman power, but was not subjected entirely to it. The year 1448, Amurath the Turkish sultan, besieged Coria, one of the strongest cities in the Roman empire. The end of the five months would come the next year. We should naturally look for some great defeat of the Christian emperor's army. But was it so? So far from it, that after a long summer's siege and a great loss of men, the fall coming on and rains setting in, the Turks raised the siege and retired. The empire was now left in peace. One would be almost inclined to think the word of prophecy must now fail.

But the time came, and the word of God was confirmed by the event. "John Paleologus emperor of Constantinople, was dead, and his brother, Constantine Deacozes, would not venture to ascend the throne without the permission of Amurath, the Turkish sultan. He sent ambassadors to ask his consent before he presumed to call himself [155] sovereign. This happened A.D. 1449. This shameful proceeding seemed to presage the approaching downfall of the empire. Ducas, the historian, counts John Paleologus for the last Greek emperor, without doubt, because he did not consider as such, a prince who had not dared to reign without the permission of his enemy." *Hawkins' Otto. Emp.* P. 113. Gibbon, an infidel, is so struck with the singular accuracy of the record of the origin of this empire, that he attributes it to some foresight in the historian, of the rapid growth of the monster. But would it not become Christians better, to attribute it to the superintending providence of that Being who had set a bound for that and other empires, which they may not pass? who had *given* them power to harass and torment the empire of Constantinople five months; and to kill or subject it to their own sway, an hour, a day, a month, and a year; the whole being five hundred and forty-one years and fifteen days.

The sixth trumpet sounded; and a voice from the four horns of the golden altar which is before God, said to the sixth angel which had the trumpet - "Loose the four angels which are bound in the great river Euphrates." And the four angels were loosed which were prepared for an hour, a day, and a month, and a year, for to slay the third part of men. The four angels denote ministers of judgment. They refer to the four nations of the Seljukan Turks of which the Ottoman empire was composed, [156] located near the river Euphrates, at Aleppo, Iconium, Damascus and Bagdat. Up to the period of 1449, they had indeed tormented the Christian empire, but could not subject it. When the sixth trumpet sounded, God seems to have overawed the Greek emperor, and all power of independence seems, as in a moment, to have fled. He, in the most strange and unaccountable manner, voluntarily acknowledged that he reigned by the permission of the Turkish sultan. The Turks very soon after this addressed themselves to the work of reducing Constantinople. This they effected, A.D. 1453, four years after the emperor obtained permission to ascend the throne. The last third of the ancient Roman empire was now reduced by Turkish arms. The number of horsemen *were* two hundred thousand thousand; what this number means, expositors have been at a loss to determine. But I am inclined to believe with Mr. Miller, that it means two hundred thousand twice told, making four hundred thousand in all. What makes this probable, is the fact, that the Turks usually had from three to four hundred thousand horsemen in their army. They had, when Constantinople was taken, three hundred thousand, and some say four hundred thousand horsemen, beside many foot, and a fleet.

Since the fifth trumpet sounded, there has been an astonishing change in the arms of the Turks. They then had breastplates of iron, and were armed with dirks and scimeters. Now the scene is [157] changed, and they are prepared with breastplates of fire, and of jacinth and brimstone. And out of the mouths of the horses, proceeded fire, and smoke, and brimstone. Their power was in their mouth and tail; their tails were like serpents; long cylindrical instruments like serpents with heads in them, (bullets) with which they did hurt. This description has long been considered by expositors as a description of fire arms and gunpowder. And, indeed, I do not know how any one who knew nothing of such instruments, could describe them more clearly. The design of these plagues is stated in the twentieth verse. It was to lead the people on whom these plagues were inflicted, to repent of their sins and break them of devil worship, &c. But they did not repent, neither fornications, nor of their thefts, They, like most on whom the judgments of God fall, remain impenitent to this day; and the Turks continue to oppress them.

But when will this power be overthrown? According to the calculations already made, that the five months ended 1449, the hour, fifteen days, the day, one year, the month, thirty years, and the year, three hundred and sixty years; in all, three hundred and ninety-one years and fifteen days will end in A.D. 1840, some time in the month of August. The prophecy is the most remarkable and definite, (even descending to the days) of any in the Bible, relating to these great events. It is as singular as the record [158] of the time when the empire rose. The facts are now before the reader, and he must make what disposition of them he thinks best. The sixth woe yet continues, and will till the great river Euphrates is dried up, and the seventh trumpet sounds.

Chapter x. We are here presented with new scenes. A mighty angel from heaven, clothed with a cloud; and a rainbow on his head, and his face shining as the sun, and his feet as pillars of fire. In his hand was a little book open; he set his right foot on the sea and his left on the land, and cried as when a lion roareth. Seven thunders then uttered their voices, and John was about to write. But a voice from heaven said – "Seal up those things which the seven thunders uttered, and write them not." "And the angel which I saw stand on the sea and upon the earth lifted up his hands to heaven, and sware by him that liveth for ever and ever, who created heaven and the things that there are therein, and the earth and the things that therein are, and the sea and the things which are therein, that there should be time no longer. But in the days of the voice of the seventh angel, when he shall begin to sound, the mystery of God should be finished, as he hath declared to his servants the prophets."

There shall be time no longer. This scene is to take place immediately after the end of the three hundred and ninety-one years and fifteen days, or the drying up of the great river Euphrates. There [159] shall be no more season of mercy; for in the days of the seventh angel, when he shall begin to sound, the mystery of God shall be finished. The great mystery of salvation by faith shall be ended, and the year of his redeemed will come.

Reader, are you prepared for that event? Have you on a wedding garment? Have you your lamp trimmed and oil in your vessel? O be wise now, *for* THEN *the* MASTER *will have shut to the* DOOR.

The divine apostle now almost began to imagine his work done. But he heard the voice from heaven the second time, saying, "Go and take the little book, which is open in the hand of the angel which standeth upon the sea and upon the earth. And I went unto the angel and said, Give me the little book. And he said unto me, Take it, and eat it up; and it shall make thy belly bitter, but it shall be in thy mouth sweet as honey. And I took the little book out of the angel's hand, and ate it up; and it was in my mouth sweet as honey, and as soon as I had eaten it, my belly was bitter. And he said unto me, Thou must prophecy again before many peoples and nations and tongues and kings." These events were distant, and John's prophecy of them must go through all the earth.[285]

[59] As the spring opened, and the summer came, the entire community were excited, and expectation on tiptoe, in reference to the 11th of August and its anticipated events, the fall of the Ottoman empire, &c. &c. Many were the predictions that when that day should have passed by, as it certainly would do, without the event being realized, that then the spell would be broken, and Adventism would die. But the time came; and it must be confessed it was for a few weeks a time of trial to many. Yet "He who tempers the wind to the shorn lamb," had compassion on his little ones and did not suffer them to be tempted above what they were able to bear. And few, very few, even under that trial, shrunk from their faith. The time came and passed by; and, as a matter of [60] course, the distance from Constantinople could not be passed without consuming some considerable period of time. But when the fact did reach us, it was found that on the very day anticipated, the 11th of August, a transfer was made of the supremacy of that empire from Mahomedan hands. This fact entirely discomfited the hosts of the enemy. The cause again revived, and careered on its way with still greater power than ever before.[286]

THE FIFTH TRUMPET, OR FIRST WO.

"There is scarcely so uniform an agreement among interpreters concerning any part of the apocalypse as respecting the application of the fifth and sixth trumpets, or the first and second wo, to the Saracens and Turks. It is so obvious that it can scarcely be

---

[285] J. Litch, *The Probability of the Second Coming of Christ* (Boston: David H. Ela., 1838)146-159.
[286] J.V. Himes, S. Bliss, & A. Hale, *The Advent Shield and Review* (Boston: Joshua V. Himes, 1844)59-60.

misunderstood. Instead of a verse or two designating each, the whole of the ninth chapter of the Revelation, in equal portions, is occupied with a description of both.

"The Roman empire declined, as it arose, by conquest; but the Saracens and the Turks were [162] the instruments by which a false religion became the scourge of an apostate church; and, hence, instead of the fifth and sixth *trumpets*, like the former, being marked by that name alone, they were called *woes*. It was because the laws were transgressed, the ordinances changed, and the everlasting covenant broken, that the curse came upon the earth or the land.

"We have passed the period, in the political history of the world, when the western empire was extinguished; and the way was thereby opened for the exaltation of the papacy. The imperial power of the city of Rome was annihilated, and the office and the name of emperor of the west was abolished for a season. The trumpets assume a new form, as they are directed to a new object, and the close coincidence, or rather express identity between the king of the south, or the king of the north, as described by Daniel, and the first and second wo, will be noted in the subsequent illustration of the latter. The spiritual supremacy of the pope, it may be remembered, was acknowledged and maintained, after the fall of Rome, by the emperor Justinian. And whether in the character of a trumpet or a wo, the previous steps of history raise us, as on a platform, to behold in a political view the judgments that fell on apostate Christendom, and finally led to the subversion of the eastern empire."

Chapter ix., verse 1. *"And the fifth angel sounded, and I saw a star fall from heaven unto the earth: and to him was given the key of the bottomless pit."*

"Constantinople was besieged for the first time after the extinction of the western empire, by Chosroes, the king of Persia."

[163] *"A star fell from heaven unto the earth: and to him was given the key of the bottomless pit."*

"While the Persian monarch contemplated the wonders of his art and power, he received an epistle *from an obscure citizen of Mecca,* inviting him to acknowledge *Mahomet as the apostle of God.* He rejected the invitation, and tore the epistle. "It is thus," exclaimed the Arabian prophet, "that God will tear the kingdom, and reject the supplication of Chosroes." Placed on the verge of these two empires of the east, *Mahomet observed with secret joy the progress of mutual destruction;* and in the midst of the Persian triumphs he ventured to foretell, that, before many years should elapse, victory should again return to the banners of the Romans.' 'At the time when this prediction is said to have been delivered no prophecy could be more distant from its accomplishment (!) since the first twelve years of Heraclius announced the *approaching dissolution of the empire.'*

"It was not, like that designative of Attila, on a single spot that the star fell, but upon the *earth.*

"Chosroes subjugated the Roman possessions in Asia and Africa. And 'the Roman empire,' at that period, 'was reduced to the walls of Constantinople, with remnant of Greece, Italy, and Africa, and some maritime cities, from Tyre to Trebisond, of the Asiatic coast. The experience of six years at length persuaded the Persian monarch to renounce the conquest of Constantinople, and to specify the *annual tribute or the ransom of the* ROMAN EMPIRE:a thousand talents of gold, a thousand talents of silver, a [164] thousand silk robes, a thousand horses, and a thousand virgins.

Heraclius subscribed these ignominious terms. But the time and space which he obtained to collect those treasures from the poverty of the east, was industriously employed in the preparations of a bold and desperate attack.'

"The king of Persia despised the obscure Saracen, and derided the message of the pretended prophet of Mecca. Even the overthrow of the Roman empire would not have opened a door for Mahometanism, or for the progress of the Saracenic armed propagators of an imposture, though the monarch of the Persians and chagan of the Avars (the successor of Attila) had divided between them the remains of the kingdom of the Caesars. Chosroes himself *fell*. The Persian and Roman monarchies exhausted each other's strength. And before a sword was put into the hands of the false prophet, it was smitten from the hands of those who would have checked his career, and crushed his power.

"'Since the days of Scipio and Hannibal, no bolder enterprise has been attempted than that which Heraclius achieved for the deliverance of the empire. He permitted the Persians to oppress for a while the provinces, and to insult with impunity the capital of the east; while the Roman emperor explored his perilous way through the Black Sea and the mountains of Armenia, penetrated *into the heart of Persia,* and recalled the armies of the *great king* to the defence of their *bleeding country.* The revenge and ambition of Chosroes exhausted his kingdom. The whole city of Constantinople was invested, - and [165] the inhabitants descried with terror the flaming signals of the European and Asiatic shores. In the battle of Nineveh, which was fiercely fought from daybreak to the eleventh hour, twenty-eight standards, besides those which miht be broken, or torn, were taken from the Persians; the greatest part of their army was cut in pieces, and the victors, concealing their own loss, passed the night on the field. The cities and palaces of Assyria were open for the first time to the Romans.

"'The Greeks and modern Persians minutely described how Chosroes was insulted, and famished, and tortured by the command of an inhuman son, who so far surpassed the example of his father: but at the time of his death, what tongue could relate the story of the parricide? what eye could penetrate into the *tower of darkness? The glory of the house of Sassan ended with the life of Chosroes;* his unnatural son enjoyed only eight months' fruit of his crimes; and in the space of four years the regal tide was assumed by nine candidates, who disputed, with the sword or dagger, the fragments of an *exhausted monarchy.* Every province and every city of Persia was the scene of independence, of discord, and of blood, and the state of anarchy continued about eight years longer, *till the factions were silenced and united under the common yoke of the* ARABIAN CALIPHS.'

"The Roman emperor was not strengthened by the conquests which he achieved; and a way was prepared at the same time, and by the same means, for the multitudes of Saracens from Arabia, like locusts from the same region, who, propagating in their course the dark and delusive [166] Mahometan creed, speedily overspread both the Persian and Roman empires.

"More complete illustration of this fact could not be desired that is supplied in the concluding words of the chapter from Gibbon, from which the preceding extracts are taken."

"'Yet the deliverer of the east was indigent and feeble. Of the Persian spoils the most valuable portion had been expended in the war, distributed to the soldiers, or buried by an unlucky tempest in the waves of the Euxine. The loss of two hundred thousand soldiers, who had fallen by the sword, was of less fatal importance than the decay of arts, agriculture, and population, in this long and destructive war: and although a victorious army had been formed under the standard of Heraclius, the unnatural effort seems to have exhausted rather than exercised their strength. While the emperor triumphed at Constantinople of Jerusalem, an obscure town on the confines of Syria was pillaged by the Saracens, and they cut in pieces some troops who advanced to its relief - an ordinary and trifling occurrence, had it not been *the prelude of a mighty revolution.* These robbers were the *apostles of Mahomet*; THEIR FANATIC VALOR HAD EMERGED FROM THE DESERT; and in the last eight years of his reign, Heraclius lost to the Arabs the same provinces which he had rescued from the Persians.'

"'The spirit of fraud and enthusiasm, whose abode is not in the heavens,' was let loose on earth. The bottomless pit needed but a key to open it; and that key was the fall of Chosroes. He had contemptuously torn the letter of an obscure citizen of Mecca. But when from his [167] 'blaze of glory' he sunk into 'the tower of darkness' which no eye could penetrate, the name of Chosroes was suddenly to pass into oblivion before that of Mahomet; and the cresent seemed but to wait its rising till the falling of the star. Chosroes, after his entire discomfiture and loss of empire, was murdered in the year six hundred and twenty-eight; and the year six hundred and twenty-nine is marked by 'the conquest of Arabia,' 'and the first war of the Mahometans against the Roman empire.' - *And the fifth angel sounded, and I saw a star fall from heaven unto the earth: and to him was given the key of the bottomless pit. And he opened the bottomless pit. He fell unto the earth.* When the strength of the Roman empire was exhausted, and the great king of the east lay dead in his tower of darkness. The pillage of an obscure town on the borders of Syria was 'the prelude of a mighty revolution.' '*The robbers were the apostles of Mahomet, and their* FANATIC *valor* EMERGED *from the desert.*'

"A more succinct, yet ample, commentary may be given in the words of another historian.

"'While Chosroes of Persia was pursuing his dreams of recovering and enlarging the empire of Cyrus, and Heraclius was gallantly defending the empire of the Caesars against him; while IDOLATRY and metaphysics were diffusing their baleful influence through the church of Christ, and the simplicity and purity of the gospel were nearly lost beneath the mythology which occupied the place of that ancient Greece and Rome, the seeds of a new empire, and of a new religion, were sown in the inaccessible deserts of Arabia.'

[168] "The first wo arose at a time when transgressors had come to the full, when men had changed the ordinances and broken the everlasting covenant, when idolatry prevailed, or when tutelary saints were honored – and when the 'mutual destruction' of the Roman and Persian empires prepared the way of the fanatic robbers, - or opened the bottomless pit, from whence an imposture, which manifests its origin from the 'father of liars,' spread over the greater part of the world.

"And there arose a smoke out of the pit, as the smoke of a great furnace, and the sun and the air were darkened by reason of the smoke of the pit. Like the noxious and even deadly vapor which the winds, particularly from the south-west, diffuse in Arabia, Mahometanism spread from thence its pestilential influence – and arose as suddenly, and spread as widely, as smoke arising out of the pit, the smoke of a great furnace. Such is a suitable symbol of the religion of Mahomet, of itself, or as compared with the pure light of the gospel of Jesus. It was not, like the latter, a light from heaven; but a smoke out of the bottomless pit.

"'Mahomet alike instructed to preach and to fight; and the union of these opposite qualities, while it enhanced his merit, contributed to his success; the operation of force and persuasion, of enthusiasm and fear, continually acted on each other, till every barrier yielded to their irresistible power.' 'The first caliphs ascended the pulpit to persuade and edify the congregation.'

"'While the state was exhausted by the Persian war, and the church was distracted by the Nestorian and Monophysite sects, Mahomet, *with the* SWORD *in one hand,* and *the* KORAN *in the other,* [169] erected his throne on the ruins of Christianity and of rome. The genius of the Arabian prophet, the manners of his nation, and *the spirit of his religion,* involve the causes of the decline and fall of the eastern empire; and our eyes are curiously intent on one of the most memorable revolutions which have impressed a new and most lasting character on the *nations of the globe.*'

"Mahomet, it may be said, has heretofore divided the world with Jesus. He rose up against the Prince of princes. A great sword was given him. His doctrine, generated by the spirit of fraud and enthusiasm, whose abode is not in the heavens, as even an unbeliever could tell, arose out of the bottomless pit, spread over the earth like the *smoke of a great furnace,* and *the sun and the air were darkened by reason of the smoke of the pit.* It spread from Arabia, over great part of Asia, Africa, and Europe. The Greeks of Egypt, whose numbers could scarcely equal a tenth of the nation, were overwhelmed by the *universal defection.* And even in the farthest extremity of continental Europe, the decline of the French monarchy invited the attacks of these insatiate fanatics. The smoke that arose from the cave of Hera was diffused from the Atlantic to the Indian Ocean. But the prevalence of their faith is best seen in the extent of their conquests."

Verse 3: *"And there came out of the smoke locusts upon the earth; and unto them was given power, as the scorpions of the earth have power."*

"A false religion was set up, which, although the scourge of transgressions and idolatry, filled the world with darkness and delusion; and swarms of Saracens, like locusts, overspread the earth, [170] and speedily extended their ravages over the Roman empire, from east to west. The hail descended from the frozen shores of the Baltic; the burning mountain fell upon the sea, from Africa: and the locusts, (the fit symbol of the Arabs,) issued from Arabia, their native region. They came, as destroyers, propagating a new doctrine, and stirred up to rapine and violence by motives of interest and religion.

"'In the ten years of the administration of Omar, the Saracens reduced to his obedience thirty-six thousand cities or castles, destroyed four thousand churches or temples of the unbelievers, and erected fourteen hundred mosques, for the exercise of the religion of Mahomet. One hundred years after his flight from Mecca, the arms and the reign of his successors extended from India to the Atlantic Ocean.

"'At the end of the first century of the Hegira, the caliphs were the most potent and absolute monarchs of the globe. The regal and sacerdotal characters were united in the successors of Mahomet. Under the last of the Ommiades, the Arabic empire extended two hundred days' journey from east to west, from the confines of Tartary and India to the shores of the Atlantic Ocean. And if we retrench the sleeve of the robe, as it is styled by their writers, the long and narrow province of Africa, the solid and compact dominion from Fargana to Aden, from Tarsus to Surat, will spread on every side to the measure of four or five months of the march of a caravan. The progress of the Mahometan religion diffused over this ample space a general resemblance of manners and opinions: the language and laws of the Koran were studied with equal devotion at [171] Sarmacand and Seville: the Moor and the Indian embraced as countrymen and brothers in the pilgrimage of Mecca; and the Arabian language was adopted as the popular idiom in all the provinces to the westward of the Tigris.'

"A still more specific illustration may be given, of the power, like unto that *of scorpions,* which was given them. Not only was their attack *speedy and vigorous,* but 'the nice sensibility of honor, which weighs the insult rather than the injury, sheds *its deadly venom* on the quarrels of the Arabs: - an indecent action, a contemptuous word, can be expiated only by the blood of the offender; and such is their patient *inveteracy,* that they expect whole months and years the opportunity of revenge.' "

Verse 4: "*And it was commanded them that they should not hurt the grass of the earth, neither any green thing, neither any tree; but only those men which have not the seal of God in their foreheads.*"

On the sounding of the first angel, *the third part of the trees was burnt up, and all green grass was burnt up.*

After the death of Mahomet, he was succeeded in the command by Abubeker, A.D. 632; who as soon as he had fairly established his authority and government, despatched a circular letter to the Arabian tribes, of which the following is an extract: - "This is to acquaint you that I intend to send the true believers into Syria to take it out of the hand of the infidels, and I would have you know that the fighting for religion is an act of obedience to God."

"His messengers returned with the tidings [172] of pious and martial ardor, which they had kindled in every province; the camp of Medina was successively filled with the intrepid bands of the Saracens, who panted for action, complained of the heat of the season and the scarcity of provisions, and accused, with impatient murmurs, the delays of the caliph. As soon as their numbers were complete, Abubeker ascended the hill, reviewed the men, the horses, and the arms, and poured forth a fervent prayer for the success of their undertaking. His *instructions* to the chiefs of the Syria were inspired by the *warlike fanaticism* which advances to seize, and affects to despise, the objects of earthly ambition. 'Remember," said the successor of the prophet, 'that you are always in the presence of God, on the verge of death, in the assurance of judgment, and the hope of Paradise: avoid injustice and oppression; consult with your brethren, and study to preserve the love and confidence of your troops. When you fight the battles of the Lord, acquit yourselves like men, without turning your backs;

but let not your victory be stained with the blood of women or children. Destroy NO *palm-trees, nor burn any fields of corn.* Cut down *no* fruit trees, nor do any mischief to cattle, only such as you kill to eat. When you make any covenant or article, stand to it, and be as good as your word. As you go on, you will find some religious persons who live retired in monasteries, and propose to themselves to serve God that way; let them alone, and *neither kill* them nor destroy their monasteries; and you will find another sort of people that belong to the synagogue of Satan, who have shaven crowns; be *sure you cleave* [173] *their skulls,* and give them no quarter till they either turn Mahometans or pay tribute.'

"It is not said in prophecy or in history that the more humane injunctions were as scrupulously obeyed as the ferocious mandate. But it was so *commanded* them. And the preceding are the only instructions recorded by Gibbon, as given by Abubeker to the chiefs whose duty it was to issue the commands to all the Saracen hosts. The commands are alike discriminating with the prediction; as if the caliph himself had been acting in known as well as direct obedience to a higher mandate than that of mortal man – and in the very act of going forth to fight against the religion of Jesus, and to propagate Mahometanism in its stead, he repeated the words which it was foretold in the Revelation of Jesus Christ, that he would say."

Verse 5: "*And to them it was given that they should not kill them, but that they should be tormented five months; and their torment was as the torment of a scorpion when he striketh a man.*"

"Their constant incursions into the Roman territory, and frequent assaults on Constantinople itself, were an unceasing torment throughout the empire, which yet they were not able effectually to subdue, notwithstanding the long period, afterwards more directly alluded to, during which they continued, by unremitting attacks, grievously to afflict an idolatrous church, of which the pope was the head. Their charge was to torment, and then to hurt, but not to kill, or utterly destroy. The marvel was that they did not. To repeat the words of Gibbon – 'The calm historian of the present hour must study to explain by what [174] means the church and state were *saved* from this *impending, and, as it should seem, from this inevitable danger.* In this inquiry I shall unfold the events that rescued our ancestors of Britain, and our neighbors of Gaul, from the civil and religious yoke of the Koran; that protected the majesty of Rome, and *delayed* the servitude of Constantinople; that invigorated the defence of the Christians, and scattered among their enemies the seeds of division and decay.' Ninety pages of illustration follow, to which we refer the readers of Gibbon.

Verse 6: "*And in those days shall men seek death, but they shall not find it; and shall DESIRE to die, but death shall flee from them.*"

"Men were weary of life, when life was spared only for a renewal of wo, and when all that they accounted sacred was violated, and all that they held dear constantly endangered; and when the savage Saracens domineered over them, or left them only to a momentary repose, ever liable to be suddenly or violently interrupted, as if by the sting of a scorpion. They who *tormented* men were commanded *not* to kill them. And death might thus have been sought even where it was not found. 'Whosoever falls in battle,' says Mahomet, 'his sins are forgiven at the day of judgment: at the day of judgment his wounds shall be resplendent as vermilion, and odoriferous as musk, and the loss of his limbs shall be supplied by the wings of angels and cherubim.' The intrepid souls of the Arabs were fired with enthusiasm: the picture of the invisible world was strongly painted on their imagination; *and* [175] *the* DEATH *which they always despised became an object of hope and* DESIRE."

Verse 7: "*And the shapes of the locusts were like unto* HORSES PREPARED UNTO BATTLE."

"Arabia, in the opinion of the naturalist, is the genuine and original country of the *horse*; the climate most propitious, not indeed to the size, but to the *spirit and swiftness* of that generous animal. The merit of the Barb, the Spanish, and the English breed, is derived from a mixture of the Arabian blood; the Bedouins preserve with superstitious care the honors and the memory of the purest race. These horses are educated in the tents, among the children of the Arabs, with a tender familiarity, which trains them in the habits of gentleness and attachment. They are accustomed only to walk and to gallop: their sensations are not blunted by the incessant use of the spur and the whip; their powers are reserved for the *moments* of flight and pursuit; but *no sooner* do they feel the touch of the hand or the stirrup, than they DART AWAY *with the swiftness of the wind.*

"The Arabian horse takes the lead throughout the world; and skill in horsemanship is the art and science of Arabia. And the barbed Arabs, swift as locusts and armed like scorpions, ready to *dart away* in a moment, were ever *prepared unto battle.*

"*And on their heads were, as it were, crowns like gold.* When Mahomet entered Medina, (A.D. 622,) and was first received as its prince, 'a *turban* was unfurled before him to supply the deficiency of a standard.' The turbans of the Saracens, like unto a coronet, were their ornament [176] and their boast. The rich booty abundantly supplied and frequently renewed them. To assume the turban, is proverbially to turn Mussulman. And the Arabs were anciently distinguished by the mitres which they wore.

"*And their faces were as the faces of* MEN. 'The gravity and firmness of the mind of the Arab is conspicuous in his outward demeanor, - his only gesture is that of stroking his beard, the venerable symbol of *manhood.*' 'The honor of their beards is most easily wounded.'"

Verse 8: "*And they had hair as the hair of women.*"

"Long hair is esteemed an ornament by women. The Arabs, unlike to other men, had their hair as the hair of women, or uncut, as their practice is recorded by Pliny and others. But there was nothing effeminate in their character, for, as denoting their ferocity and strength to devour, *their teeth were as the teeth of lions.*

Verse 9: "*And they had breastplates, as it were breastplates of iron.*"

"The cuirass (or breastplate) was in use among the Arabs in the days of Mahomet. In the battle of Ohud (the second which Mahomet fought) with the Koreish of Mecca, (A.D. 624) 'seven hundred of them were armed with cuirasses.' And in his next victory over the Jews, 'three hundred *cuirasses,* five hundred pikes, a thousand lances, composed the most *useful* portion of the spoil.' After the defeat of the imperial army of seventy thousand men, on the plain of Aiznadin, (A.D. 633,) the spoil taken by the Saracens 'was inestimable; many banners and crosses of gold and silver, precious stones, [177] silver and gold chains, and *innumerable suits of the richest armor* and apparel. The seasonable supply of arms became the *instrument of new victories.'*"

Verse 9: *"And the sound of their wings was as the sound of chariots of many horses running to battle."*

"The charge of the Arabs was not like that of the Greeks and Romans, the efforts of a firm and compact infantry: their military force was chiefly formed of *cavalry and archers;* and the engagement was often interrupted, and often renewed by single combats and flying skirmishes, &c. The periods of the battle of Cadesia were distinguished by their peculiar appellations. The first, from the well-timed appearance of six thousand of the Syrian brethren, was denominated the day of *succor.* The day of *concussion* might express the disorder of one, or perhaps of both the contending armies. The third, a nocturnal *tumult,* received the whimsical name of the night of *barking,* from the *discordant clamors, which were compared to the inarticulate sounds of the fiercest animals.* The morning of the succeeding day determined the fate of Persia.' With a touch of the hand, the Arab horses *dart away with the swiftness of the wind.* The *sound* of their wings was as the sound of chariots of many horses *running* to battle. Their conquests were marvelous, both in rapidity and extent, and their attack was instantaneous. Nor was it less successful against the Romans than the Persians. 'A religion of peace was incapable of withstanding the *fanatic cry* of "Fight, fight! Paradise, [178] paradise!" that *re-echoed* in the ranks of the Saracens.'"

Verse 10: *"And they had tails like unto scorpions; and there were stings in their tails; and their power was to hurt men five months."*

"The authority of the compassions of Mahomet expired with their lives: and the chiefs or emirs of the Arabian tribes *left behind* in the desert the spirit of equality and independence. The legal and sacerdotal characters were united in the successors of Mahomet; and if the Koran was the rule of their actions, they were the supreme judges and interpreters of that divine book. They reigned by the right of conquest over the nations of the east, to whom the name of liberty was unknown, and who were accustomed to applaud in their *tyrants* the acts of *violence* and *severity* that were exercised at *their own expense.'"

Thus far Keith has furnished us with illustrations of the sounding of the first five trumpets. But here we must take leave of him, and, in applying the prophetic periods, pursue another course.

THE TORMENT OF THE GREEKS ONE HUNDRED AND FIFTY YEARS.

Verse 10: "Their power was to hurt men five months."

1. The question arises, What men were they to hurt five months? Undoubtedly, the same they were afterwards to slay; [see verse 15.] "The third part of men," or third of the Roman empire – the Greek division of it.

[179] 2. When were they to begin their work of torment? The 11th verse answers the question: - "They had a king over them, which is the angel of the bottomless pit, whose name in the Hebrew tongue is *Abaddon,* BUT IN THE Greek hath his name *Apollyon.*"

1. *"They had a king over them."* From the death of Mahomet until near the close of the 13th century, the Mahommedans were divided into various factions, under several leaders, with no general civil government extending over them all. Near the close of the 13th century, Othman founded a government, which has since been known as the Ottoman government, or empire, extending over all the principal Mahommedan tribes, consolidating them into one grand monarchy.

2. The character of the king. *"Which is the angel of the bottomless pit."* An angel signifies a messenger, or minister, either good or bad; not always a spiritual being. "The angel of the bottomless pit," or chief minister of the religion which came from thence when it was opened. That religion is Mahommedism, and the Sultan is its chief minister. "The Sultan, or Grand Signior, as he is indifferently called, is also Supreme Caliph, or high priest, uniting in his person the highest spiritual dignity with the supreme secular authority."

When the address of "The World's AntiSlavery Convention" was presented to Mehemet Ali, he expressed his willingness to act in the matter, but said he could do nothing; they "must [180] go to the head of religion at Constantinople," that is, the Sultan.

3. *His name.* In Hebrew, *"Abaddon,"* the destroyer; in Greek, *"apollyon,"* one that *exterminates or destroys.* Having two different names in the two languages; it is evident that the character, rather than the name of the power, is intended to be represented. If so, in both languages he is a destroyer. Such has always been the character of the Ottoman government.

Says *Perkins,* - "He," the Sultan, "has unlimited power over the lives and property of his subjects, especially of the high officers of state, whom he can remove, plunder or put to death at pleasure. They are required submissively to kiss the bow-string which sends them wherewith they are to be strangled."

All the above marks apply to the Ottoman government in a striking manner.

But when did Othman make his first assault on the Greek empire? According to Gibbon, (*Decl. and Fall,"* &c.) "Othman first entered the territory of Nicomedia on the 27th day of July, 1299."

The calculations of some writers have gone upon the supposition that the period should begin with the foundation of the Ottoman empire; but this is evidently an error: for they not only were to have a king over them, but were to torment men *five months.* But the period of torment could not begin before the first attack of the tormentors, which was as above, July 27th, 1299.

The calculation which follows founded on this starting-point, was made and published in [181] "CHRIST'S SECOND COMING," &c., by the author, in 1838.

"And their power was to torment men five months." Thus far their commission extended, to torment, by constant depredations, but not politically to kill them. *"Five months;"* that is, one hundred and fifty years. Commencing July 27th, 1299, the one hundred and fifty years reach to 1449. During that whole period the Turks were engaged in an almost perpetual war with the Greek empire, but yet without conquering it. They seized upon and held several of the Greek provinces, but still Greek independence was maintained in Constantinople. But in 1449, the termination of the one hundred and fifty years, a change came. Before presenting the history of that change, however, we will look at verses 12-15.

THE OTTOMAN SUPREMACY IN CONSTANTINOPLE THREE HUNDRED AND NINETY-ONE YEARS AND FIFTEEN DAYS.

Verse 12: "One wo is past; and behold, there come two woes more hereafter."

Verse 13: "And the sixth angel sounded, and I heard a voice, from the four horns of the golden altar which is before God."

Verse 14: "Saying to the sixth angel which had the trumpet, Loose the four angels which are bound in the great river Euphrates."

Verse 15: "And the four angels were loosed, which were prepared for an hour, a day, a month, and a year, for to slay the third part of men."

[182] The first wo was to continue from the rise of Mahommedism until the end of the five months. Then the first wo was to end, and the second begin. And when the sixth angel sounded, it was commanded to take off the restraints which had been imposed on the nation, by which they were restricted to the work of *tormenting* men, and their commission extended to *slay* the third part of men. This command came from the four horns of the golden altar which is before God. "The four angels," are the four principal sultanies of which the Ottoman empire is composed, located in the country of the Euphrates. They had been restrained; God commanded, and they were loosed.

In the year 1449, John Paleologus, the Greek emperor, died, but left no children to inherit his throne, and Constantine Deacozes succeeded to it. But he would not venture to ascend the throne without the consent of Amurath, the Turkish Sultan. He therefore sent ambassadors to ask his consent, and obtained it, before he presumed to call himself sovereign.

"This shameful proceeding seemed to presage the approaching downfall of the empire. Ducas, the historian, counts John Paleologus for the last Greek emperor, without doubt, because he did not consider as such a prince who had not dared to reign without the permission of his enemy."

Let this historical fact be carefully examined in connection with the prediction above. This was not a violent assault made on the Greeks, by which their empire was overthrown and their independence taken away, but simply a voluntary surrender of that independence into the [183] hands of the Turks, by saying, "I cannot reign unless you permit."

The four angels were loosed for an hour, a day, a month, and a year, to slay the third part of men. This period amounts to three hundred and ninety-one years and fifteen days; during which Ottoman supremacy was to exist in Constantinople.

But; although the *four angels* were thus loosed by the voluntary submission of the Greeks, yet another doom awaited the *seat of empire*. Amurath, the sultan to whom the submission of Deacozes was made, and by whose permission he reigned in Constantinople, soon after died, and was succeeded in the empire, in 1451, by Mahomet II., who set his heart on Constantinople, and determined to make it a prey. He accordingly made preparations for besieging and taking the city. The siege commenced on the 6th of April, 1453, and ended in the taking of the city, and death of the last of the Constantines, on the 16th day of May following. And the eastern city of the Caesars became the seat of the Ottoman empire.

The arms and mode of warfare by which the siege of Constantinople was to be overthrown, and held in subjection were distinctly noticed by the revelator. – 1. The army.

Verse 16: *"And the number of the army of the horsemen were two hundred thousand thousand: and I heard the number of them."*

Innumerable hordes of horses and them that sat on them. Gibbon describes the first invasion of the Roman territories by the Turks, thus: -- *"The myriads of Turkish horse* overspread a frontier of six hundred miles from Tauris to Azeroum, [184] and the blood of 130,000 Christians was a grateful sacrifice to the Arabian prophet." Whether the number is designed to convey the idea of any definite number, the reader must judge. Some suppose 200,000 twice told is meant, and then following some historians, find that number of Turkish warriors in the siege of Constantinople. Some think 200,000,000 to mean all the Turkish warriors during the 391 years, fifteen days of their triumph over the Greeks. I confess this to me appears the most likely. But as it cannot be ascertained whether that is the fact or not, I will affirm nothing on the point.

Verse 17: *"And thus I saw the horses in the vision, and them that sat on them, having breastplates of fire, and of jacinth and brimstone: and the heads of the horses were as the heads of lions; and out of their mouths issued fire, and smoke, and brimstone."*

On this text I shall again refer to Mr. Keith for an illustration of it: --

"The color of fire is *red*, of hyacinth or jacinth *blue*, and of brimstone *yellow*, and this, as Mr. Daubuz observes, 'has a literal accomplishment; for the Othmans, from the first time of their appearance, have affected to wear such warlike apparel of scarlet, blue, and yellow. Of the Spahis, particularly, some have red and some have yellow standards, and others red or yellow mixed with other colors. In appearance, too, the heads of the horses were as the heads of lions, to denote their strength, courage and fierceness.' Without rejecting so plausible an interpretation, the suggestions may not be unwarrantable, that a still closer and more direct exposition may be [185] given of that which the prophet saw in the vision. In the prophetic description of the fall of Babylon, they who rode on horses are described as holding the bow and the lance; but it was with other arms than the arrow and the spear that the Turkish warriors encompassed Constantinople; and the breastplates of the horsemen, in reference to the more destructive implements of war, might then, for the first time, be said to be fire, and jacinth, and brimstone. The musket had recently supplied the place of the bow. *Fire* emanated from their breasts. *Brimstone*, the flame of which is *jacinth*, was an ingredient both of the *liquid fire* and of gunpowder. Congruity seems to require this more strictly literal interpretation, as conformable to the significancy of the same terms in the immediately subsequent verse, including the same general description. A new mode of warfare was at that time introduced, which has changed the nature of war itself, in regard to the form of its instruments of destruction; and sounds and sights unheard of and unknown before, were the death-knell and doom of the Roman empire. Invention outrivaled force, and a new power was introduced, that of musketry as well as of artillery, in the art of war, before which the old Macedonion phalanx would not have remained unbroken, nor the Roman legions stood. That which John saw 'in the vision,' is read in the history of the times."

Verse 18: *"By these three was the third part of men killed, by the fire, and by the smoke, and by the brimstone, which issued out of their mouths."*

"'Among the implements of destruction, he studied with peculiar care the *recent* and tremendous [186] discovery of the Latins, and *his artillery* surpassed *whatever had yet appeared in the world*. A founder of cannon, a Dane or Hungarian, who had been almost starved in the Greek service, deserted to the Moslems, and was liberally entertained by the Turkish sultan. Mahomet was satisfied with the answer to his first question, which he eagerly pressed on the artist, -- "Am I able to cast a cannon capable of throwing a ball or stone of sufficient size to batter the walls of Constantinople?" "I am not ignorant of their strength, but were they more solid than those of Babylon, I could oppose an engine of superior power; the position and management of that engine must be left to your engineers." On this assurance a foundery was established at Adrianople; the metal was prepared; and at the end of three months Urban produced a piece of brass ordnance of stupendous and almost incredible magnitude. A measure of twelve palms was assigned to the bore, and the stone bullet weighed about six hundred pounds. A vacant place before the new palace was chosen for the *first experiment;* but to prevent the sudden and mischievous effects of astonishment and fear, a proclamation was issued that the cannon would be discharged the ensuing day. The explosion was felt or heard in a circuit of a hundred furlongs; the ball, by force of the gunpowder, was driven about a mile, and on the spot where it fell, it buried itself a fathom deep in the ground. For the conveyance of this destructive engine, a frame or carriage of thirty wagons was linked together, and drawn along by a train of sixty oxen; two hundred men on both sides were stationed to poise or support the rolling weight; two hundred [187] and fifty workmen marched before to smooth the way and repair the bridges, and near two months were employed in a laborious journey of a hundred and fifty miles. I dare not reject the positive and unanimous evidence of contemporary writers. A Turkish cannon, more enormous than that of Mahomet, still guards the entrance of the Dardanelles, and if the use be inconvenient, it has been found, on a late trial, that the effect is far from contemptible. A stone bullet of eleven hundred pounds weight was once discharged with three hundred and thirty pounds of powder; at the distance of six hundred yards it shivered into three rocky fragments, traversed the strait, and leaving the waters in a foam, again rose and bounded against the opposite hill.'

"In the siege, 'the incessant volleys of lances and arrows were accompanied with the SMOKE, the sound, and the FIRE of their *musketry* and *cannon.* Their *small arms* discharged at the same time five or even ten balls of lead of the size of a walnut, and according to the closeness of the ranks, and the force of the powder, several breastplates and bodies were transpierced by the same shot. But the Turkish approaches were soon sunk in trenches, or covered with ruins. Each day added to the science of the Christians, but their inadequate stock of gunpowder was wasted in the operations of each day. Their ordnance was not powerful either in size or number, and if they possessed some heavy cannon, they feared to plant them on the walls, lest the aged structure should be shaken and overthrown by the explosion. The same destructive secret had been revealed to the Moslems, by whom it was employed [188] with the superior energy of zeal, riches and despotism. The great cannon of Mahomet has been separately noticed; *an important and visible object in the history of the times;* but that enormous engine was flanked by two fellows almost of equal magnitude; *the long order of the Turkish artillery* was pointed against the walls; fourteen batteries thundered at once on the most accessible places, and of *one* of these it is ambiguously expressed that it was mounted with one hundred and thirty guns, or that it discharged one hundred and thirty bullets. Yet in the power and activity of the sultan we may discern *the infancy of the new science;* under a master who counted the moments, the *great cannon* could be loaded and fired no more than seven times in

213

one day. The heated metal unfortunately burst; several workmen were destroyed; and the skill of an artist was admired who bethought himself of preventing the danger and the accident by pouring oil after each explosion into the mouth of the cannon.'"

This historical sketch from Gibbon, of the use of gunpowder, fire-arms and cannon, as the instrumentality by which the city was finally overcome, is so illustrative of the text, that one can hardly imagine any other scene can be described.

The specified time for the continuance of Turkish of Mahometan supremacy over the Greeks, was an hour, day, month, and year. A *prophetic* year, three hundred and sixty days; a month, thirty days; one day; and an hour, or the twenty-fourth part of a day. Three hundred and sixty, the number of days in a prophetic year, divided by twenty-four, the number of hours in a [189] day, gives us fifteen days. Three hundred and ninety-one years and fifteen days.

Commencing when the one hundred and fifty years ended, in 1449, the period would end August 11th, 1840. Judging from the manner of the commencement of the Ottoman supremacy, that it was by a voluntary acknowledgement on the part of the Greek emperor that he only reigned by permission of the Turkish sultan, we should naturally conclude that the fall or departure of the Ottoman independence would be brought about in the same way; that at the end of the specified period, *the Sultan would voluntarily surrender his independence into the hands of the Christian powers, from whom he received it.*

When the foregoing calculation was made, it was purely a matter of calculation on the prophetic periods of Scripture. Now, however, the time has passed by, and it is proper to inquire what the result has been – whether it has corresponded with the previous calculation.

I SHALL NOW PASS TO THE QUESTION, HAS THAT SUPREMACY DEPARTED FROM THE MAHOMETANS INTO CHRISTIAN HANDS, SO THAT THE TURKS NOW EXIST AND REIGN BY THE SUFFERANCE AND PERMISSION OF THE CHRISTIAN POWERS, AS THE CHRISTIANS DID FOR SOME TWO TO THREE YEARS BY THE PERMISSION OF THE TURKS?

First Testimony.—The following is from Rev. Mr. Goodell, missionary of the American Board at Constantinople, addressed to the Board, and by them published in the Missionary Herald, for April, 1841, p. 160: -

"The power of Islamism is broken forever; [190] and there is no concealing the fact even from themselves. They exist now by mere sufferance. And though there is a mighty effort made by Christian governments to sustain them, yet at every step they sink lower and lower with fearful velocity. And though there is a great endeavor made to graft the institutions of civilized and Christian countries upon the decayed trunk, yet the very root itself is fast wasting away by the venom of its own poison. How wonderful it is, that, when all Christendom combined together to check the progress of Mahommedan power, it waxed exceedingly great in spite of every opposition; and now, when all the mighty potentates of Christian Europe, who feel fully competent to settle all the quarrels, and arrange all the affairs of the whole world, are leagued together for its protection and defence, down it comes, in spite of all their fostering care."

Mr. Goodell has been for years a missionary in the Turkish dominions, and is competent to judge of the state of the government. His deliberate and unequivocal testimony is, that "the *power of Islamism* is broken forever." But it is said the Turks yet reign! So also says our witness – "but it is by MERE SUFFERANCE." They are at the mercy of the *Christians.* Their independence is broken.

Another Witness. – Rev. Mr. Balch, of Providence, R.I., in an attack on Mr. Miller for saying that the Ottoman empire fell in 1840, says: -- "How can an honest man have the hardihood to stand up before an intelligent audience, and make such an assertion, when the most authentic [191] version of the change of the Ottoman empire is that it has not been on a better foundation in fifty years, for it is now *re-organized* by the European kingdoms, and is honorably treated as such."

But how does it happen that Christian Europe *re-organized the government?* What need of it, if it was not *disorganized?* If Christian Europe has done this, then it is now, to all intents and purposes, a Christian government, and is only ruled nominally by the sultan, as their vassal.

This testimony is the more valuable for having come from an opponent. We could not have selected and put together words more fully expressive of the idea of the present state of the Ottoman empire. It is true the Christian governments of Europe have re-organized the Turkish empire, and it is their creature. From 1840 to the present time, the Ottoman government has been under the dictation of the great powers of Europe; and scarcely a measure of that government has been adopted and carried out without the interference and dictation of the allies; and that dictation has been submitted to by them.

It is in this light politicians have looked upon the government since 1840, as the following item will show: --

The London Morning Herald, after the capture of St. Jean d'Acre, speaking of the state of things in the Ottoman empire, says: -- "We (the allies) have conquered St. Jean d'Acre. We have dissipated into thin air the *prestige* that lately invested as with a halo the name of Mehemet Ali. We have in all probability [192] destroyed forever the power of that hitherto successful ruler. *But have we done aught to restore strength to the Ottoman empire?* WE FEAR NOT. WE FEAR THAT THE SULTAN HAS BEEN REDUCED TO THE RANK OF A PUPPET; AND THAT THE SOURCES OF THE TURKISH EMPIRE'S STRENGTH ARE ENTIRELY DESTROYED.

"If the supremacy of the Sultan is hereafter to be maintained in Egypt, it must be maintained, we fear, by the *unceasing intervention* of England and Russia."

What the London Morning Herald last November feared, has since been realized. The Sultan has been entirely, in all the great questions which have come up, under the dictation of the Christian kingdoms of Europe.

WHEN DID MAHOMMEDAN INDEPENDENCE IN CONSTANTINOPLE DEPART?

In order to answer this question understandingly, it will be necessary to review briefly the history of that power for a few years past.

For several years the Sultan has been embroiled in war with Mehemet Ali, Pacha of Egypt. In 1838 there was a threatening of war between the Sultan and his Egyptian vassal. Mehemet Ali Pacha, in a note addressed to the foreign consuls, declared that in future he would pay no tribute to the Porte, and that he considered himself independent sovereign of Egypt, Arabia, and Syria. The Sultan, naturally incensed at this declaration, would have immediately commenced hostilities, had he not been restrained by the influence of the foreign ambassadors, and persuaded to delay. This war, however, was [193] finally averted by the announcement of Mehemet, that he was ready to pay a million of dollars, arrearages of tribute which he owed the Porte, and an actual payment of $750,000, in August of that year.

In 1838 hostilities again commenced, and were prosecuted, until, in a general battle between the armies of the Sultan and Mehemet, the Sultan's army was entirely cut up and destroyed, and his fleet taken by Mehemet and carried into Egypt. So completely had the Sultan's fleet been reduced, that, when hostilities commenced in August, he had only two first-rates and three frigates, as the sad remains of the once powerful Turkish fleet. This fleet Mehemet positively refused to give up and return to the Sultan, and declared, if the powers attempted to take it from him, he would burn it.

In this posture affairs stood, when, in 1840, England, Russia, Austria and Prussia interposed, and determined on a settlement of the difficulty; for it was evident, if let alone, Mehemet would soon become master of the Sultan's throne.

The following extract from an official document, which appeared in the *Moniteur Ottoman,* Aug. 22, 1840, will give an idea of the course of affairs at this juncture. The conference spoken of was composed of the four powers above named, and was held in London, July 15th, 1840: --

"Subsequent to the occurrence of the disputes alluded to, and after the reverses experienced, as known to all the world, the ambassadors of the great powers at Constantinople, in a collective official note declared that their governments were unanimously agreed upon taking measures to [194] arrange the said differences. The Sublime Porte, with a view of putting a stop to the effusion of Mussulman blood, and to the various evils which would arise from a renewal of hostilities, ACCEPTED *the intervention of the great powers.* "

Here was certainly a voluntary surrender of the question into the hands of the great powers. But it proceeds: --

"His Excellency, Sheikh Effendi, the Bey Likgis, was therefore despatched as plenipotentiary to represent the Sublime Porte at the conference which took place in London, for the purpose in question. It having been felt that all the zealous labors of the conferences of London in the settlement of the Pacha's pretensions were useless, and that the only public way was to have recourse to coercive measures to reduce him to obedience in case he persisted in not listening to pacific overtures, the powers have, together with the OTTOMAN PLENIPOTENTIARY, drawn up and signed a treaty, whereby the *Sultan offers* the Pacha the hereditary government of Egypt, and all that part of Syria extending from the gulf of Suez to the lake of Tiberias, together with the province of Acre, for life; the Pacha, on his part, evacuating all other parts of the Sultan's dominions now occupied by him, and returning the Ottoman fleet. A certain space of time has been granted him to accede to these terms; and, as the proposals of the Sultan and his allies, the four powers, do not admit of any change or qualification, if the Pacha refuse to accede to them, it is evident that the evil consequences to fall upon him will be attributable solely to his own fault.

"His Excellency, Rifat Bey, Musleshar for foreign affairs, has been despatched in a government [195] steamer to Alexandria, to communicate the ultimatum to the Pacha."

From these extracts it appears, --

1. That the Sultan, conscious of his own weakness, did voluntarily accept the intervention of the great Christian powers of Europe to settle his difficulties, which he could not settle himself.

2. That they (the great powers) were agreed on taking measures to settle the difficulties.

3. That the ultimatum of the London conference left it with the Sultan to arrange the affair with Mehemet, if he could. The Sultan was to offer to him the terms of settlement. So that if Mehemet accepted the terms, there would still be no actual intervention of the powers between the Sultan and Pacha.

4. That if Mehemet rejected the Sultan's offer, the ultimatum admitted of no change or qualification; *the great powers* stood pledged to coerce him into submission. So long, therefore, as the Sultan held the ultimatum in his own hands, he still maintained the independence of his throne. But that document once submitted to Mehemet, and it would be forever beyond his reach to control the question. It would be for Mehemet to say whether the powers should interpose or not.

5. The Sultan did despatch Rifat Bey, in a government steamer, (which left Constantinople Aug. 5,) to Alexandria, to communicate to Mehemet the ultimatum.

This was a voluntary governmental act of the Sultan.

The question now comes up, WHEN WAS THAT DOCUMENT PUT OFFICIALLY UNDER THE CONTROL OF MEHEMET ALI?

[196] The following extract of a letter from a correspondent of the *London Morning Chronicle,* of Sept. 18, 1840, dated "Constantinople, Aug. 27th, 1840," will answer the question: --

"By the French steamer of the 24th, we have advices from Egypt to the 16th. They show no alteration in the resolution of the Pacha. Confiding in the valor of his Arab army, and in the strength of the fortifications which defend his capital, he seems determined to abide by the last alternative; and as recourse to this, therefore, is now inevitable, all hope may be considered as at an end of a termination of the affair without bloodshed. Immediately on the arrival of the Cyclops steamer with the news of the convention of the *four powers*, Mehemet Ali, it is stated, had quitted Alexandria, to make a short tour through Lower Egypt. The object of his absenting himself at such a moment being partly to avoid conferences with the European consuls, but principally to endeavor, by his own presence, to arouse the fanaticism of the Bedouin tribes, and facilitate the raising of his new levies. During the interval of his absence, the *Turkish government steamer,* WHICH HAD REACHED ALEXANDRIA ON THE 11TH, WITH THE ENVOY RIFAT BEY ON BOARD, had been by his orders placed in quarantine, and she was not released from it till the 16th. Previous, however, to the Porte's leaving, and on the very day on which he had been admitted to pratique, the abovenamed functionary had had an audience of the Pacha, and had communicated to him the command of the Sultan, with respect to the evacuation of the Syrian provinces, appointing another audience for the next day, when, in the [197] presence of the consuls of the European powers, he would receive from him his definite answer, and inform him of the alternative of his refusing to obey; giving him the ten days which have been allotted him by the convention to decide on the course he should think fit to adopt."

According to the foregoing statement, the ultimatum was *officially put into the power of Mehemet Ali, and was disposed of by his orders, viz., sent to quarantine,* ON THE ELEVENTH DAY OF AUGUST, 1840.

But have we any evidence, beside the fact of the arrival of Rifat Bey at Alexandria with the ultimatum on the 11th of August, that Ottoman supremacy died, or was dead, that day?

Read the following, from the same writer quoted above, dated "Constantinople, August 12, 1840:" –

"I can add but little to my last letter, on the subject of the plans of the *four powers*; and I believe the details I then gave you comprise everything that is yet decided on. The portion of the Pacha, as I then stated, is not to extend beyond the line of Acre, and does not include either Arabia or Candia. Egypt alone is to be hereditary in his family, and the province of Acre to be considered as a pachalic, to be governed by his son during his lifetime, but afterward to depend on the will of the Porte; and even this latter is only to be granted him on the condition of his accepting these terms, and delivering up the Ottoman fleet within ten days. In the event of his not doing so, this pachalic is to be cut off. Egypt is then to be offered him, [198] with another ten days to deliberate on it, before actual force is employed against him.

"The manner, however, of applying the force, should he refuse to comply with these terms, -- whether a simple blockade is to be bombarded, and his armies attacked in the Syrian provinces, -- is the point which still remains to be learned; nor does a note delivered yesterday by the four ambassadors, in answer to a question put to them by the Porte, as to the plan to be adopted in such an event, throw the *least light* on this subject. It simply states that provision has been made, and there is no necessity for the Divan alarming itself about any contingency that might afterwards arise."

Let us now analyze this testimony.

1. The letter is dated "Constantinople, Aug. 12."

2. "Yesterday," the 11th of August, the Sultan applied, in his own capital, to the ambassadors of four *Christian nations,* to know the measures which were to be taken in reference to a circumstance vitally affecting his empire; and was only told that "provision had been made," but he could not know what it was; and that he need give himself no alarm *"about any contingency which might* AFTERWARDS ARISE!!" From that time, then, *they,* and not *he,* would manage that.

Where was the Sultan's independence that day? GONE. Who had the supremacy of the Ottoman empire in their hands? *The great powers.*

According to previous calculation, therefore, [199] OTTOMAN SUPREMACY *did depart on the* ELEVENTH OF AUGUST *into the hands of the great Christian powers of Europe.*

Then the second wo is past, and the sixth trumpet has ceased its sounding; and the conclusion is now inevitable, because the word of God affirms the fact in so many words, *"Behold, the third wo cometh quickly."* And "in the days of the voice of the seventh angel, when he shall be finished." But what will take place when the seventh angel sounds? I answer, Great voices will be heard in heaven, saying, "The kingdoms of this world have become the kingdoms of our Lord and his Christ, and he shall reign forever and ever." Nor is this event a mere spiritual reign over the kingdoms of this world; but the Revelator goes on to say, "and thy wrath is come, and the time of the dead, that they should be judged; and that thou shouldest give reward unto thy servants the prophets, the saints, and them that fear thy name, small and great, and shouldest destroy them that destroy the earth." This, then, is the consummation, when every one shall receive his retribution, according to what he has done.

"The third wo cometh quickly." It cannot be afar off; it is nigh, even at the door. Men may scornfully inquire, "Where is the promise of his coming? for since the fathers fell asleep, all things continue as they were from beginning." "But the day of the Lord will come as a thief in the night." There are abundant promises of his coming, and that speedily. But I do not expect another sign equal in strength and conclusiveness to the one now spread out before us in the present [200] article. The present calculation was before the world two years and more before the time of fulfilment; and the attention of the whole community was turned toward it. There are few persons, in New England at least, whose minds were not arrested and turned to the 11th of August; and vast multitudes were ready to say, ay, did say. If this event takes place according to the calculation, at the time specified, we will believe the doctrine of the *advent near*. But how is it with them now? Why, just as it was with the old Jews in the days of Christ; when he was every day performing the most stupendous miracles in their sight, they said to him, "Master, we would see a sign of thee." So now: men desire a sign from heaven. But let them be assured, they can never have a more convincing one than this; -- the last great prophecy with which a prophetic period is connected, except the concluding period, when Christ will come, has been filled up in the exact time, and has brought us to the very verge of eternity. There is no time to be whiled away in idleness or indifference by those who love the Lord Jesus Christ. They have a great work to do, both for themselves and others. Nor should the sinner delay to awake from his slumbers, and lay hold on eternal life. Grace be with all who love the Lord Jesus Christ.[287]

---

[287] Josiah Litch, *Prophetic Exposition; Or A Connected View Of The Testimony Of The Prophets Concerning The Kingdom Of God And The Time Of Its Establishment.* (Boston: Joshua V. Himes, 1842), 161-200.

APPENDIX VI

The Morning Chronicle

Oct. 3, 1840

"The five powers had by the collective note which was presented to the Port on the 27th of July, 1839, by their representative at Constantinople, declared to the Sultan that their union was assured, and they had requested him to abstain from any direct negotiation with Mehemet Ali, and to make no arrangement with the Pasha without the concurrence of the five powers, and yet her Majesty's government have good reason to believe that for many months past the French representative at Constantinople has with respect to the matters from the other four powers, and has earnestly and repeatedly pressed the Porte to negotiate directly with Mehemet Ali, and to make an arrangement with the Pasha, not only without the concurrence of the other four powers, but under the single mediation of France, and according to the particular views of the French therefore that has separated herself from the four powers and not the four powers that have separated themselves from France. (Signed) Palmerston.[288]

[A note showing how France separated herself from the other four great powers.]

---

[288] *The Morning Chronicle*, London, Saturday, Oct. 3, 1840. Pg. 2. Col. 5.

APPENDIX VII

The Morning Chronicle

September 7, 1840

EGYPT

ALEXANDRIA, August 17.

[From our own correspondent.]

"At length "The Eastern Question" seems to have reached a crisis. On the morning of the 11th a steamer of the Sultan arrived here from Constantinople, having on board Rifaat Bey, on a special mission to present to the Pacha the *ultimatum* of the Porte, with the convention signed by the Four Powers. Although the envoy was not out of quarantine, and, of course, his communication not made until yesterday, yet the object of his mission soon became very generally known here; nor would it be easy to give you an idea of the anxiety and excitement which is created. These were, if possible, increased by the arrival on the following day from Toulon of the French war-steamer the Tartaras, having on board Count Walewski, upon a secret mission from M. Thiers, to the rumoured object of which I shall advert presently. Another, and a not less important cause of disqufet was the view taken of the state of affairs by the Consul-General, Colonel Hodges, and which induced him to address the following letter to the British Consul, Mr. Larking: --

[Our correspondent encloses the letter of Colonel Hodges, dated the 11th of August, and which, as it was published in the *Chronicle* of Saturday, it is unnecessary to repeat.]

Then came the French steam-packet from Marseilles, bringing Clot-Bey and a bag full of newspapers, filled with those falsehoods and exaggerations which I dare say, or at least hope, your readers have already forgotten, with the passing feeling of indignation which they were so calculated to excite. To give a climax to the public anxiety, it only required that a British ship of war should appear off the coast, and accordingly the Bellerophon cast anchor yesterday under the very guns of the palace.

Men of all colours of opinion, harassed and worn out by the contunation of the *status quo*, seem to rejoice at the prospect of any termination. What that particular termination will be, however, it really seems more difficult to anticipate when one is upon the very stage than when at a distance. I can do no more than give you the opinions of others as well as my own, with the grounds upon which it rests.

Whether it results from the peculiar position in which the diplomatic body, such as it is, is placed towards the inhabitants, necessarily holding free and frequent intercourse with them, and that intercourse as often through a medium as directly, or whether it results from the easy access of the respectable Frank population to the minister and the palace, or from the dragoman channel through which diplomatic communications are made, I know not; but I do not believe there is a city in the world in which diplomacy has fewer secrets than in Alexandria. The communication which the Consul has made in the morning the merchant will detail to you in the afternoon, and the views and intentions of the Pacha even upon important subjects are frequently known in the counting-house before they have found their way to the consulate. Exaggerations and untruths of course one must expect, and bore you have them in abundance. But along with them I find that one also gets the principal facts. Thus, out of all that is said of the proceedings and intentions of the different consuls, I think you may rely upon this as all that is yet known: -- When the envoy of the Sultan has presented the ultimatum, he waits for ten days, that is, to the 26th, for the answer of the Pacha. The Consuls of the four nations communicating to the Pacha the convention signed at London, will urge upon him the acceptance of the proposed terms. If rejected at the end of ten days, the second proposition will be made; and if that be rejected at the end of ten days, the four consuls will strike their flags and leave Alexandria. But will the proposals of the Sultan be accepted or not? In the first place, I believe it to be the unanimous feeling – or rather apprehension – of the consuls that they will be obliged to leave Alexandria. I have myself heard persons thoroughly acquainted with the views and character of Mehemet Ali declare their conviction that the Pacha will not yield. Indeed, I hear this from so many and such sources, that I participate in the general feeling that the Four Powers will be driven to extremities. It was late on the evening of the 14th when the Pacha returned from an excursion he had been making up the Nile. When informed that a British ship had anchored off the palace, he took immediate precautions, ordering the gunners to remain at the batteries through the night. In the morning a transport was dispatched with ammunition for Syria. Indeed, everything indicates an intention on the part of the Pacha to meet force by force.

It is scarcely possible to believe that a man of Mehemet Ali's shrewdness and selfish prudence would enter into such a struggle as that which resistance is certain to provoke if he depended merely upon the resources at his own command. These resources are undoubtedly considerable, but no man dreams of their being sufficient to resist the efforts of any one of the powers which have jointly undertaken to oppose them. It is unquestionable that the Pacha calculates upon the support of France. His reliance upon this it is that has been betrayed him into his present embarrassment. I shall take another opportunity of adverting to the reprehensible means adopted to produce this mischievous effect upon the Pacha's mind, and to the still more reprehensible motives in which the efforts of the French agents – authorized or not – have originated. There is no doubt, however, that the Pacha, his ministers, his partisans – all have been induced to believe that France will actively interfere. What is the object of Count Walewski's mission? Is it to dispel or to realize this impression? Nominally, I have reason to believe it is to endeavour to prevail upon the Pacha to yield. But can this be the real object of a mission which, while counseling obedience, puts into the Pacha's hands a demi-official newspaper, containing a direct promise of aid if he resist? What can be the object of France in this? You can make nothing definite out of anything she says or does in this matter. The question asked by every second man you meet here is, "What will France do? Will she support the Pacha, or will she leave him to be coerced by the other powers?" And the only answer that can be given would seem to be – Without committing herself to the promise of support, she will yet induce the Pacha to believe he will obtain it, and thus betray him into a conflict which she will watch, and in which she will become actor or spectator, as the opportunity may present itself, of doing either to her own advantage. If her ministers should think it more prudent for her "de retirer dans sn force," and to stay there, - why they have violated no engagement, for did they not send Count Walewski to Alexandria to counsel the Pacha to obedience. If, on the other hands, the chapter of accidents should present some tempting opportunity of interference with a prospect of profit from it, then "the honour and the dignity of France will have imperatively demanded her interference." When it is asked, then, "What will the French government do?" I do not believe that even themselves can answer. Is this be the policy of the French government, it would require one of those gentlemen who are so liberal of their abuse of England to characterize it as it deserves; if it be not, then I can only say the French government has been grievously wronged, and is so still, by many even of its own partisans.

As to the means of giving effect to the policy of the Four Powers, you have probably much better information in England than I should be able to send you from Alexandria. Here it is generally believed that in the first place a sufficient force (it requires but a small one) will appear before Alexandria, to blockade it. The town and the combined fleet (the whole of the fleet is now within the bar and not a ship of them could pass out in the face of a single seventy-four and an armed steamer) would be completely at the mercy of a few line-of-battle-ships lying in the roadstead. A few thousand disciplined troops (Austrians, it is said) will probably be landed on the coast of Syria, and arms distributed to the tribes, who only seek the opportunity of rising in revolt against the terrible tyranny under which they labour.

Many people here imagine that the Pacha will give an immediate answer in the negative. This of course the consuls will not notice – waiting for the explanation of the ten days. One contingency, however, may arise to compel a more speedy solution of the affair; and one can observe some indication that it will arise. Mehemet Ali is busily engaged raising money to pay troops and I should not be at the slightest degree surprised to hear that he had ordered Ibrahim to advance towards Constantinople. Should this be so, the question will be brought to an immediate crisis.

In the beginning of this letter I have given you a letter addressed by Colonel Hodges for the information of the British merchants. In consequence of this letter, a meeting of the merchants was immediately called at which the following resolutions were paused. [Here follow the resolutions which we published on Saturday.] The object of these proceedings on the part of the British merchants is very clear and very natural. In case of any destruction of property or loss from unnecessary alarm, they would doubtless wish to have the best title to indemnity. Their complaint at being left without more specific information seems to me to be exceedingly unreasonable.

I shall conclude my notice of these transactions by simply stating, that since the signature of the convention in London, no despatches have been received by Colonel Hodges; and the merchants who signed the preceding document know perfectly well that the government despatches always arrive by the British steamer, which is hourly expected. But no – it is not information which the British merchants require, but something which may serve as an authority and guarantee for whatever may befall. I have no hesitation in expressing my conviction, that the merchants would not act upon any information they received from Colonel Hodges, unless they saw that by doing so they could establish a claim upon Government. If Colonel Hodges is obliged to quit Alexandria, the British merchants will not accompany him. They will remain, and put themselves under the protection of the Pacha. It would too much extend this letter to enter into the cause of this resolution upon the part of the British merchants, and of the diversity of views of the merchants and the Consul-general. But the subject is of sufficient interest, and has sufficient connection with the general questions, to induce me to call your attention to it on another occasion.[289]

---

[289] The Morning Chronicle, September 7, 1840, pg. 1, col. 5-6.

APPENDIX VIII

Possini's Observationum

Chronological Tables

Observations of Pachymer, Book 3 Chronologicus

847

1298; 4; 16, 5 of Michael

John the prince of the Lazi dies, with his son Alexius succeeding him.

This one proposes that the mother, Eudocia, of this one (Alexius?), since she set out because of the death of her husband for his/her brother Andronicus the emperor, settle in marriage with the cralis of Serbia.

John Veccus once a patriarch dies in prison at the citadel of S. Gregorius, at the end of March.

Eudocia resolved to remain in widowhood refuses matrimony to the cralis of Serbia.

Emperor Andronicus, disappointed with this hope, since he thought it necessary to conquer the cralis with a close relationship to himself, offers his own daughter Simonides, not much older than six, to him in betrothal.

The sister of Maria, the spouse of Michael Augustus the younger, Theodora, who was named in the memory of the mother of Andronicus thus

848

spoken of, is betrothed to Theophanus, the son of John the sebastocrator, likewise named for John.

But she/he dies before the marriage.

The Persians, when they are incited by the slaughter of their men who had stuck with Philanthropenus the insurgent, forsake all the Oriental regions with savage excursions.

Observations of Pachymer, Book 3 Chronologicus

1299 of the Year of Christ, 5 of Boniface VIII of the Roman Pontiffs, Of the Roman Emperors 17 of Andronicus, 6 of Michael

The greatest and most unbending winter of all which humans have remembered raged violently for the first months of this year. Whence it happened that the journey destined for the emperor to Thessalonica was of necessity delayed.

At last at the beginning of February on the day of preparation (Good Friday/day before Sabbath), this is the sixth day of the week, which it was proper that it fell upon in that year, which had the cycle of the sun at 20 and index letter of Sunday as D, on the sixth day of its month, near/before evening the emperor Andronicus going out of the city takes himself to Dripea, whence he prepared the rest of the journey, with some delay there.

The patriarch John attempts at Dripea to dissuade Andronicus, since he wants the marriage of Simonides with the cralis: but through those sent to meet he is asked by the emperor, who knows to what purpose he came, to precede to Selybria.

At Selybria after John was mocked by Andronicus, not having been allowed to discuss the things which he wanted about/concerning the marriage of Simonides, he decided to stay there while the emperor was absent, and not to return into the city, until that one (Andronicus) had returned from Thessalonica.

From the emperor's Thessalonica Andronicus sends Radosthlab back into Bulgaria with Roman troops, whence he had been beaten back by Osphentisthlab.

Eltimeres while fighting on behalf of Osphentisthlab takes possession of Radosthlab who was conquered in battle, and sends him blinded back to his wife.

Osphentisthlabus returns the father Terteren who had been detained in custody by Andronicus the emperor with the exchange of Roman generals who were captured by Eltimeres; nevertheless he does not return to him the kingdom of Bulgaria, but attributed it as a citystate, where he may live as a free and private citizen.

849

1299 of the Year of Christ, 5 of Boniface VIII of the Roman Pontiffs, of the Roman Emperors 17 of Andronicus, 6 of Michael

The emperor at Thessalonica, after the management of the union by marriage with the cralis of Serbia was concluded, receives from him Cotanitza as a deserter and the former wife of the cralis, the daughter of Terter, and in turn authenticates his own daughter Simonides espoused to the cralis, a little girl scarcely 8 to a man nearly fifty and the husband of many wives already, of course with her being guarded as a virgin until the age of puberty (which however Gregoras 1.7 writes he had returned, incapable of bearing children afterwards, because the deflowering of the little girl was hastened through the intemperate impatience of the one awaiting (with desire) it.

A legation of Veneti meet/met with Andronicus the emperor at Thessalonica, seeking that much of the city of Constantinople which had been appointed to tenants be allowed to go back to the Veneti, and that the pledge/mortgage of property which had been made now for some ago because of the fire of Galata be eased: but it accomplished nothing.

The emperor Andronicus in vain attempts to bring about the marriage of Alexius the prince of the Lazi, his own nephew from his sister, and an orphan/ward by the last will of the father, with the daughter of the prefect for canicleo, and to nullify by a tutorial (concerning the legal guardian) law the earlier marriage which had been contracted by the same Alexius without the mother or uncle as originators with a certain daughter of one of the most distinguished of the Iberi.

Hence dejected without good reason he tries to arrange in marriage the same daughter of the prefect for canicleo, to his own son John, a despot, even though the mother of the youth, the August Irene, was opposed to it.

On November 22 Andronicus the emperor, returned from Thessalia, was carried/brought into the city of Constantinople by a solemn occurrence.

Atman the satrap of the Persians, said by others to be Ottomans, the originator of the house which today rules among the Turks, becomes strong with resources, when there were joined to him numerous troops of fierce bandits from Paphlagonia.

850.

1300 of the Year of Christ, 6 of Boniface VIII of the Roman Pontiffs, of the Roman Emperors 18 of Andronicus and 7 of Michael.

John the patriarch with the grief of the injurious and wicked, as he saw it, union undertaken by Andronicus, without his advice, with the cralis of Serbia, spent time in the monastery of Pammacarist as a private man.

The emperor after he (E) had tried in vain to placate him (J) through many who had been sent from himself (E), at last on the calends of February late at night himself summons him (J); and gives satisfaction to him (J) fully about three reasons of the complaints concerning himself (E), and persuades him to return into the patriarchal churches and return to the government of the Church.

After the Paschal holidays the emperor Andronicus publicly revoked the opinion/statement which had been brought by him against John of Ephesus, and declared him innocent of the crime on account of which agreement he had been thrown out fraudulently from the throne and given into custody/confinement.

Nevertheless John the patriarch with the bishops opposes the Philadelphiense and Smyrnense restoration of John of Ephesus.

Thence offended by the complaints which appeared John the patriarch again departed from the patriarchal district into the monastery of Pammacaristus.

Against him the bishops bring a written accusation full of complaints to the emperor.

John the patriarch approaching voluntarily the emperor on October 25 the third day of the week, in that year numbering 21 cycle of the sun with the letter of Sunday C B, returns from his (emperor's) desire with/for the functions of the patriarchal district, a thing which he said was commanded to himself through an angel.

1301, 7, Andron. 19, Michael. 8

Michael the despot married the daughter, who had been repudiated by the cralis, of the Serbian Terteris.

In this year at/near the equinox of autumn, when the sun had entered into the Virgin, a comet appears at Constantinople, which has been described by Pachymer.

An unaccustomed dryness had preceded the appearance/rising of the comet, because of which (dryness) the perpetual fountains dried up; whence it happened that the earth's fruits and grasses perished, and with frequent winds

851

that were arid and stormy returning scarcely breathable air.

1301 of the Year of Christ, 7 of Boniface VIII of the Roman Pontiffs, of the Roman Emperors 19 of Andronicus, 8 of Michael

The Alans who were fighting under/near Noga, in the number of 16 thousand, cross over into parts of the emperor.

Having been sent into Asia they harass and plunder the Romans; nevertheless after they were joined by/to the imperial troops at the place called Chena they conquer illustriously the enemy of the empire, thereby enriched not immoderately by booty.

About this time Atman or Ottomanes took up the name of the kings, and after Prusa was later occupied placed there the seat of the kingdom. Then dying in the year of Hegira, according to Al Iannabius the Arabian chronologer, 726, this is in the year of Christ about 1327, he left his son Urchanes as the heir of the kingdom which was begun in the recently captured city Prusa. Pachymer gives a sign to the siege of Prusa 1.5 c.21 p.296, [that it was] but also a taking by storm at 1.7 c.27.

1302, 8, Andron. 20/Michael.9

On January 14th a horrifying eclipse of the moon was seen at Constantinople.

Michael Augustus the younger moves into the Orient with a strong army in the beginning of spring about the Paschal holidays, and the fame of himself causes the Persians great consternation [by the fame of himself].

The Persians at length are elicited to the contest: but in the preparation for departure of the battle the emperor was persuaded by the Roman generals to refuse an listless battle. Whence he comes into the contempt by the enemy; by which all of the Roman regions of those (presently) districts were soon laid waste by their savage and avaricious attacks.

The Hetaeriarch [official of a confraternity] Muzalo the leader of the Roman troops in Bithynia, while he endeavors himself in opposition--to withstand Osman who is devastating everything, is conquered by an ignoble languor of the Roman soldiers, who were fighting with a weariness, spite, and listless despair; and by the strong effort of the Alans he scarcely conceals the rest of the scattered army within Nicomedia. This defeat happened on the 27th day of the month of July around Bapheum close to Nicomedia.

852

1302 of the Year of Christ, 8 of Boniface VIII of the Roman Pontiffs, of the Roman Pontiffs 20 of Andronicus , 9 of Michael.

Thirteen Venetan triremes with seven piratical ships are brought in aggressively at noon at Constantinople, enter the port called *Ceras*, proceed hostilely in regard to the region of the imperial palace with an immoveable post, when fire and weapons have been sent into the obvious things (that are in the way). And thus they force the emperor to concede what he had denied to the Venetan legates of Thessalonica, namely a letting go back of many a thing and a (ex)pledge/mortgage of occupied possessions.

At this time the pirates, after the island of the Princes was occupied, force the emperor to redeem/ransom with ready/at hand money the very many captives, which they had made there.

When the August Michael the junior was shut in at Magnesia, the Alans who were fighting under him, seek a mission. Unwillingly at length with the blandishments of words there is gained by them the space of a delay of three months. Having been advised about these things, Andronicus is unable to supply to his son the things which he lacks, even though he wants to very much.

P 618/ The things which prevented Andronicus from providing for the things which were necessary for the army of the August Michael, were, besides the Venetan war just now recalled (mentioned), the crowds of ecclesiastical people (of the church) which had at that time broken out in the city, which things are told (in) l.4 from c.27 nearly to the end of the book.

In this year peace between Carol/Charles the Neapolitan king and Frideric who was ruling in Sicily grew united after a war of long duration, when Elenora the daughter of Carol was given for a wife to Frideric. Pachymer wrongly calls this daughter of Carol Ecatherine; the occasion of which error I refer/relate in the notes. Pontifex Boniface confirms this marriage and the peace, although he wanted something to be changed in the stipulations. See the most accurate Odoricus Raynaldus in/for this year from the number 1 to 8.

Roger Lauris, whom Pachymer calls Rontzerius, who had served in the army fought usefully when Frideric was preparing for war [*or:* for Frideric in a preceding war], after he was received eagerly by the emperor Andronicus, to whom he had offered that he would come as to aid, and summoned by a letter of introduction (conferring privileges) which was protected with a golden seal (of a papal document) for abundant hopes, prepares a fleet and troops to set out to him there.

853

The Alans, after the three-month period of time which they had agreed to with emp. Michael elapsed, extort a mission forth, with armed requests."[290]

---

[290] Georgius Pachymeres, *Corpus Scriptorum Historiae Byzantinae* (Bonn ed., 1835), Vol. Alt., p. 847-851. (Petri Possini Observationum.)

CPSIA information can be obtained at www.ICGtesting.com
Printed in the USA
BVOW02s1700100714

358607BV00009B/444/P